Luxury Yarn ONE-SKEIN WONDERS

101 Small Indulgences

EDITED BY JUDITH DURANT

Storey Publishing

OCT   2008

The mission of Storey Publishing is to serve our customers by
publishing practical information that encourages
personal independence in harmony with the environment.

Edited by Judith Durant and Gwen Steege
Art direction and book design by Mary Winkelman Velgos
Text production by Jennifer Jepson Smith

Photography by © Kate Sears
Photo styling by Victoria Petro Conroy

How-to illustrations by Alison Kolesar
Charts by Leslie Anne Charles/LAC Design
Diagrams by Ilona Sherratt

Indexed by Christine R. Lindemer, Boston Road Communications

Special thanks to our models: Kenneth Harris, Laura Kavanaugh, Lilia Polacheck, and Victoria Wall

Printed in the United States by Walsworth Publishing Company
10 9 8 7 6 5 4 3 2 1

Library of Congress Cataloging-in-Publication Data

Luxury yarn one-skein wonders / edited by Judith Durant.
    p. cm.
  Includes index.
  ISBN 978-1-60342-079-2 (pbk. : alk. paper)
   1. Knitting—Patterns. I. Durant, Judith, 1955–
TT820.L89 2008
746.43'2041—dc22
                                      2008031975

This book is dedicated to those who raise the animals,
those who grow the plants, and those who spin the resulting fibers
into luscious yarns for our knitting pleasure.

CONTENTS

Medium Weight

Bulky Weight

An Invitation to Indulge

Luxury. Just reading the word makes some of us giddy. Couple that "luxury" with "yarn," and we're beside ourselves. We've all been there — walking through a yarn shop, touching and feeling our way up the aisles or along the walls, when suddenly, we're overwhelmed by the feel of something special. We've been seduced by silk, awed by alpaca, or captivated by cashmere. We want to indulge the sensation by claiming it as our own.

Thus was born the inspiration for this third collection of one-skein wonders, 101 things to do with that one truly special, if possibly outrageously expensive, skein of yarn. In addition to the familiar luxury yarns such as silk, cashmere, and alpaca, we've included yarns from exotic fibers such as soy, qiviut, bison, and corn. We also offer designs for projects knitted in ecofriendly fibers like linen, organic cotton, and organic wool.

If it's luxury you're after, consider silk, a rich and shiny natural protein fiber that's been cultivated for textiles for thousands of years. Once reserved for royalty, silk and silk-blend yarns are widely available to today's knitter. Pure silk, silk blended with cashmere, silk blended with alpaca, lace-weight silk, silk ribbon — it's all out there, in every color imaginable, including hand-painted varieties. Check out the Sweet Violet Silk-Cashmere Scarf on page 52, the Caravan Silk-Wool Socks on page 83, and the Silk Purses on page 128, for three widely different yarns and projects for silk or silk blends.

For luxurious warmth, alpaca is an excellent choice. Shorn from the animal of the same name, which is native to South America, the fiber is lightweight, warm, and very, very soft. It is available pure and in blends, spun in thicknesses from lace weight to bulky. The Top-down Alpaca Mitts on page 63, Arachne's Alpaca Lace Ring on page 226, and the Heirloom Merino-Alpaca Baby Hat on page 245 all use alpaca yarn.

Also lightweight and soft, though usually more expensive than alpaca, is cashmere. Produced by cashmere goats mainly in China and Mongolia, but also in India, Pakistan, Turkey, and other countries, the textile fiber comes from the soft undercoat of hair that's found beneath an outer growth of guard hair.

Cashmere is used for the Beaded Cashmere Wristlets on page 125, the Cashmere Baby Leg Warmers on page 140, and the Diamond and Crystal Cashmere Evening Bag on page 165.

Exotic yarns abound, coming from both animal and plant fibers. The Qiviut Neck Muff on page 124 was knitted with yarn spun from the down of the arctic musk ox. Pygora goat hair combines with merino wool in the Nancy Pygora-Merino Lace Scarf on page 56, and the Vicuña Scarf on page 59 uses a small amount of the expensive but delicious yarn from the rare South American relative of the alpaca. The fur is said to be the softest in the world. From the plant world comes yarn made from corn, like that used in the Corn Fiber Lace Bath Cloth on page 146; yarn made from flax makes the Linen Bag on page 136; and even soybeans get into the act in Soy Beanie on page 173.

We also sought out natural and ecofriendly fibers. Bamboo is the fiber of the moment; it is wonderfully soft and shiny like silk, has a lovely drape when knitted, and is completely green and biodegradable. We've included several projects in bamboo: Baby's Bamboo Singlet in fingering-weight yarn appears on page 74, Beautiful Baby Bamboo-Merino Sweater on page 144 uses a DK weight, and worsted-weight bamboo yarn is used for the Sueño Bamboo Spa Mask on page 208. The Blossom Silk-SeaCell Shawl on page 106 uses silk blended with SeaCell, which is made from wood pulp and seaweed. Organic cotton is a popular and safe fabric for babies; check out the Inca-Dincadoo Organic Cotton Baby Cardigan on page 204 and the Organic Cotton Bunnies on page 168.

On the following pages, you'll find 101 one-skein projects organized by weight of yarn. We've used the Craft Yarn Council of America's standards to classify each yarn, and you'll find a chart of these weights in the techniques section at the back of the book. Also in this section, you'll find instructions for all the techniques you'll need to complete the projects, as well as a list of the abbreviations we've used. Any special instruction or abbreviation is included with the individual project.

With this collection, we hope you'll agree that you no longer need to consider passing by the next to-die-for yarn you encounter. Go ahead and buy a skein — you're sure to find something to do with it here.

Project Photos

Vicuña Scarf, *page 59*

Sweet Violet Silk-Cashmere Scarf, *page 52*

CASHMERE BANGLES, *page 58*

JOEL BISON LACE SCARF, *page 50*

NANCY PYGORA-MERINO LACE SCARF, *page 56*

Bison Shawlette, *page 54*

Falling Leaves Mohair-Silk Scarf, *page 80*

DIAMONDS AND SHELLS ALPACA SCARF, *page 86*

SEASIDE COTTAGE ALPACA-SILK STOLE, *page 88*

SILK WEDDING RING PILLOW, *page 98*

Top-down Alpaca Mitts, *page 63*

Parisian Alpaca-Wool Scarf, *page 85*

Wool and Camel-Down Ripple Scarf, *page 62*

Tiffany Cashmere Socks, *page 103*

Alpaca-and-Silk Baby Cap, *page 67*

SILK-MERINO TWISTED GLOVES, *page 69*

WHISPER RIB AND LACE ALPACA SOCKS, *page 78*

QUEEN OF DIAMONDS MERINO-SILK GLOVES, *page 9*

Baby's Bamboo Singlet, *page 74*

CARAVAN SILK-WOOL SOCKS, *page 83*

STELLA BAMBOO LACE SCARF, *page 77*

SILK-MERINO FINGERLESS GLOVES, *page 87*

Blossom Silk-SeaCell Shawl, *page 106*   Alpaca-Silk Christening Blanket, *page 101*

LACY GRAY ALPACA SCARF, *page 120*

A PAIR OF SILK PURSES, *page 128*

MOCK CABLE ALPACA TAM, *page 115*

BEADED CASHMERE WRISTLETS, *page 125*

QIVIUT NECK MUFF, *page 124*

STARFISH OF YAK, *page 121*

ANGORA BRIDAL GARTER, *page 127*

FRILLY MERINO-ANGORA BOOTIES, *page 130*

LINEN BAG, page 136

ANGORA PENDANT NECKLACE, page 126

ANGORA PENDANT NECKLACE, page 126

LACY LINEN TABLE LAYER, *page 133*

ALPACA ELEPHANT HAT, *page 110*

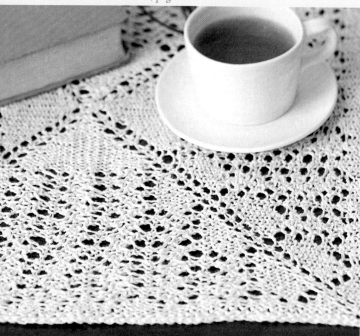

SILK-MERINO LEAF LACE HAT, *page 117*

ALPACA GATOR SOCKS, *page 113*

Lacy Cotton-Hemp Blend Vase, *page 171*

Ocean Wave Merino-Bamboo Vest, *page 161*

DOWNTOWN LAMB'S WOOL CLUTCH, *page 186*

SILK OPERA CLUTCH, *page 185*

DIAMOND AND CRYSTAL CASHMERE EVENING BAG, *page 165*

Angora Beaded Hat, *page 176*

Silk Fountain Hood, *page 153*

Sarena Cashmere Cowl, *page 158*

SIOSTRA MOHAIR-WOOL HAT, *page 182*

ORGANIC COTTON BUNNIES, *page 168*

SOY BEANIE, *page 173*

LAOTIAN SILK NECKLACE WITH BEADS, *page 148*

SILK-CASHMERE DOMINOES, *page 180*

Bamboo Napkin Rings, *page 164*

Silk-Wool Horseshoe Lace Scarf, *page 152*

Merino-Silk Shrug for Baby, *page 151*

MERINO-SILK CABLES FOR BABY, page 174

CORN FIBER LACE BATH CLOTH, page 146

WISTERIA WAVES SILK-MERINO BEANIE, page 162

BEAUTIFUL BABY BAMBOO-MERINO SWEATER, *page 144*

SILK-MERINO DOLL SWEATER, *page 154*

ALPACA BROADWAY GLOVES, *page 142*

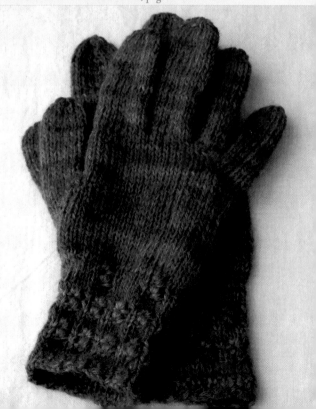

Cashmere Baby Leg Warmers, page 140

ANGORA BABY BUNNY CAP, page 149

Reversible Cable and Eyelet Wool-Silk Scarf, *page 159*   Ailish's Alpaca-Merino Crush Hat, *page 156*

Boise Cashmere Scarf, *page 141*

Baby's Cabled Milk-Silk Cap, *page 178*

Big-Kid Wool-Soy Mittens, *page 183*

RECLAIMED CASHMERE MITTENS, *page 234*

ARACHNE'S ALPACA LACE RING, *page 226*

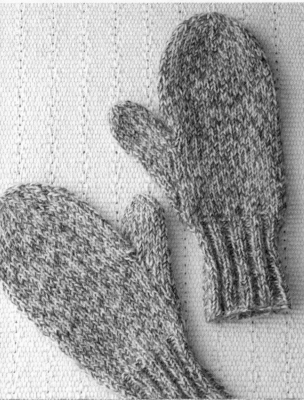

COOL LITTLE LLAMA-SILK MITTENS, *page 198*

Felted-Merino Treasure Cozy!, *page 215*

Reclaimed Cashmere Lacy Scarf, *page 224*

Merino-and-Glass Love Bag, page 197

Baby's Wool-Tencel Booties, page 222

Silk Berry Jewelry Bag, page 230

YAK NECK CUFF, *page 237*

STORMY CASHMERE PURSE, *page 190*

CASHMERE-SILK NECK CANDY, *page 202*

WINTER WINDOWS SILK SCARF, *page 192*

Elizabeth's Wool-Angora Diagonal Scarf, *page 217*

Lacy Leaf Alpaca-Angora Hat, *page 220*

Ruffled Merino-SeaCell Bias Scarf, *page 195*

Yak Hat, *page 194*

Inca-Dincadoo Organic Cotton Baby Cardigan, *page 204*

Lyra Wool-Soy Cabled Baby Bonnet, *page 201*

Seed Stitch Wool-Soy Hat, *page 223*

MOJITO ALPACA NECKTIE, *page 228*

PAMPER-YOURSELF SILK-LINEN SPA SET, *page 232*

LLAMA-WOOL SLIPPER SOCKS, *page 211*

Button-down Alpaca-Wool Hat, *page 236*

Flirty Merino-Silk Neck Warmer, *page 206*

Sueño Bamboo Spa Mask, *page 208*

CROSSROADS SOY-WOOL HAT, *page 207*

SILK DELIGHT SCARF, *page 218*

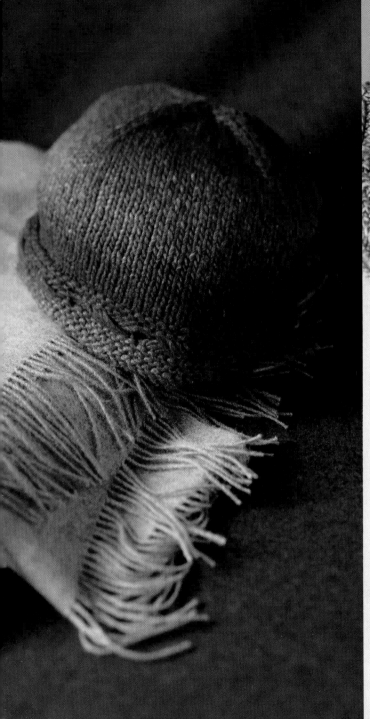

CASHMERE NECK WARMER, *page 203*

SEAMAN-STYLE CASHMERE SCARF, *page 213*

ANGORA AND PEARLS FOR SARAH, *page 199*

MERMAID ORGANIC BLEND NECK WARMER, *page 240*

HEIRLOOM MERINO-ALPACA BABY HAT, *page 245*

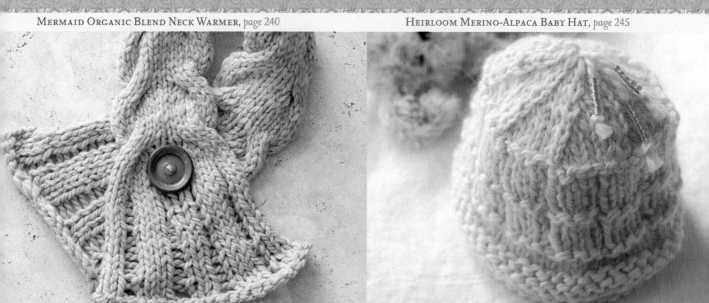

CROPPED ECOFRIENDLY VEST, *page 241*

LEAF BAND ALPACA-MERINO HAT, *page 246*

Joel Bison Lace Scarf

DESIGNED BY MYRNA A. I. STAHMAN, photo on page 11

This lovely scarf is knitted with Buffalo Gold yarn, and it is softer than soft. The lovely brown is a natural bison color and would perfectly complement your camel dress coat.

FINISHED MEASUREMENTS	Approximately 7" (18 cm) wide and 72" (183 cm) long
YARN	Buffalo Gold Lace Weight 11, 100% bison, 1.5 oz (40 g)/ 400 yds (366 m), Natural
NEEDLES	US 1 (2.5 mm) straight needles *or size you need to obtain correct gauge*
GAUGE	Not crucial to project, approximately 28 sts and 30 rows = 4" (10 cm) in pattern stitch, after blocking
OTHER SUPPLIES	Scrap yarn for cast-on, tapestry needle, lace blocking wires

Getting Started

❉ Using a provisional method (see page 265), cast on 45 stitches. Work the Set-up Row from the chart. You now have 49 stitches.

Knitting the Scarf

❉ Following the chart, repeat Rows 1–24 for desired length. (The scarf shown has 23 repeats.)

Finishing

❉ Bind off using the 3-stitch I-cord method (see page 266), working the final cable twist in each border while binding off and keeping the three-to-one vertical decrease in line with each three-to-one vertical decrease worked in Row 23 of final repeat before binding off those stitches. Carefully remove provisional cast-on and place stitches on needle. Bind off using the 3-stitch I-cord method.

❉ Weave in ends. Wash and block scarf using blocking wires.

Joel Bison Lace Scarf

☐ knit on RS rows, purl on WS rows

• purl on RS rows, knit on WS rows

○ yarn over

5 work the number of stitches, knit on RS rows, purl on WS rows

⬛ slip 2 stitches to cable needle and hold in front, K2, K2 from cable needle

⬛ slip 2 stitches to cable needle and hold in back, K2, K2 from cable needle

⋏ slip 2tog kwise, K1, p2sso

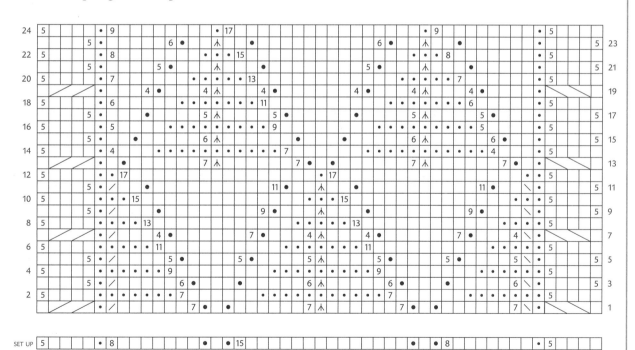

SWEET VIOLET SILK-CASHMERE SCARF

DESIGNED BY JOLENE TREACE, *photo on page 10*

The lace stitch used here is similar to the five petals of a violet. The scarf is knitted with a silk-and-cashmere blend and has an edging that is applied to the main body of the scarf as it is knitted.

FINISHED MEASUREMENTS	Approximately 6.5" (16.5 cm) wide and 62" (157.5 cm) long after blocking
YARN	Treenway Silks Silk/Cashmere, 80% silk/20% cashmere, 3.5 oz (100 g)/1662 yds (1520 m), Ecru
NEEDLES	US 2 (2.75 mm) straight needles, US 2 (2.75 mm) circular needle 24" (60 cm) long, and two US 2 (2.75 mm) double-point needles *or size you need to obtain correct gauge*
GAUGE	Approximately 18 stitches = 2" (5 cm) in lace, blocked
OTHER SUPPLIES	Tapestry needle

Knitting the Main Body

❋ With straight needles, cast on 29 stitches loosely. Note: Slip the first stitch of every row purlwise to create a chain stitch edge of 1 chain for every 2 rows. The first and last stitch of each row are *not* included on the chart; begin the chart after slipping the first stitch and knit the last stitch of each row after completing the charted row.

❋ Begin with Row 1 of Main Body chart and work the A section once, work the B section twice, and work the C section once. Continuing in this manner, repeat Rows 1–16 of the chart a total of 21 times, ending with Row 16. Work Rows 1–8 once more. You now have 172 chained stitches on each side.

Knitting the Edging

❋ Note: The edging will be attached to the main body as it is knit.

❋ With circular needle and working on the RS of the 29 main body stitches, M1, K29. Pick up and knit (see page 264) along the side of the scarf, increasing every fourth stitch as follows: *K into front loop of next 3 chain stitches, Kfb into next chain stitch; repeat from * to cast-on edge. You now have 245 stitches. M1, pick up 1 stitch for each cast-on stitch along the bottom of the scarf, then pick up along the second long side as for the first long side. You now have 490 stitches.

With RS of scarf still facing and using the same ball of yarn, cast on 5 stitches onto a double-point needle at the end of the pick-up round. Turn the work so the WS is facing you.

SET-UP ROW (WS): K4, K2tog (last edging stitch with first scarf stitch).

Note: The last edging stitch will always be worked together with 1 stitch from the edge of the scarf on even-numbered rows, with WS facing.

Turn the work and work Row 1 of Edging chart. Turn the work and work Row 2 of Edging chart, knitting the last stitch together with the next scarf stitch.

Continue in this manner until all picked-up stitches around the edge of the scarf have been worked, ending with Row 10 of Edging chart. Bind off remaining 5 edge stitches loosely.

Finishing

Sew the bind-off and cast-on ends of the edging together neatly. Weave in ends. Block.

Sweet Violet Silk-Cashmere Scarf

- ☐ knit on RS rows, purl on WS rows
- ⊡ purl on RS rows, knit on WS rows
- ⊙ yarn over
- ⊠ ssk
- ⊠ K2tog
- ⊠ slip 1, K2tog, psso
- ▨ no stitch
- Ⓐ attach edging to scarf
- Ⓢ slip
- ⊓ bind off

EDGING

MAIN BODY

C (end)   B (repeat)   A (begin)

Bison Shawlette
DESIGNED BY RENÉ E. WELLS, *photo on page 12*

Three triangles knitted simultaneously combine to make this lovely shaped "shawlette." It is light and airy, making it appropriate for any occasion in any weather. Who would have thought buffalo could be so versatile?

FINISHED MEASUREMENTS	Approximately 26" (66 cm) wide and 26" (66 cm) deep
YARN	Buffalo Gold Lace Weight 11, 100% bison, 1.5 oz (40 g)/ 400 yds (366 m), Natural
NEEDLES	US 6 (4 mm) straight needles *or size you need to obtain correct gauge*
GAUGE	25 stitches = 4" (10 cm) in stockinette stitch, 19 stitches = 4" (10 cm) in pattern
OTHER SUPPLIES	Scrap yarn for provisional cast-on, markers, tapestry needle

Knitting the Border

❊ Using a provisional method (see page 265), cast on 5 stitches. Knit 30 rows. Pick up and knit (see page 264) 15 stitches along the stitch band (pick up 1 stitch for every garter ridge). Remove provisional cast-on and knit the 5 stitches. You now have 25 stitches.

❊ SET-UP ROW: K5, place marker (pm), P5, pm, P5, pm, P5, pm, K5.

Beginning the Lace

❊ Note: Throughout the knitting, the first and last 5 stitches are knitted on both RS and WS rows, forming a garter stitch border. These stitches are not shown on the charts. Only RS rows are charted; except for the 5 border stitches at the beginning and end of every row, WS rows are purled.

❊ Work Rows 1–22 of Set-up chart, repeating the chart 3 times in each row. When you have completed the chart, you will have 93 stitches.

❊ Work Rows 1–16 of chart A 4 times.

❊ Work Rows 1–16 of chart B once.

❊ Work Rows 1–4 of chart C. Bind off loosely on WS, knitting all stitches.

Finishing

❊ Weave in ends. Hand wash gently in warm water and lay flat to dry.

Bison Shawlette

☐	knit on RS rows, purl on WS rows
⊙	yarn over
⟍	ssk
⟋	K2tog
⅄	slip 1, K2tog, psso
⋏	slip 2tog kwise, K1, p2sso

Chart C

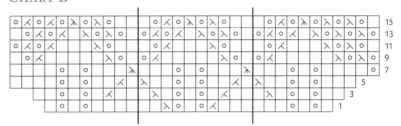

Chart B

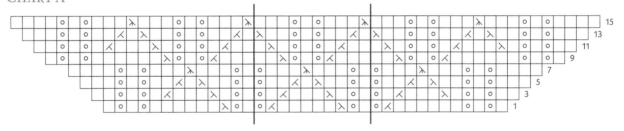

Chart A

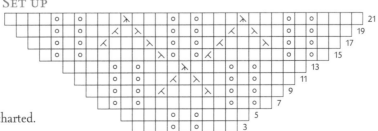

Set up

Note: Only RS rows are charted.
Purl all WS rows.

Nancy Pygora-Merino Lace Scarf

DESIGNED BY MYRNA A. I. STAHMAN, *photo on page 11*

This lovely lace scarf is knitted in a Pygora-merino blend. If you've ever seen a Pygora goat, you can imagine what this yarn feels like. The scarf begins and ends with a seed stitch border and has a six-stitch seed stitch border at each side.

FINISHED MEASUREMENTS	Approximately 8" (20.5 cm) wide and 65" (165 cm) long
YARN	Rainbow Yarns Northwest Laceweight, 70% Pygora/ 30% merino, 1.8 oz (80 g)/400 yds (366 m), Brown
NEEDLES	US 4 (3.5 mm) straight needles *or size you need to obtain correct gauge*
GAUGE	20 stitches = 4" (10 cm) in lace pattern, blocked
OTHER SUPPLIES	Tapestry needle, lace blocking wires

Knitting the Beginning Border

❋ Cast on 41 stitches.

❋ ROW 1: K2, *P1, K1; repeat from * to last stitch, K1.

❋ ROWS 2–6: Slip 1 pwise wyif, bring yarn to back between the needles, *K1, P1; repeat from * to last 2 stitches, K2.

Beginning the Lace Pattern

❋ Follow chart, working seed stitch border on first and last 6 stitches and lace on 29 center stitches. Repeat Rows 1–36 until scarf is desired length. (The scarf shown has 12 repeats.)

Knitting the Ending Border

❋ ROWS 1–6: Repeat Row 2 of beginning border.

Finishing

❋ Bind off in pattern. Weave in ends. Block, using lace dressing wires.

Nancy Pygora-Merino Lace Scarf

☐   knit

⊡   yarn over

⑤   knit the number of stitches

⟍   ssk

⟋   k2tog

⋏   slip 2tog kwise, K1, p2sso

6 seed-stitch border at beginning of each row as slip 1 pwise, (K1, P1) twice, K1, and at the end of each row as (K1, P1) twice, K2

Pattern (⟍ = ssk, ⟋ = k2tog, ⋏ = slip 2tog kwise K1 p2sso, o = yarn over)	Row
# ⟍ o 11 o ⋏ o 11 o ⟋ #	35
# ⟍ o o ⋏ o o ⟋ ⟍ o o ⋏ o o ⟋ #	33
# ⟍ o ⟍ o o ⟋ ⟍ o o ⟋ o ⋏ o ⟍ o o ⟋ ⟍ o o ⟋ o ⟍ o ⟋ #	31
# ⟍ o ⟍ o 5 o ⟋ o ⟍ o ⟋ ⟍ o ⟍ o 5 o ⟋ o ⟍ o ⟋ #	29
# ⟍ o ⟍ o ⟍ o o ⟋ o ⟍ o ⋏ o ⟋ o ⟍ o 5 o ⟋ o ⟋ o ⟋ #	27
# ⟍ o ⟍ o ⟍ o o ⟋ o ⟍ o ⟋ o ⟍ o ⟍ o ⟍ o o ⟋ o ⟍ o ⟋ o ⟍ o ⟋ #	25
# ⟍ o ⟍ o o ⟋ o ⟍ ⟍ o ⟍ o o ⟋ o ⟍ #	23
# o ⋏ o ⟍ o o ⟋ o ⋏ o o ⋏ o ⟍ o o ⟋ o ⋏ o #	21
# o ⟋ ⟍ o o ⟋ ⟍ o o ⟋ ⟍ o o ⟋ ⟍ o #	19
# 6 o ⋏ o 11 o ⋏ o 6 #	17
# ⟍ o o ⟋ ⟍ o o ⟋ o ⟍ #	15
# ⟍ o o ⟋ o ⋏ o ⟍ o o ⟋ o ⋏ o ⟍ o #	13
# o ⟋ o ⟋ ⟍ o ⟍ o o ⟋ o ⟋ ⟍ o ⟍ o #	11
# o ⟋ o ⟋ o ⋏ o ⟍ o ⟍ o o ⟋ o ⟋ o ⋏ o ⟍ o ⟍ o #	9
# o ⟋ o ⟋ o ⟋ ⟍ o ⟍ o ⟍ o o ⟋ o ⟋ o ⟋ ⟍ o ⟍ o ⟍ o #	7
# o ⟋ o ⟋ ⟍ o ⟍ o o ⟋ o ⟋ ⟍ o ⟍ o #	5
# o ⟋ o ⋏ o o ⋏ o ⟍ o o ⟋ o ⋏ o o ⋏ o ⟍ o #	3
# o ⟋ ⟍ o o ⟋ ⟍ o o ⟋ ⟍ o o ⟋ ⟍ o #	1

Note: Only RS rows are charted. Purl all WS rows.

CASHMERE BANGLES

DESIGNED BY JUDITH DURANT, *photo on page 11*

If you can imagine it, you can knit it! Worked in a yarn that is the height of luxury — a blend of cashmere and silk — this chic jewelry doubles as wrist warmers. One ball of this luscious yarn covers about 10 bangles.

FINISHED MEASUREMENTS	Approximately 2.5" (6.5 cm) interior diameter, 1.5" and 1" (4 and 2.5 cm) wide
YARN	Filatura De Crosa Superior, 70% cashmere/30% silk, 0.88 oz (25 g)/328 yds (300 m), 0010 Chartreuse
NEEDLES	Set of five US 0 (2 mm) double-point needles *or size you need to obtain correct gauge*
GAUGE	40 stitches = 4" (10 cm) in stockinette stitch
OTHER SUPPLIES	Cable needle, 64 size 10° seed beads, US 13 (0.85 mm) crochet hook, tapestry needle, plastic bangle bracelets as specified in Finished Measurements, above
ABBREVIATIONS	**C6F** slip 3 stitches to cable needle and hold in front, K3, K3 from cable needle **PBS** place bead and slip: pick up bead with crochet hook, remove next stitch from needle with hook, slide bead onto stitch, replace the stitch and slip it to the right needle

Knitting the Cabled Bangle

※ Cast on 80 stitches and divide onto 4 double-point needles so there are 16 stitches on needles 1, 2, and 3 and 32 stitches on needle 4. Join into a round, being careful not to twist the stitches.

※ Work Round 1 only of Simple Cable pattern until piece measures 1.25" (3 cm). Work Rounds 6–10 of Simple Cable pattern once, then work Rounds 1–10 twice. Bind off in pattern, leaving a 12" (30.5 cm) tail.

FINISHING

※ Thread the tail onto a tapestry needle. Wrap knitted piece around bangle and join the cast-on to the bind-off edge, stitch for stitch.

Knitting the Beaded Bangle

※ Cast on 80 stitches and divide evenly onto 4 double-point needles. Join into a round, being careful not to twist the stitches.

STITCH PATTERNS

simple cable

ROUNDS 1–5: *K6, P2; repeat from *.

ROUND 6: *C6F, P2; repeat from *.

ROUNDS 7–10: Repeat Round 1.

REPEAT ROUNDS 1–10 FOR PATTERN.

beaded rib

ROUNDS 1–3: K3, P2; repeat from *.

ROUND 4: *K1, PBS, K1, P2; repeat from *.

REPEAT ROUNDS 1–4 FOR PATTERN.

❄ Work Round 1 only of Beaded Rib pattern until piece measures 0.75" (2 cm). Work Round 4 of Beaded Rib pattern once, then work Rounds 1–4 three times and then work Rounds 1–3 once more. Bind off in pattern, leaving a 12" (30.5 cm) tail.

FINISHING

❄ Finish as for Cabled Bangle.

VICUÑA SCARF

DESIGNED BY MARY MCGURN, photo on page 10

The vicuña is a relative of the llama and the alpaca, residing exclusively in South America. Vicuñas produce extremely fine wool; it is softer and warmer than that from any other animal, having a diameter that is less than half that of the finest sheep's wool. Because the vicuña produces only about 1 pound of wool per year, among other reasons, the yarn is very expensive. So here's a small and simple scarf that can be knit with just 1 ounce. But the pattern's reversible, so you get double the pleasure.

FINISHED MEASUREMENTS	Approximately 4.5" (11.5 cm) wide and 28" (71 cm) long
YARN	Jacques Cartier Vicuna, 100% vicuna, 1 oz (28.5 g)/217 yds (198 m), Natural
NEEDLES	US 4 (3.5 mm) straight needles *or size you need to obtain correct gauge*
GAUGE	45 stitches = 4" (10 cm) in pattern stitch
OTHER SUPPLIES	Tapestry needle

STITCH PATTERN
slip-stitch rib

ROW 1: K3, *slip 1 wyif, K3; repeat from * to end of row.

ROW 2: K1, *slip 1 wyif, K3; repeat from * to last 2 stitches, slip 1 wyif, K1.

REPEAT ROWS 1 AND 2 FOR PATTERN.

Knitting the Scarf

❄ Cast on 51 stitches.

❄ Work Rows 1 and 2 of Slip-Stitch Rib pattern until you have only enough yarn to bind off (approximately 20" [51 cm]). Bind off in pattern.

Finishing

❄ Weave in ends. Block lightly with steam.

WOOL AND CAMEL-DOWN RIPPLE SCARF

DESIGNED BY MARLAINE DESCHAMPS, *photo on page 14*

A luxurious blend of wool and camel down is used for this scarf with a ripple pattern. The yarn is light, lofty, and warm, and the colors are beautiful.

FINISHED MEASUREMENTS	Approximately 6" (15 cm) wide and 68" (173 cm) long
YARN	Just Our Yarn Caravan, 65% wool/35% camel down, 2 oz (57 g)/300 yds (274 m), Color CW07W-22
NEEDLES	US 6 (4 mm) straight needles *or size you need to obtain correct gauge*
GAUGE	20 stitches = 4" (10 cm) in garter stitch
OTHER SUPPLIES	Tapestry needle

Knitting the Scarf

❀ Cast on 40 stitches.

❀ ROW 1: K1, *K2tog, K7, yo, K1, yo, K7, K2tog; repeat from * to last stitch, K1.

❀ ROW 2: Knit.

❀ Repeat Rows 1 and 2 until piece measures 68" (173 cm), ending with Row 1. Bind off in pattern.

Finishing

❀ Weave in ends. Wet scarf and lay flat to finished measurements. When scarf is nearly dry, put in cool dryer for 15 minutes to fluff the camel down. Finish drying flat.

TOP-DOWN ALPACA MITTS
DESIGNED BY ANN MCCLURE, photo on page 14

These lovely mitts are about as feminine as they come. Knitted with a blend of alpaca, silk, and cashmere, they feature a lace and cable pattern on the back of the hand, and a rib and cable on the palm. The cuff has smocking and ends with a ruffle.

FINISHED MEASUREMENTS	Approximately 8" (20.5 cm) circumference
YARN	Knit One Crochet Two Ambrosia, 70% baby alpaca/20% silk/10% cashmere, 1.75 oz (50 g)/137 yds (125 m), 767 Purple Heather
NEEDLES	Set of four US 2 (2.75 mm) double-point needles *or size you need to obtain correct gauge*
GAUGE	28 stitches = 4" (10 cm) in stockinette stitch
OTHER SUPPLIES	Cable needle, scrap yarn for holders and cast-on, size E/4 (3.5 mm) crochet hook
ABBREVIATIONS	**C4B (cable 4 back)** place next 2 stitches on cable needle and hold in back, K2, K2 from cable needle **C4F (cable 4 front)** place next 2 stitches on cable needle and hold in front, K2, K2 from cable needle

STITCH PATTERNS
lace and cable

ROUND 1: P2, K5, yo, K2tog tbl, K3, K2tog, yo, K5, P2.

ROUND 2: P2, K4, P1, K7, P1, K4, P2.

ROUND 3: P2, K6, yo, K2tog tbl, K1, K2tog, yo, K6, P2.

ROUND 4: Repeat Round 2.

ROUND 5: P2, C4F, K3, yo, sl 1, K2tog, psso, yo, K3, C4B, P2.

ROUND 6: Repeat Round 2.

ROUND 7: P2, K17, P2.

ROUND 8: Repeat Round 2.

REPEAT ROUNDS 1–8 FOR PATTERN.

wrap 3

With yarn in back, slip 3 stitches purlwise, bring yarn to front, slip 3 stitches back to left needle, bring yarn to back, slip 3 stitches to right needle again.

Knitting the Right Mitt

※ Cast on 45 stitches. Place 21 stitches on needle 1, 12 stitches on needle 2, and 12 stitches on needle 3. Join into a round, being careful not to twist the stitches.

※ ROUND 1: P2, K4, P2, K5, P2, K4, P2, K3, P3, K3, P1, K4, P1, K3, P3, K3.

※ ROUNDS 2–6: Repeat Round 1.

※ ROUND 7: Work 31 stitches in pattern as established, C4B (palm cable; C4F for left mitt), P1, K3, P3, K3.

※ ROUNDS 8–10: Repeat Round 1.

BEGINNING LACE AND CABLE PATTERN

※ ROUNDS 11–14: Work Rounds 1–4 of Lace and Cable pattern on needle 1 (back-of-hand stitches), continue in pattern as established on needles 2 and 3 (palm stitches). (For pattern, see box above left and chart, page 64.)

※ ROUND 15: Work Round 5 of Lace and Cable pattern on needle 1, continue in pattern as established on needles 2 and 3, remembering to C4B (C4F on left mitt) over the 4 knit stitches as before.

TOP-DOWN ALPACA MITTS *continued*

Top-down Alpaca Mitts

·	purl
	knit
○	yarn over
⟍	K2tog tbl
⟋	K2tog
⅄	slip 1, K2tog, psso
⟋⟍	C4F
⟍⟋	C4B
⬭	wrap 3

LACE AND CABLE

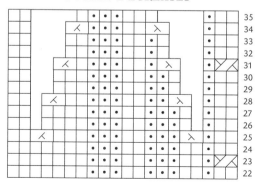

SMOCKING

THUMB GUSSET DECREASES

❋ ROUNDS 16–20: Work Rounds 6–8, then Rounds 1 and 2 of Lace and Cable pattern on needle 1, continue in pattern as established on needles 2 and 3.

KNITTING THE THUMB GUSSET

❋ With scrap yarn and crochet hook, chain 20 and fasten off for provisional cast-on (see page 265). Set aside until Round 22.

❋ Continue in pattern as established on needles 1 and 2 (back-of-hand and half the palm stitches), remembering to C4B (C4F on left mitt) as established every 8th round, and work stitches on needle 3 as follows:

❋ ROUND 21 (NEEDLE 3): K2, P1, K3, P3, K1, place last 5 stitches worked on a holder, K2.

❋ ROUND 22 (NEEDLE 3): K2, P1, K2, pick up 13 stitches from the crochet chain, K2. You now have 21 stitches on needle 1, 12 stitches on needle 2, and 20 stitches on needle 3.

❋ ROUND 23 (NEEDLE 3): Work first 2 stitches in the C4B (C4F on left mitt) with last 2 stitches of needle 2, P1, K2, P3, K2, P3, K7.

❋ ROUND 24: Work in pattern as established.

❋ ROUND 25 (NEEDLE 3): K2, P1, K2tog tbl, P3, K2, P3, K3, K2tog, K2. You now have 18 stitches on needle 3.

❋ ROUNDS 26 AND 27: Work in pattern as established.

❋ ROUND 28 (NEEDLE 3): K2, P1, K2tog tbl, P2, K2, P3, K2, K2tog, K2. You now have 16 stitches on needle 3.

❋ ROUNDS 29 AND 30: Work in pattern as established.

❋ ROUND 31 (NEEDLE 3): K2, P1, K2tog tbl, P1, K2, P3, K1, K2tog, K2. You now have 14 stitches on needle 3.

❋ ROUNDS 32 AND 33: Work in pattern as established.

❋ ROUND 34 (NEEDLE 3): K2, P1, K2tog tbl, K2, P3, K2tog, K2. You now have 12 stitches on needle 3 and 45 total stitches.

❋ ROUND 35 (NEEDLE 3): K2, P1, K3, P3, K3.

❋ ROUNDS 36–42: Work all stitches on all needles in patterns as established: 4 repeats of Lace and Cable pattern completed.

KNITTING THE CUFF

❋ ROUND 1: *P1, K1; repeat from * to last 3 stitches, P1, K2tog. You now have 44 stitches.

❋ ROUND 2: *P1, K1; repeat from *.

❋ ROUND 3: *P1, work. Wrap 3 pattern (see page 63); repeat from *.

❋ ROUNDS 4–6: Repeat Round 2.

Top-down Alpaca Mitts *continued*

* **ROUND 7:** P1, K1, *P1, work. Wrap 3 pattern (see page 63); repeat from * to last 2 stitches, P1, use last stitch of round and first 2 stitches of next round to complete final Wrap 3. Do not change starting point of rounds; just continue with following round from this point.
* **ROUNDS 8–10:** Repeat Round 2.
* **ROUND 11:** Repeat Round 3.
* **ROUNDS 12–14:** Repeat Round 2.
* **ROUND 15:** Repeat Round 7.
* **ROUNDS 16–19:** Repeat Round 2.
* **ROUND 20:** *Pfb, Kfb; repeat from *. You now have 88 stitches.
* **ROUNDS 21–22:** Knit.
* Bind off.

Knitting the Thumb

* Pick up and knit (see page 264) 13 stitches from crochet chain, removing scrap yarn. Pick up 5 stitches from holder, and pick up 1 extra stitch on the palm and 2 extra stitches on the back of hand as needed to close the gaps. You now have 21 stitches.
* Work 6 rounds in pattern as established.
* Bind off.

Knitting the Left Mitt

* Work as for right mitt through Round 20.
* **ROUND 21 (NEEDLE 2):** K3, P3, K1, place last 5 stitches worked on a holder, K2, P1, K2.
* **ROUND 22 (NEEDLE 2):** K2, pick up 13 stitches from crochet chain as for right mitt, K2, P1, K2.
* Continue as for right mitt, reversing shaping.

Finishing

* Weave in ends. Block.

ALPACA-AND-SILK BABY CAP

DESIGNED BY EDIE ECKMAN, *photo on page 15*

Alpaca and silk, perfect together in this adorable crocheted cap for baby. This is one that should be worn for generations to come.

SIZES AND FINISHED MEASUREMENTS	To fit an infant, approximately 14" (35.5 cm) circumference
YARN	Plymouth Yarn/Bristol Yarn Gallery Buckingham, 80% baby alpaca/20% silk, 1.75 oz (50 g)/218 yds (199 m), 100 Natural
CROCHET HOOK	US D/3 (3.25 mm) *or size you need to obtain correct gauge*
GAUGE	24 stitches = 4" (10 cm) in double crochet
OTHER SUPPLIES	Tapestry needle
ABBREVIATIONS	**dc2tog** double crochet 2 together: yarn over, insert hook into next space and pull up a loop, yarn over, pull through 2 loops, yarn over, insert hook into same space and pull up a loop, yarn over, pull through 2 loops, yarn over, and pull through all 3 loops on hook **dc3tog** double crochet 3 together: yarn over, insert hook into next space and pull up a loop, yarn over, pull through 2 loops, (yarn over, insert hook into same space and pull up a loop, yarn over, pull through 2 loops) 2 times, yarn over, and pull through all 4 loops on hook

Crocheting the Hat

❋ ROUND 1: Ch 4, 11 dc in fourth chain from hook, join with a slip stitch to top of ch-4. You now have 12 dc.

❋ ROUND 2: Ch 6 (counts as dc and ch-3), *dc in next dc, ch 3; repeat from * around, join with a slip stitch to third chain of ch-6.

❋ ROUND 3: Ch 3, dc2tog in first ch-3 space, ch 4, *dc3tog in next ch-3 space, ch 5; repeat from * around, join with a slip stitch to top of ch-3, slip stitch in next ch-5 space.

❋ ROUND 4: Ch 3 (counts as dc) 6 dc in same space, (7 dc in next ch-5 space) around, join with a slip stitch to top of ch-3.

❋ ROUND 5: *Ch 7, sc between next two 7-dc groups; repeat from * around, ending with last sc between last 7-dc group and ch-3, ch 1.

❋ ROUND 6: 9 sc in each ch-7 space around, join with a slip stitch to first sc.

❋ ROUND 7: Ch 6 (counts as dc and ch-3), *skip 4 sc, sc in next sc, ch 3, skip 4 sc**, dc between last sc and next sc (between the sc-9 groups), ch 3; repeat from * around, ending last repeat at **, join with a slip stitch to third chain of ch-6, ch 1.

ALPACA-AND-SILK BABY CAP *continued*

- ❊ ROUND 8: 3 sc in next ch-3 space, ch 1, *skip 1 st, 3 sc in next ch-3 space, ch 1; repeat from * around, join with a slip stitch to first sc.
- ❊ ROUND 9: Ch 6 (counts as dc and ch-3), *dc in next ch-1 space, ch 3; repeat from * around, join with a slip stitch to ch-3, ch 1.
- ❊ ROUND 10: *3 sc in next ch-3 space, ch 1; repeat from * around, join with a slip stitch to first sc.
- ❊ ROUND 11: Ch 3 (counts as dc), dc in next 2 sc, ch 1, *dc in next 3 sc, ch 1; repeat from * around, join with a slip stitch to top of ch-3.
- ❊ ROUND 12: Ch 6 (counts as dc and ch-3), *dc in next ch-1 space, ch 3; repeat from * around, join with a slip stitch to third chain of ch-6, slip stitch in next ch-3 space.
- ❊ ROUND 13: Ch 3 (counts as dc), 2 dc in next ch-3 space, ch 1, *3 dc in next ch-3 space, ch 1; repeat from * around, join with a slip stitch to top of ch-3.
- ❊ ROUNDS 14–17: Repeat Rounds 12 and 13 twice.
- ❊ ROUND 18: *Ch 6, sc in next ch-1 space; repeat from * around, join with slip stitch to first chain.
- ❊ ROUND 19: 7 sc in each ch-6 space around, join with slip stitch to first sc.

Finishing

- ❊ Cut yarn and pull through last stitch. Weave in ends.

Silk-Merino Twisted Gloves

DESIGNED BY LAURA NELKIN, *photo on page 16*

If you've resisted knitting gloves because of the effort it takes, resist no more. These are too lovely to pass by. Once you get the hang of it, you'll want to knit them for everyone. Included are instructions for three sizes.

STITCH PATTERN
mock cable ribbing

ROUND 1: *K2, P2; repeat from *.

ROUND 2: *K2tog and leave stitches on left needle, knit first stitch again, drop both stitches from needle, P2; repeat from *.

ROUNDS 3 AND 4: Repeat Round 1.

WORK ROUNDS 1–4 FOR PATTERN.

SIZES AND FINISHED MEASUREMENTS	To fit adult small (medium, large), approximately 7" (7.5", 8") (18 [19, 20.5] cm) palm circumference
YARN	Schaefer Yarn Company Heather, 55% superwash merino/ 30% silk/15% nylon, 4 oz (113 g)/400 yds (366 m), Burgundy
NEEDLES	Sets of five US 2 (2.75 mm) double-point needles and US 1 (2.25 mm) double-point needles *or size you need to obtain correct gauge*
GAUGE	29 stitches and 40 rows = 4" (10 cm) in stockinette stitch on larger needles
OTHER SUPPLIES	Stitch markers (one color A, two color B), cable needle, scrap yarn for holders, tapestry needle
ABBREVIATIONS	**C4B (cable 4 back)** slip 2 stitches to cable needle and hold in front, K2, K2 from cable needle **C4F (cable 4 front)** slip 2 stitches to cable needle and hold in back, K2, K2 from cable needle **T3B (twist 3 back)** slip 1 stitch onto cable needle and hold in back, K2, P1 from cable needle **T3F (twist 3 front)** slip 2 stitches onto cable needle and hold in front, P1, K2 from cable needle

Knitting the Cuff

❋ With smaller needles cast on 52 (56, 60) stitches. Place marker A and join into a round, being careful not to the twist the stitches. Work Mock Cable Ribbing until piece measures 3.5" (4", 4.5") (9 [10, 11.5] cm), ending with Round 1, 3, or 4.

Knitting the Right Glove

❋ Knit 1 round, dividing stitches as follows:
  ❋ NEEDLE 1: 14 (15, 16) back-of-hand stitches.
  ❋ NEEDLE 2: 14 (15, 16) back-of-hand stitches.
  ❋ NEEDLE 3: 4 palm stitches.
  ❋ NEEDLE 4: 20 (22, 24) palm stitches.

SILK-MERINO TWISTED GLOVES *continued*

SHAPING THE THUMB GUSSET AND KNITTING THE CABLE

❉ Increase for thumb gusset as directed below, and at the same time begin chart (page 71) on Round 3 (4, 6).

❉ ROUND 1: K28 (30, 32) pm B, M1L, K1, M1R, pm B, knit to end of round. You now have 54 (58, 62) stitches.

❉ ROUND 2: Knit.

❉ ROUND 3 (BEGIN CABLE FOR SMALL SIZE): K0 (30, 32), work chart over next 28 (0, 0) stitches, sm, M1L, knit to next marker, M1R, sm, knit to end of round.

❉ ROUND 4 (BEGIN CABLE FOR MEDIUM SIZE): K0 (1, 32), work chart over next 28 (28, 0) stitches, K0 (1, 0), knit to end of round.

❉ ROUND 5: For sizes S and M, continue established pattern and knit remaining stitches; for size L, knit all stitches.

❉ ROUND 6 (BEGIN CABLE FOR LARGE SIZE): K0 (1, 2), work chart over next 28 stitches, K0 (1, 2), knit to end of round.

❉ ROUND 7: K0 (1, 2), work chart over next 28 stitches, K0 (1, 2), sm, M1L, knit to next marker, M1R, sm, knit to end of round.

❉ ROUNDS 8–10: K0 (1, 2), work chart over next 28 stitches, knit to end of round.

❉ Repeat Rounds 7–10 three (four, five) times more, then work Round 7 once more, continuing to work chart on back-of-hand stitches with 0 (1, 2) stitches in stockinette on each side of chart. You now have 15 (17, 19) thumb gusset stitches between B markers.

❉ NEXT ROUND: Work in established patterns to first gusset marker, place thumb gusset stitches onto a length of scrap yarn, remove gusset markers, cast on 1 stitch over gap left by gusset and knit to end of round. Redistribute palm stitches evenly onto needles 3 and 4. You now have 52 (56, 60) stitches, 14 (15, 16) stitches each on all 4 needles.

❉ Continue to work chart until complete, knitting all palm stitches.

❉ Work even in stockinette stitch until piece measures 3.25" (3.75", 4.25") (8.5 [9.5, 11] cm) from end of cuff. Remove beginning-of-round marker. Go to Knitting the Fingers on page 72 and work according to right glove directions.

Knitting the Left Glove

❉ Work cuff as for right glove.

❉ Knit 1 round, dividing stitches as follows:

❉ NEEDLE 1: 20 (22, 24) palm stitches.

❉ NEEDLE 2: 4 palm stitches.

❉ NEEDLE 3: 14 (15, 16) back-of-hand stitches.

❉ NEEDLE 4: 14 (15, 16) back-of-hand stitches.

Silk-Merino Twisted Gloves

☐	knit
·	purl
	T3B
	T3F
	C4B
	C4F

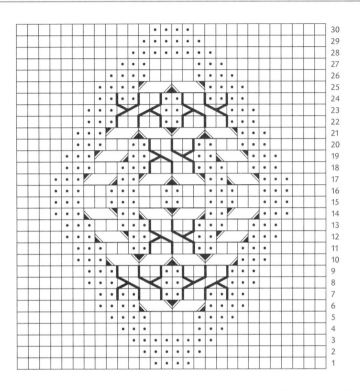

SHAPING THE THUMB GUSSET AND KNITTING THE CABLE

✢ Increase for thumb gusset as directed below, and at the same time begin chart above on Round 3 (4, 6).

✢ ROUND 1: K24 (26, 28) pm B, M1L, K1, M1R, pm B, knit to end of round. You now have 54 (58, 62) stitches.

✢ ROUND 2: Knit.

✢ ROUND 3 (BEGIN CABLE FOR SMALL SIZE): K24 (26, 28), sm, M1L, knit to next marker, M1R, sm K0 (30, 32), work chart over next 28 (0,0) stitches.

✢ ROUND 4 (BEGIN CABLE FOR MEDIUM SIZE): Knit to last 28 (30, 32) stitches, K0 (1, 32) work chart over next 28 (28, 0) stitches, K0 (1, 0).

✢ ROUND 5: For sizes S and M, continue established cable pattern and knit remaining stitches; for size L, knit all stitches.

✢ ROUND 6 (BEGIN CABLE FOR LARGE SIZE): Knit to last 28 (30, 32) stitches, K0 (1, 2), work chart over next 28 stitches, K0 (1, 2).

✢ ROUNDS 8–10: Knit to last 28 (30, 32) stitches, K0 (1, 2), work chart over next 28 stitches, K0 (1, 2).

SILK-MERINO TWISTED GLOVES *continued*

❉ Repeat Rounds 7–10 three (four, five) times more, then work Round 7 once more, continuing to work chart on back-of-hand stitches with 0 (1, 2) stitches in stockinette on each side of chart. You now have 15 (17, 19) thumb gusset stitches between B markers.

❉ NEXT ROUND: Knit to thumb gusset, place thumb gusset stitches on holder, remove gusset markers, cast on 1 stitch over gap left by gusset and work in established patterns to end of round. Redistribute palm stitches evenly onto needles 1 and 2. You now have 52 (56, 60) stitches, 14 (15, 16) stitches each on all 4 needles.

❉ Continue to work chart until complete, knitting all palm stitches.

❉ Work even in stockinette stitch until piece measures 3.25" (3.75", 4.25") (8.5 [9.5, 11] cm) from end of cuff. Remove beginning-of-round marker.

Knitting the Fingers

❉ Note: It helps to try on the glove as you work and adjust the finger length to fit the wearer's hand.

KNITTING THE LITTLE FINGER

❉ Right Glove: K6 (7, 8), place next 42 (45, 48) stitches on holder, cast on 3 stitches over gap, knit remaining 4 stitches, and join into a round. You now have 13 (14, 15) stitches.

❉ Left Glove: K4, place next 42 (45, 48) stitches on holder, cast on 3 stitches over gap, knit remaining 6 (7, 8) stitches, and join into a round. You now have 13 (14, 15) stitches.

❉ Both Gloves: Distribute stitches as evenly as possible on 3 double-point needles. Knit 21 (23, 25) rounds even or to desired length.

❉ Top of Finger: *K2tog; repeat from * to last 3 (0, 3) stitches, k3tog 1 (0, 1) time. Cut yarn, leaving a 4" (10 cm) tail. Thread tail onto tapestry needle and draw through remaining stitches. Pull up snug and fasten off.

SETTING UP FOR REMAINING FINGERS

❉ ROUND 1: Put held stitches back on needles, join yarn to beginning of cast-on stitches at base of pinky finger, leaving a long tail. Pick up and knit (see page 264) 4 tbl along cast-on edge of pinky finger; knit to end of round.

❉ ROUND 2: *K2tog twice, knit to end of round.

❉ ROUND 3: Knit. You now have 44 (47, 50) stitches.

KNITTING THE RING FINGER

❉ Right Glove: K8 (9, 10), place next 29 (31, 33) stitches on holder, cast on 1 over gap, K7. You now have 16 (17, 18) stitches.

* Left Glove: K9, place next 29 (31, 33) stitches on holder, cast on 1 over gap, K6 (7, 8) from holder. You now have 16 (17, 18) stitches.
* Both Gloves: Divide stitches as evenly as possible on 3 double-point needles. Knit 23 (26, 30) rounds even or to desired length. *K2tog; repeat from * to last 0 (3, 0) stitches, k3tog 0 (1, 0) time.

Knitting the Middle Finger

* Join yarn to beginning of cast-on stitches at base of ring finger, leaving a long tail.
* ROUND 1: Pick up and knit (see page 264) 3 tbl along cast-on edge of ring finger, K8 (9, 9) from holder, leave next 14 (15, 16) stitches on holder, cast on 1 stitch over gap, K7 (7, 8) from holder.
* Divide stitches as evenly as possible on 3 double-point needles.
* ROUND 2: K2tog twice, knit to end of round. You now have 17 (18, 19) stitches.
* Knit 26 rounds even or to desired length. Finish as for little finger (see page 72).

Knitting the Index Finger

* Join yarn to beginning of cast-on stitches at base of middle finger, leaving a long tail.
* ROUND 1: Pick up and knit 3 tbl along cast-on edge of middle finger, k14 (15, 16) from holder, join into a round. Divide stitches as evenly as possible on 3 double-point needles.
* ROUND 2: K2tog, knit to end of round. You now have 16 (17, 18) stitches.
* Knit 23 (25, 27) rounds even or to desired length. Finish as for ring finger (see page 72).

Knitting the Thumb

* Join yarn to beginning of stitch cast on over top of thumb gap, leaving a long tail.
* ROUND 1: Place the 15 (17, 19) held thumb gusset stitches onto double-point needles and pick up and knit 3 tbl from base of cast-on stitch, join into a round. Divide stitches as evenly as possible on 3 double-point needles.
* ROUND 2: K2tog, knit to end of round. You now have 17 (19, 21) stitches.
* Knit 19 (21, 23) rounds even or to desired length. *K2tog; repeat from * to last 3 sts, k3tog.

Finishing

* Weave in all loose ends, using tails to close gaps at base of thumb and fingers. Block if desired.

Baby's Bamboo Singlet

DESIGNED BY GITTA SCHRADE, *photo on page 17*

Bamboo is a wonderfully silky fiber that is very elastic when knit up, making it ideal for baby clothes. This singlet is designed with snaps at the shoulders for ease of dressing.

SIZES AND FINISHED MEASUREMENTS	To fit infant 0–3 months, approximately 16" (41 cm) chest circumference and 8" (20.5 cm) length
YARN	Fiber Trends Naturally Stella, 100% bamboo, 1.75 oz (50 g)/ 191 yds (175 m), Color 430
NEEDLES	US 3 (3.25 mm) and US 2 (2.5 mm) straight needles *or size you need to obtain correct gauge*
GAUGE	28 stitches and 36 rows = 4" (10 cm) in stockinette stitch on larger needles
OTHER SUPPLIES	Scrap yarn for holders, tapestry needle, four sets of snap fasteners, sewing needle and coordinating sewing thread, 3 mm crochet hook for flower (optional)

Knitting the Back

❊ With smaller needles, cast on 55 stitches. Work seed stitch for 8 rows.

❊ Change to larger needles and work stockinette stitch until piece measures 5" (12.5 cm) from beginning, ending with a WS row.

Shaping the Armholes

❊ ROW 1 (RS): (K1, P1) twice, sl 1, K1, psso, knit to last 6 stitches, K2tog, (P1, K1) twice.

❊ ROW 2: (K1, P1) twice, purl to last 4 stitches, (P1, K1) twice.

❊ Repeat Rows 1 and 2 five more times. You now have 43 stitches.

❊ Work even in pattern as established until piece measures 7" (18 cm) from beginning, ending with a WS row.

Shaping the Neck

❊ ROW 1 (RS): (K1, P1) twice, K12, (K1, P1) 5 times, K1; K12, (P1, K1) twice.

❊ ROW 2: (K1, P1) twice, P12, (K1, P1) 5 times, K1; P12, (P1, K1) twice.

❊ ROW 3: (K1, P1) twice, K7, K2tog, (P1, K1) 8 times, P1, sl 1, K1, psso, K7, (P1, K1) twice.

STITCH PATTERN

seed stitch

(WORKED ON AN ODD NUMBER OF STITCHES)

ROW 1: *K1, P1; repeat from * to last stitch, K1.

REPEAT ROW 1 FOR PATTERN.

The alternate, multicolored version shown on page 17 was knit with a variegated sock yarn using a technique developed by Margaret Radcliffe (see page 255): Each time the color green appeared in the variegation, the stitches were purled on the right side and knit on the wrong side, creating a lively textural effect.

❋ ROW 4: (K1, P1) twice, P8, (P1, K1) 8 times, P1; P8, (P1, K1) twice.

❋ ROW 5: (K1, P1) twice, K6, K2tog, (P1, K1) twice; place remaining 25 stitches on a holder.

KNITTING THE RIGHT SHOULDER

❋ ROW 1 (WS): (K1, P1) twice, P7, (P1, K1) twice.

❋ ROW 2: (K1, P1) twice, K5, K2tog, (P1, K1) twice.

❋ ROW 3: (K1, P1) twice, P6, (P1, K1) twice.

❋ ROW 4: (K1, P1) twice, K4, K2tog, (P1, K1) twice.

❋ ROW 5: (K1, P1) twice, P5, (P1, K1) twice.

❋ Continue in this manner, decreasing 1 stitch on RS rows and working WS rows even 2 more times, ending with a WS row. You now have 11 stitches.

❋ Work 4 rows even in seed stitch. Bind off in pattern.

KNITTING THE LEFT SHOULDER

❋ Place 25 held stitches on needles. With RS facing, join yarn and bind off 9 back neck stitches in pattern (stitch left after binding off counts as K1), P1, K1, P1, sl 1, K1, psso, K6, (P1, K1) twice.

❋ ROW 1 (WS): (K1, P1) twice, P7, (P1, K1) twice.

❋ ROW 2: (K1, P1) twice, sl 1, K1, psso, K5, (P1, K1) twice.

❋ ROW 3: (K1, P1) twice, P6, (P1, K1) twice.

❋ Continue in this manner, decreasing 1 stitch on RS rows and working WS rows even 3 more times, ending with a WS row. You now have 11 stitches.

❋ Work 4 rows even in seed stitch. Bind off in pattern.

Knitting the Front

❋ Work as for back to 4 rows before first neck-shaping row, ending with a WS row.

SHAPING THE NECK

❋ ROW 1 (RS): (K1, P1) twice, K14; (P1, K1) 3 times, P1; K14, (P1, K1) twice.

❋ ROW 2: (K1, P1) twice, P14; (P1, K1) 3 times, P1; P14, (P1, K1) twice.

❋ ROW 3: (K1, P1) twice, K8, K2tog; (P1, K1) 7 times, P1; sl 1, K1, psso, K8, (P1, K1) twice.

❋ ROW 4: (K1, P1) twice, P9; (P1, K1) 7 times, P1; P9, (P1, K1) twice.

❋ ROW 5: (K1, P1) twice, K7, K2tog; (P1, K1) twice; place remaining 24 stitches on a holder.

BABY'S BAMBOO SINGLET *continued*

KNITTING THE LEFT SHOULDER

❋ ROW 1 (WS): (K1, P1) twice, P8, (P1, K1) twice.

❋ ROW 2: (K1, P1) twice, K6, K2tog, (P1, K1) twice.

❋ ROW 3: (K1, P1) twice, P7, (P1, K1) twice.

❋ Continue in this manner, decreasing 1 stitch on RS rows and working WS rows even 4 more times, ending with a WS row. You now have 11 stitches.

❋ Work even in pattern for 2 more rows, then work 4 rows even in seed stitch. Bind off in pattern.

KNITTING THE RIGHT SHOULDER

❋ Place held stitches on needles. With RS facing, join yarn, bind off 7 stitches in pattern (stitch left after binding off counts as K1), P1, K1, P1, sl 1, K1, psso, K7, (P1, K1) twice.

❋ ROW 1 (WS): (K1, P1) twice, P8, (P1, K1) twice.

❋ ROW 2: (K1, P1) twice, sl 1, K1, psso, K6, (P1, K1) twice.

❋ ROW 3: (K1, P1) twice, P7, (P1, K1) twice.

❋ Continue in this manner, decreasing 1 stitch on RS rows and working WS rows even 4 more times, ending with a WS row. You now have 11 stitches.

❋ Work even in pattern for 2 more rows, then work 4 rows even in seed stitch. Bind off in pattern.

Finishing

❋ Sew side seams. Weave in ends.

❋ Sew two sets of snap fasteners to each shoulder, overlapping front over back.

CROCHETING THE FLOWER (OPTIONAL)

❋ Ch 5, join with a slip stitch to form a ring.

❋ *Work 1 sc, 2 ch, 2 dc, 2 ch into ring; repeat from * 4 more times. Join with slip stitch to first sc. Weave in ends.

❋ Sew flower to center front as shown in photo (see page 17).

Stella Bamboo Lace Scarf

DESIGNED BY BEV GALESKAS, *photo on page 18*

Bamboo is a wonderfully soft fiber that is made from an easily sustainable fiber. What could be better than ecofriendly luxury?

FINISHED MEASUREMENTS	Approximately 5" (12.5 cm) wide and 46" (117 cm) long
YARN	Naturally Yarns Stella, 100% bamboo, 1.75 oz (50 g)/191 yds (175 m), 428 Yellow
NEEDLES	US 8 (5 mm) straight needles *or size you need to obtain correct gauge*
GAUGE	24 stitches = 4" (10 cm) in stockinette stitch
OTHER SUPPLIES	Tapestry needle

Knitting the Border

* Loosely cast on 35 stitches.
* ROWS 1–5: Slip 1 wyif, knit to end of row.

Knitting the Lace

* ROW 1: Slip 1 wyif, K4, (yo, K2, ssk, K2tog, K2, yo, K1) 3 times, K3.
* ROW 2: Slip 1 wyif, K2, purl to last 3 stitches, K3.
* ROW 3: Slip 1 wyif, K3, (yo, K2, ssk, K2tog, K2, yo, K1) 3 times, K4.
* ROW 4: Repeat Row 2.

* Repeat Rows 1–4 for desired length or until you have about 3 yards (3 m) of yarn left, ending with Row 1 or 3 of pattern. Work 4 border rows as for beginning border. Bind off.

Finishing

* Weave in ends. Soak scarf in cool water. Roll in towel to remove excess water, then spread scarf on flat surface. Pull ends into scallops and straighten side edge. Leave until completely dry.

WHISPER RIB & LACE ALPACA SOCKS

DESIGNED BY ANNE CARROLL GILMOUR, *photo on page 16*

These socks were inspired by a hand-knitted pair from Estonia. Knitted in an alpaca blend, they are a delight both to knit and to wear. They feature a picot edge at the top of the cuff and a lacy cable down the front.

SIZES AND FINISHED MEASUREMENTS	To fit average woman, approximately 7" (18 cm) circumference
YARN	Classic Elite Alpaca Sox, 60% alpaca/20% merino wool/ 20% nylon, 3.5 oz (100 g)/450 yds (411 m), 1856 Garden
NEEDLES	Set of five US 2 (2.75 mm) double-point needles *or size you need to obtain correct gauge*
GAUGE	32 stitches = 4" (10 cm) in stockinette stitch, 26 stitches = 4" (10 cm) in pattern after blocking
OTHER SUPPLIES	Scrap yarn for holders, tapestry needle
ABBREVIATIONS	**p2sso** pass 2 slipped stitches over **sl 2tog** slip 2 stitches together

Knitting the Picot Edge

✳ Cast on 62 stitches and distribute onto 3 double-point needles so there are 20 stitches on needles 1 and 3 and 22 stitches on needle 2. Join into a round, being careful not to twist the stitches.

✳ ROUNDS 1–3: Knit.

✳ ROUND 4: *Yo, K2tog; repeat from *.

✳ ROUNDS 5–7: Knit.

✳ Turn to the inside and knit the cast-on stitches together with the live stitches, being sure you knit the first cast-on stitch together with the first live stitch, the second cast-on stitch together with the second live stitch, etc. Knit 1 more round.

Knitting the Cuff

✳ Work Whisper Rib 1 on needle 1, Lace on needle 2, and Whisper Rib 2 on needle 3 until 9 full repeats of Rounds 1–8 of Lace have been completed.

Knitting the Heel Flap

✳ With needle 3, K15 from needle 1. Place remaining 5 stitches from needle 1, 22 stitches from needle 2, and first 5 stitches from needle 3 on a holder. Work the heel flap back and forth on 30 stitches as follows:

STITCH PATTERNS

whisper rib 1
(WORKED ON NEEDLE 1)

ROUND 1: K1, *P1, K2; repeat from * to last stitch, P1.

ROUND 2: Knit.

REPEAT ROUNDS 1 AND 2 FOR PATTERN.

whisper rib 2
(WORKED ON NEEDLE 3)

ROUND 1: P1, *K2, P1; repeat from * to last stitch, K1.

ROUND 2: Knit.

REPEAT ROUNDS 1 AND 2 FOR PATTERN.

lace
(WORKED ON NEEDLE 2)

ROUND 1: K2, P2, K3, K2tog, K1, yo, P2, yo, K1, ssk, K3, P2, K2.

ROUND 2 AND ALL EVEN-NUMBERED ROUNDS THROUGH 8: K2, P2, K6, P2, K6, P2, K2.

ROUND 3: K2, P2, K2, K2tog, K1, yo, K1, P2, K1, yo, K1, ssk, K2, P2, K2.

ROUND 5: K2, P2, K1, K2tog, K1, yo, K2, P2, K2, yo, K1, ssk, K1, P2, K2.

ROUND 7: K2, P2, K2tog, K1, yo, K3, P2, K3, yo, K1, ssk, P2, K2.

REPEAT ROUNDS 1–8 FOR PATTERN.

❈ ROW 1 (WS): *Sl 1 pwise, P1; repeat from * to last 2 stitches, K1, P1.

❈ ROW 2: *Sl 1 pwise, knit to last 2 stitches, P1, K1.

❈ Repeat Rows 1 and 2 fourteen more times (30 rows total in heel flap).

Turning the Heel

❈ ROW 1 (WS): (Sl 1 pwise, p1) 9 times, P1, P2tog, turn.

❈ ROW 2: Sl 1 pwise, K8, ssk, turn.

❈ ROW 3: (Sl 1, p1) 4 times, P1, P2tog, turn.

❈ Repeat Rows 2 and 3 until 10 stitches remain, then knit 1 row.

Knitting the Gussets

❈ With needle holding heel stitches (needle 1), pick up and knit (see page 264) 15 stitches along side of heel flap; with needle 2, knit 32 held stitches, working first 5 stitches in Whisper Rib 1, center 22 stitches in Lace pattern, and last 5 stitches in Whisper Rib 2; with needle 3, pick up and knit 15 stitches along other side of heel flap and K5 from needle 1. You now have 20 stitches on needles 1 and 3 and 32 stitches on needle 2.

❈ ROUND 1: Knit to last 3 stitches on needle 1, K2tog, K1; work in patterns as established on needle 2; K1, ssk at beginning of needle 3, knit to end of round.

❈ ROUND 2: Work even in patterns as established.

❈ Repeat Rounds 1 and 2 until you have 15 stitches on needles 1 and 3.

Knitting the Foot

❈ Work even as established until foot measures 7" (18 cm) or 2" (5 cm) less than desired finished length.

Knitting the Toe

❈ You will work the toe in stockinette stitch (knit every row) on 5 double-point needles, beginning with a Set-up Row as follows:

  ❈ NEEDLE 1: Knit to last 3 stitches on needle 1, sl 2tog kwise, K1, p2sso, P2tog from needle 2.

  ❈ NEEDLE 2: K13 (to center of Lace panel), P2tog.

  ❈ NEEDLE 3: K13, P2tog.

  ❈ NEEDLE 4: K13, P2tog.

❈ You now have 56 stitches, 14 on each needle.

❈ ROUND 1: Knit.

❈ ROUND 2: Knit to last 2 stitches on each needle, P2tog.

❋ Repeat Rounds 1 and 2 until 4 stitches remain on each needle. Work Round 1 once more.

Finishing

❋ Cut yarn, leaving an 8" (20.5 cm) tail. Thread tail onto tapestry needle and draw through remaining stitches twice. Pull up snug and fasten off. Weave in ends.

FALLING LEAVES MOHAIR-SILK SCARF
DESIGNED BY HÉLÈNE RUSH, *photo on page 12*

Lofty, light, and lovely.

FINISHED MEASUREMENTS	Approximately 7" (18 cm) wide and 44" (112 cm) long
YARN	Knit One, Crochet Too Douceur et Soie, 65% baby mohair/ 35% silk, 0.88 oz (25 g)/225 yds (208 m), 8558 Spring
NEEDLES	US 7 (4.5 mm) straight needles *or size you need to obtain correct gauge*
GAUGE	18 stitches = 4" (10 cm) in stockinette stitch
OTHER SUPPLIES	Tapestry needle

Knitting the Scarf

❋ Cast on 29 stitches.
❋ ROW 1 (RS): P2, (K1, P5) 4 times, K1, P2.
❋ ROW 2: K2, (P1, K5) 4 times, P1, K2.
❋ ROW 3: Repeat Row 1.
❋ ROW 4: Repeat Row 2.
❋ ROW 5: P2, K1, yo, (P5, yo, K1, yo) 3 times, P5, yo, K1, P2. You now have 37 stitches.
❋ ROW 6: K2, P2, (K5, P3) 3 times, K5, P2, K2.
❋ ROW 7: P2, K1, yo, K1, [P5, K1, (yo, K1) 2 times] 3 times, P5, K1, yo, K1, P2. You now have 45 stitches.
❋ ROW 8: K2, P3, (K5, P5) 3 times, K5, P3, K2.
❋ ROW 9: P2, K1, yo, K2, (P5, K2, yo, K1, yo, K2) 3 times, P5, K2, yo, K1, P2. You now have 53 stitches.

- ❈ ROW 10: K2, P4, (K5, P7) 3 times, K5, P4, K2.
- ❈ ROW 11: P2, K2, K2tog, (P5, ssk, K3, K2tog) 3 times, P5, ssk, K2, P2. You now have 45 stitches.
- ❈ ROW 12: K2, P3, (K5, P5) 3 times, K5, P3, K2.
- ❈ ROW 13: P2, K1, K2tog, (P2, K1, P2, ssk, K1, K2tog) 3 times, P2, K1, P2, ssk, K1, P2. You now have 37 stitches.
- ❈ ROW 14: K2, P2, (K2, P1, K2, P3) 3 times, K2, P1, K2, P2, K2.
- ❈ ROW 15: P2, K2tog, (P2, K1, P2, sl 1, K2tog, psso) 3 times, P2, K1, P2, ssk, P2. You now have 29 stitches.
- ❈ ROW 16: K2, (P1, K2) 9 times.
- ❈ ROW 17: P2, K1, P2, (yo, K1, yo, P2, K1, P2) 4 times. You now have 37 stitches.
- ❈ ROW 18: K2, P1, K2, (P3, K2, P1, K2) 4 times.
- ❈ ROW 19: P5, [K1, (yo, K1) 2 times, P5] 4 times. You now have 45 stitches.
- ❈ ROW 20: K5, (P5, K5) 4 times.
- ❈ ROW 21: P5, (K2, yo, K1, yo, K2, P5) 4 times. You now have 53 stitches.
- ❈ ROW 22: K5, (P7, K5) 4 times.
- ❈ ROW 23: P5, (ssk, K3, K2tog, P5) 4 times. You now have 45 stitches.
- ❈ ROW 24: Repeat Row 20.
- ❈ ROW 25: P2, K1, P2, (ssk, K1, K2tog, P2, K1, P2) 4 times. You now have 37 stitches.
- ❈ ROW 26: K2, P1, K2, (P3, K2, P1, K2) 4 times.
- ❈ ROW 27: P2, K1, P2, (sl 1, K2tog, psso, P2, K1, P2) 4 times. You now have 29 stitches.
- ❈ ROW 28: Repeat Row 16.
- ❈ Repeat Rows 5–28 until you have just enough yarn left to work 8 rows (about 7 yards [6.5 m]), ending with Row 12 or Row 24.
- ❈ If ending lace pattern with Row 12, finish as follows:
- ❈ ROW 1: P2, K1, K2tog, (P5, ssk, K1, K2tog) 3 times, P5, ssk, K1, P2. You now have 37 stitches.
- ❈ ROW 2: K2, P2, (K5, P3) 3 times, K5, P2, K2.
- ❈ ROW 3: P2, K2tog, (P5, sl 1, K2tog, psso) 3 times, P5, ssk, P2. You now have 29 stitches.
- ❈ ROW 4: K2, P1, (K5, P1) 4 times, K2.
- ❈ ROW 5: P2, K1, (P5, K1) 4 times, P2.
- ❈ ROW 6: Repeat Row 4.
- ❈ Bind off loosely.
- ❈ If ending lace pattern with Row 24, finish as follows:
- ❈ ROW 1: P5, (ssk, K1, K2tog, P5) 4 times. You now have 37 stitches.

FALLING LEAVES MOHAIR-SILK SCARF *continued*

* **ROW 2:** K5, (P3, K5) 4 times.
* **ROW 3:** P5, (sl 1, K2tog, psso, P5) 4 times. You now have 29 stitches.
* **ROW 4:** K5, (P1, K5) 4 times.
* **ROW 5:** P5, (K1, P5) 4 times.
* **ROW 6:** Repeat Row 4.
* Bind off loosely.

Finishing

* Weave in ends. Block to finished size.

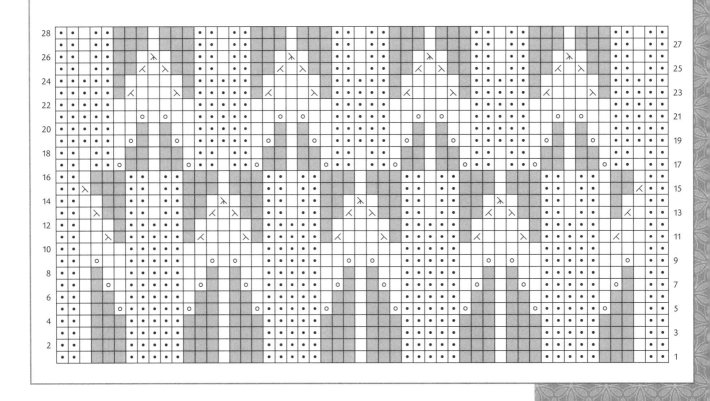

Falling Leaves Mohair-Silk Scarf

☐	knit on RS rows, purl on WS rows
•	purl on RS rows, knit on WS rows
○	yarn over
⅄	ssk
⋏	K2tog
⅄	slip 1, K2tog, psso
▨	no stitch

CARAVAN SILK-WOOL SOCKS

DESIGNED BY MELISSA MORGAN-OAKES, *photo on page 18*

Knitted at 10 stitches to the inch, this sock is fine for comfortable use with your favorite shoes. The sole is worked in reverse stockinette stitch, and the twist stitch pattern of the leg continues along the top of the foot.

SIZES AND FINISHED MEASUREMENTS	To fit small adult woman's foot, approximately 6.5" (16.5 cm) foot circumference and 8" (20.5 cm) foot length
YARN	Hand Maiden Mini Maiden, 50% silk/ 50% wool, 3.5 oz (100 g)/546 yds (500 m), Paris
NEEDLES	Set of four US 0 (2 mm) double-point needles *or size you need to obtain correct gauge*
GAUGE	40 stitches and 56 rounds = 4" (10 cm) in stockinette stitch
OTHER SUPPLIES	One spool (5 g) sock reinforcing yarn, tapestry needle

Knitting the Leg

❋ Cast on 72 stitches. Divide stitches onto 3 double-point needles so there are 36 stitches on needle 1, 14 stitches on needle 2, and 22 stitches on needle 3. Begin pattern on Row 1 of chart (page 84) and continue until sock measures 6" (15 cm). Make a note of the last chart round worked; this will be important when you begin the instep.

Knitting the Heel Flap

❋ With reinforcing thread held together with working yarn, work back and forth on 36 stitches on needle 1 as follows:

❋ ROW 1 (RS): *Slip 1 pwise wyib, K1; repeat from *.

❋ ROW 2: Slip 1 pwise wyib, purl to end of row.

❋ Repeat Rows 1 and 2 until heel flap measures 2" (5 cm), end having worked Row 1.

Turning the Heel

❋ Continue working heel flap stitches only.

❋ ROW 1 (WS): P20, P2tog, P1, turn.

❋ ROW 2: Slip 1 pwise, K5, K2tog tbl, K1, turn.

❋ ROW 3: Slip 1 pwise, P6, P2tog to close gap, P1, turn.

❋ ROW 4: Slip 1 pwise, K7, K2tog tbl to close gap, K1, turn.

CARAVAN SILK-WOOL SOCKS *continued*

❅ Continue in this manner, working 1 more stitch before the decrease on each row, until 20 stitches remain, ending with a RS row.

Knitting the Gusset

❅ With needle holding 20 heel stitches (needle 1), pick up and knit (see page 264) 18 stitches along side of heel flap. Continue with next row of charted pattern on 36 instep stitches (place all instep stitches on needle 2). With new needle (needle 3) pick up and knit 18 stitches along other side of heel flap and K10 from needle 1. You now have 28 stitches on needles 1 and 3 and 36 stitches on needle 2.

❅ ROUND 1: On needle 1, purl to last 3 stitches, P2tog, P1; on needle 2, continue even with charted pattern; on needle 3, P1, ssp, purl to end.

❅ ROUND 2: On needle 1, purl; on needle 2, continue charted pattern; on needle 3, purl.

❅ Repeat Rounds 1 and 2 until 18 stitches remain on each of needles 1 and 3.

Knitting the Foot

❅ Continuing in reverse stockinette stitch on needles 1 and 3 and charted pattern on needle 2, work even until foot measures 6" (15 cm) from back of heel or 2" (5 cm) less than desired finished length.

Shaping the Toe

❅ ROUND 1: On needle 1, purl to last 3 stitches, P2tog, P1; on needle 2, P1, ssp, purl to last 3 stitches, P2tog, P1; on needle 3, P1, ssk, purl to end.

❅ ROUND 2: Purl.

❅ Repeat Rounds 1 and 2 until 8 stitches remain.

Caravan Silk-Wool Socks

☐ knit

• purl

⬜ slip the first stitch, knit second stitch and leave it on the needle, knit the first stitch, slip both stitches off needle

Finishing

❧ Cut yarn, leaving a 10" (25 cm) tail. Use kitchener stitch (see page 262) to graft stitches together. Weave in ends.

PARISIAN ALPACA-WOOL SCARF

DESIGNED BY JUDITH L. SWARTZ, *photo on page 14*

This scarf is modeled after one that came from Paris. Knitted with a blend of alpaca and wool, the crocheted stitch complements the block of color produced by the space-dyed yarn. Elle est belle, non?

FINISHED MEASUREMENTS	Approximately 8" (20.5 cm) wide and 60" (152.5 cm) long
YARN	Classic Elite Alpaca Sox, 60% alpaca/20% merino wool/ 20% nylon, 3.5 oz (100 g)/450 yds (411 m), 1815 Emeralds
CROCHET HOOK	Size F/5 (3.75 mm) *or size you need to obtain correct gauge*
GAUGE	18 stitches and 8 rows = 4" (10 cm) in double crochet
OTHER SUPPLIES	Tapestry needle

Crocheting the Scarf

❧ FOUNDATION ROW: Loosely ch 271, turn. Starting in second ch from hook, work 1 sc in each ch (270 sc), ch 6, turn.

❧ ROW 1: Starting in second ch from hook, work 1 sl st in each of next 5 ch, work 1 sl st in first sc, ch 3 (counts as 1 dc), work 1 dc in each of next 5 sc, *ch 6, skip next 6 sc, work 1 dc in each of next 6 sc; repeat from * to end of row, ch 6, turn.

❧ ROW 2: Starting in second ch from hook, work 1 sl st in each of next 5 ch, work 1 sl st in first dc, ch 3 (counts as 1 dc), work 1 dc in each of next 5 dc, *ch 6, skip over ch from previous row, work 1 dc in each of next 6 dc; repeat from * to end of row, ch 6, turn.

❧ Repeat Row 2 fourteen more times.

❧ FINAL ROW: Starting in second ch from hook, work 1 sl st in each of next 5 ch, work 1 sl st in first dc, then work 1 sc in same dc, work 1 sc in each of next 5 dc, *work 1 sc in each of next 6 ch, work 1 sc in each of next 6 dc; repeat from * to end of row, fasten off.

Finishing

❧ Weave in ends. Steam, gently pulling chain sections vertically.

DIAMONDS AND SHELLS ALPACA SCARF

DESIGNED BY AMY O'NEILL HOUCK, *photo on page 13*

Diamonds and Shells is knit from one skein of Royal Alpaca, a rare alpaca fiber that's softer and has more bounce and memory than other alpaca, making for a supersoft, squishy wrap.

FINISHED MEASUREMENTS	Approximately 8" (20.5 cm) wide and 60" (152 cm) long
YARN	Blue Sky Royal Alpaca, 100% alpaca, 3.5 oz (100 g)/288 yds (263 m), Spanish Leather
CROCHET HOOK	US H/8 (5 mm) *or size you need to obtain correct gauge*
GAUGE	4 repeats = 8" (20 cm) after blocking
OTHER SUPPLIES	Tapestry needle
ABBREVIATIONS	**ch-sp** space created by chains from the previous row **shell** work 4 dc in the space indicated **sk** skip **tch** turning chain made at the beginning of a row

Crocheting the Scarf

❋ Chain 38.

❋ ROW 1: Sc in the tenth ch from hook, *ch 4, sk 3 ch, sc in the next ch, repeat from * across, turn.

❋ ROW 2: Ch 3, *shell in next ch-sp, ch 2, sc in next ch-sp, ch 2, repeat from *; end with dc after final ch 2 in last ch-sp. Turn.

❋ ROW 3: Ch 5, sk first ch-sp, sc in next ch-sp, *ch 4, sc in next ch-sp, repeat from *; end with sc in tch. Turn.

❋ ROW 4: Ch 5, sk first sc, sc in next sc, *ch 4, sc in next sc, repeat from *; end with sc in last sc. Turn.

❋ Repeat Rows 2–4 until scarf is desired length, or you run out of yarn, ending on Row 3. Fasten off.

Finishing

❋ Weave in ends. Steam block to measurements.

SILK-MERINO FINGERLESS GLOVES

DESIGNED BY ANDRA ASARS, *photo on page 18*

The Petite Cables pattern used in these gloves has a lot of stretch, making one size fit many. To increase or decrease the circumference, add or subtract stitches by multiples of four. The stitch is lovely on the wrong side as well, making the gloves reversible.

SIZES AND FINISHED MEASUREMENTS	To fit average woman, approximately 6" (15 cm) circumference stretching to 8.5" (21.5 cm)
YARN	Lang Merino Seta, 70% extra fine merino wool/30% silk, 1.75 oz (50 g)/164 yds (150 m), 731.0070 Gray
NEEDLES	Set of four US 3 (3.25 mm) double-point needles *or size you need to obtain correct gauge*
GAUGE	36 stitches = 4" (10 cm) in pattern
OTHER SUPPLIES	Stitch marker, tapestry needle

Knitting the Cuff

✳ Cast on 60 stitches and divide evenly onto 3 double-point needles. Join into a round, being careful not to twist the stitches. Note: To minimize the looseness that can occur in the stitches between double-point needles, position the P2 part of the rib at these places, purling the first and last stitch on each needle, (i.e., work Row 1 as follows on all needles: P1, *K2, P2; repeat from * to last 3 stitches, K2, P1).

✳ Begin Petite Cables pattern and work until piece measures 2.5" (6.5 cm). On the last round, slip the last stitch from needle 3 onto needle 1.

Knitting the Thumb Gusset

✳ ROUND 1: P1, M1L, M1R, P1. These 4 stitches start the gusset. Place marker, work remaining stitches in pattern as established.

✳ ROUND 2: P1, K2, P1, slip marker, work remaining stitches in pattern as established.

✳ Continue in this manner, increasing 2 stitches on both sides of the gusset every other round, incorporating the increased stitches into the cable pattern, until you have 26 gusset stitches.

✳ NEXT ROUND: P1, bind off 24 in pattern, P1, remove marker, work remaining stitches in pattern as established.

Completing the Hand

❋ Work even in pattern as established for 1" (2.5 cm), ending with Round 2 of pattern.

Finishing

❋ Bind off in pattern. Weave in ends. Make second glove.

SEASIDE COTTAGE ALPACA-SILK STOLE

DESIGNED BY ANNE CARROLL GILMOUR, *photo on page 13*

The lace patterns in this light and airy stole take their inspiration from seaside villages of the Hebrides. The yarn is as light and airy as the patterns, and this is sure to become one of your favorite wardrobe items.

FINISHED MEASUREMENTS	Approximately 18" (45.5 cm) wide and 78" (198 cm) long
YARN	Alpaca with a Twist Fino, 70% baby alpaca/30% silk, 3.5 oz (100 g)/875 yds (800 m), 2002 Dry Grape
NEEDLES	Two US 4 (3.5 mm) circular needles 24" (60 cm) long and set of US 4 (3.5 mm) straight needles *or size you need to obtain correct gauge*
GAUGE	22 stitches = 4" (10 cm) in stockinette stitch, blocked; 22 stitches = 4" (10 cm) in pattern, blocked
OTHER SUPPLIES	Stitch markers, point protectors, blocking pins

Knitting the Main Panel (make 2)

❋ Cast on 128 stitches and knit 1 row.

❋ Note: Slip the first stitch and knit the last stitch of every row. These stitches do not appear on the Seaweed Lace Border chart (page 89).

❋ ROW 1 (RS): Slip 1 (edge stitch), pm, work Row 1 of Seaweed Lace Border chart for 9 repeats, pm after each 14-stitch repeat, pm, K1.

❋ Work Rows 2–4 of chart, then work Rows 1–4 ten more times.

❋ Reduce the stitch count by working 2 exit rows.

Seaweed Lace Border

	knit on RS rows, purl on WS rows
▪	purl on RS rows, knit on WS rows
▫	yarn over
⟋	K2tog
人	slip 1, K2tog, psso

- ❈ **EXIT ROW 1:** Slip 1 (edge stitch), *K2tog, K1, P2, sl 1, k2tog, psso, P2, K1, P2, K1; repeat from * to last stitch, K1.
- ❈ **EXIT ROW 2:** Slip 1 (edge stitch), P1, *K2tog, P1, K2, P1, K2, P3; repeat from *. You now have 92 stitches.
- ❈ Work 2 rows of garter stitch, removing markers.

Setting up for the Next Pattern

- ❈ **SET-UP ROW (RS, COUNTS AS ROW 1 OF PATTERN):** K4, pm, *K3, P7, pm; repeat from * to last 8 stitches, K3, pm, K2tog, K3. You now have 91 stitches: 83 pattern stitches flanked by 4-stitch garter borders.
- ❈ Continue to work 4-stitch garter borders at beginning and end of each row, and follow Seaside Cottage Lace chart (page 91), beginning with Row 2, until you have completed 11 full repeats of Rows 1–18. Leave stitches on needle.

Joining the Main Panels

- ❈ Lay the 2 panels RS up with live stitches facing each other (see illustration on page 90).

SEASIDE COTTAGE ALPACA-SILK STOLE *continued*

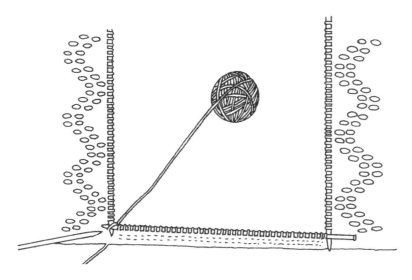

* With yarn attached to the bottom of the left panel, use straight needles and the knitted-on method (see page 262) to cast on 44 stitches. Knit the first live stitch from the right panel. *With RS facing and yarn at back, slip this stitch knitwise, knit 43 cast-on stitches, ssk the last cast-on stitch with the first live stitch from the left panel. Turn work to WS and with yarn in front, slip the first stitch purlwise, bring yarn to back and K43, bring yarn forward, and purl the last stitch together with the next live stitch of the right panel. Turn work and repeat from * until you have used all stitches of the garter stitch border, ending with a WS row.

* Continuing to join this new center panel to the 2 main panels as outlined above, begin working Seachange Lace chart (page 92). Work Rows 1 and 2, then begin again at Row 1. Repeat Rows 1–40 four times. Be careful to absorb the edge stitches from the main panels evenly; 20 rows of the joining panel should equal 1 full repeat on main panel. After completing the last row of the fourth repeat, work 8 rows of garter stitch as for the beginning. Bind off loosely.

Finishing

* Weave in ends. Wet block with blocking pins and allow to dry.

Seaside Cottage Lace

☐ knit on RS rows, purl on WS rows

• purl on RS rows, knit on WS rows

○ yarn over

⟋ K2tog

⟍ ssk

⅄ slip 1, K2tog, psso

⚥ K1 through the back loop

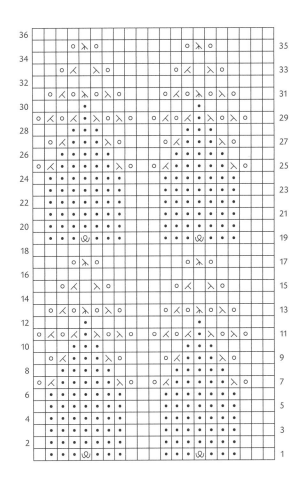

SEASIDE COTTAGE ALPACA-SILK STOLE continued

Seachange Lace

- ☐ knit on RS rows, purl on WS rows
- · purl on RS rows, knit on WS rows
- ○ yarn over
- ⟨ K2tog
- ⟩ ssk
- ⋋ slip 1, K2tog, psso
- S slip 1 kwise wyib on RS rows, pwise wyif on WS rows

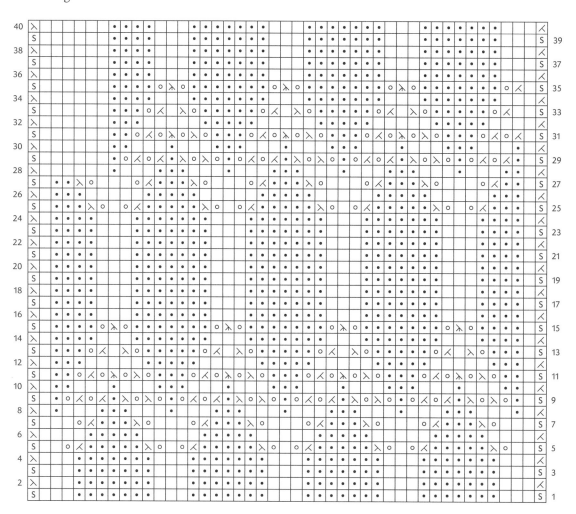

QUEEN OF DIAMONDS MERINO-SILK GLOVES

DESIGNED BY MELISSA BURT, *photo on page 16*

A perfect gift for Mother's Day or any other special occasion, these soft gloves are lightweight and warm while still allowing full use of the hands. The silk-and-merino combination makes them very comfortable to wear.

SIZES AND FINISHED MEASUREMENTS	To fit small/medium woman's hand, approximately 7" (18 cm) circumference
YARN	Knit Picks Gloss Sock, 70% merino wool/30% silk, 1.75 oz (50 g)/220 yds (201 m), Dusk
NEEDLES	Sets of four US 1 (2.5 mm) and US 0 (2 mm) double-point needles *or size you need to obtain correct gauge*
GAUGE	28 stitches and 40 rows = 4" (10 cm) in stockinette stitch on larger needle
OTHER SUPPLIES	Stitch markers, scrap yarn for holders, tapestry needle

Knitting the Right Glove

❋ With smaller needles, cast on 60 stitches and divide evenly onto 3 double-point needles. Work Rounds 1–9 of Cobweb Frill Edging pattern. You now have 40 stitches. Change to larger needles and work Rounds 1–10 of Chevron pattern twice.

INCREASING FOR THE HAND

❋ Place marker for beginning of round and thumb. You will begin at the thumb, work the palm stitches, then the back-of-hand stitches.

❋ **ROUND 1:** M1R, K16, M1L, pm for side of hand at end of palm stitches, knit to end of round. You now have 42 stitches.

❋ **ROUNDS 2, 4, 6 AND 8:** Knit.

❋ **ROUND 3:** M1R, knit to side marker, M1L, sm, knit to end. You now have 44 stitches.

❋ **ROUND 5:** Repeat Round 3. You now have 46 stitches.

❋ **ROUND 7:** Repeat Round 3. You now have 48 stitches.

❋ **ROUND 9:** M1R, knit to end. You now have 49 stitches.

❋ **ROUND 10:** Knit to end, M1L. You now have 50 stitches.

QUEEN OF DIAMONDS MERINO-SILK GLOVES *continued*

❈ ROUND 11: Knit.

❈ ROUND 12: M1R, knit to end, M1L. You now have 52 stitches.

❈ ROUNDS 13 AND 14: Repeat Rounds 11 and 12. You now have 54 stitches, 27 stitches for thumb and palm, 27 stitches for back of hand.

KNITTING THE EYELET ROUNDS

❈ ROUND 15: Knit to side marker, sm, K14, K2tog, yo, knit to end.

❈ ROUND 16 (AND ALL EVEN-NUMBERED ROUNDS THROUGH 28): Repeat Round 12.

❈ ROUND 17: Knit to side marker, sm, K13, (K2tog, yo) 2 times, knit to end.

❈ ROUND 19: Knit to side marker, sm, K12, (K2tog, yo) 3 times, knit to end.

❈ ROUND 21: Repeat Round 17.

❈ ROUND 23: Repeat Round 19.

❈ ROUND 25: Repeat Round 17.

❈ ROUND 27: Repeat Round 15.

❈ ROUND 29: Knit. You now have 68 stitches.

KNITTING THE THUMB

❈ ROUND 1: K10, slip next 48 stitches (including side marker) onto holder, cast on 4 stitches with the backward loop method (see page 261), rejoin into a round and knit to end. You may remove the thumb marker at this point. You now have 24 stitches.

❈ ROUND 2: Knit.

❈ ROUND 3: K9, ssk, K2, K2tog, knit to end. You now have 22 stitches.

❈ Knit 5 rounds and bind off loosely.

KNITTING THE HAND

❈ Place 48 held stitches back onto needles. Join yarn to beginning of these stitches with RS facing and knit to end. When you get to the thumb, pick up and knit (see page 264) 8 stitches from the base of the thumb, picking up these stitches by inserting your needle between the stitches under 2 strands of yarn. You now have 56 stitches.

❈ ROUND 1: Knit to 1 stitch before 8 picked-up stitches, ssk, K6, K2tog (joining the last picked up stitch and the first stitch of the round). Place marker for end of round. You now have 54 stitches.

❈ ROUND 2: Knit.

❈ ROUND 3: Knit to 2 stitches before side marker, ssk, sm, K2tog, knit to end. You now have 52 stitches.

❈ ROUNDS 4–7: Knit.

* ROUND 8: Repeat Round 3. You now have 50 stitches.
* ROUNDS 9–12: Knit.

KNITTING THE FINGERS

* Knit to 6 stitches before side marker, slip next 11 stitches onto holder (this will be the pinky), cast on 6 stitches, join, and knit to end of round. You now have 45 stitches.
* Knit 1 round even.

Index Finger

* K7, place the next 27 stitches onto holder, cast on 4 stitches, join, and knit to end. You now have 22 stitches on needles.
* NEXT ROUND: K6, ssk, K2, K2tog, knit to end. You now have 20 stitches.
* NEXT ROUND: K5, ssk, K2, K2tog, knit to end. You now have 18 stitches.
* Knit 4 more rounds even, then bind off loosely.

Middle Finger

* Place the next 6 palm stitches and next 6 back stitches on the needles. Join yarn to beginning of stitches on palm side with RS facing, K6, cast on 4 stitches, join, K6, pick up 6 stitches from the index finger. You now have 22 stitches on needles.
* NEXT ROUND: K15, ssk, K4, K2tog (joining the first and last stitches in the round). You now have 20 stitches.
* NEXT ROUND: K5, ssk, K2, K2tog, knit to end. You now have 18 stitches.
* Knit 5 more rounds even, then bind off loosely.

Ring Finger

* Place remaining 15 stitches on needles (ignoring pinky stitches). Join yarn with RS facing at beginning of stitches cast on for middle finger, pick up 6 stitches from middle finger, K4, ssk, K2, K2tog, knit to 1 stitch before the end.
* NEXT ROUND: Ssk (joining beginning and end of round), K4, K2tog, knit to end. You now have 17 stitches.
* Knit 5 more rounds even, then bind off loosely.

Pinky Finger

* Place 11 remaining held stitches on needles. Join yarn to beginning of these stitches with RS facing and knit them, then pick up and knit (see page 264) 8 stitches from ring finger. You now have 19 stitches.

❈ NEXT ROUND: K10, ssk, K5, K2tog. You now have 17 stitches.

❈ Knit 1 round even.

❈ NEXT ROUND: K4, K2tog, knit to end. You now have 16 stitches.

❈ Knit 2 more rounds even, then bind off loosely.

FINISHING

❈ Weave in ends and block (if desired).

Knitting the Left Glove

❈ Work Cobweb Frill Edging and Chevron patterns as for right glove.

INCREASING FOR THE HAND

❈ Place marker for beginning of round. (You will be knitting from the side of the hand across the palm to the thumb, then across the back of the hand.)

❈ ROUND 1: M1R, K16, M1L, pm at thumb, knit to end. You now have 42 stitches.

❈ ROUNDS 2, 4, 6 AND 8: Knit.

❈ ROUND 3: M1R, knit to thumb marker, M1L, sm, knit to end. You now have 44 stitches.

❈ ROUND 5: Repeat Round 3. You now have 46 stitches.

❈ ROUND 7: Repeat Round 3. You now have 48 stitches.

❈ ROUND 9: Knit to thumb marker, M1L, sm, knit to end. You now have 49 stitches.

❈ ROUND 10: Knit to thumb marker, sm, M1R, knit to end. You now have 50 stitches. Round 11: Knit.

❈ ROUND 12: Knit to thumb marker, M1L, sm, M1R, knit to end. You now have 52 stitches.

❈ ROUNDS 13 AND 14: Repeat Rounds 11 and 12. You now have 54 stitches, 27 stitches before side marker for thumb and palm, 27 stitches after side marker for back of hand.

KNITTING THE EYELET ROUNDS

❈ ROUND 15: Knit to 16 stitches before end of round, K2tog, yo, knit to end.

❈ ROUND 16 (AND ALL EVEN-NUMBERED ROUNDS THROUGH 28): Repeat Round 12.

❈ ROUND 17: Knit to 17 stitches before end of round, (K2tog, yo) 2 times, knit to end.

❈ ROUND 19: Knit to 18 stitches before end of round, (K2tog, yo) 3 times, knit to end.

❈ ROUND 21: Repeat Round 17.

❈ ROUND 23: Repeat Round 19.

❈ ROUND 25: Repeat Round 17.

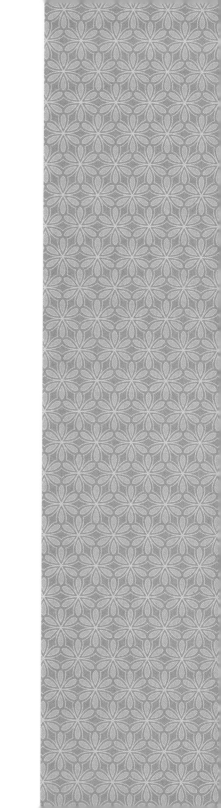

✻ ROUND 27: Repeat Round 15.

✻ ROUND 29: Knit. You now have 68 stitches.

KNITTING THE THUMB

✻ ROUND 1: Knit to 10 stitches past thumb marker, slip next 48 stitches (and side marker) onto holder. Using the backward loop method (see page 261), cast on 4 stitches, rejoin into a round and knit to end. You may remove the thumb marker at this point. You now have 24 stitches.

✻ Complete as for right thumb.

KNITTING THE HAND

✻ Place 48 held stitches onto needles. Join yarn to beginning of these stitches with RS facing and knit to end. When you get to the thumb, pick up 8 stitches from the base of the thumb. You now have 56 stitches.

✻ Complete as for right hand.

KNITTING THE FINGERS

✻ Complete as for right hand.

Middle Finger

✻ Place the next 6 palm stitches and next 6 back stitches on needles. Join yarn to beginning of stitches on back of hand with RS facing, K6, cast on 4 stitches, join, K6, pick up 6 stitches from index finger. You now have 22 stitches. Complete as for right hand.

Ring Finger

✻ Place remaining 15 stitches on needles (ignoring pinky stitches). Join yarn with RS and palm facing at beginning of stitches cast on for middle finger, pick up 6 stitches from middle finger, K4, ssk, K2, K2tog, knit to 1 stitch before end. Complete as for right hand.

Pinky Finger

✻ Complete as for right hand.

FINISHING

✻ Weave in ends and block (if desired).

SILK WEDDING RING PILLOW

DESIGNED BY GWEN STEEGE, photo on page 13

Every bride and groom will treasure this very special silk pillow knit to bear their wedding rings safely up the aisle. Use a loosely tied bow to fasten the rings to the center of the heart so they can be easily removed by pulling gently on the ribbon end. The needle size is smaller than recommended for this yarn, in order to give the fabric stability and to better show off the seed-stitch heart motif.

FINISHED MEASUREMENTS	Approximately 5" (12.5 cm) square
YARN	Halcyon 2/5 Gemstone Silk, 100% silk, 3.5 oz (100 g)/260 yds (238 m), 110 Cream
NEEDLES	US 2 (2.55 mm) straight needles *or size you need to obtain correct gauge*
GAUGE	26 stitches = 4" (10 cm) in stockinette stitch
OTHER SUPPLIES	Blocking pins, US C/2 (2.5 mm) crochet hook, tapestry needle, polyester fiberfill, 1 yd (91.5 cm) ³⁄₈" (1 cm) white satin ribbon

Knitting the Pillow
(Make 2)

* Note: If you wish, you can omit the heart motif on the back piece of the pillow. Work stockinette stitch throughout, or work the seed stitch border all around with plain stockinette in the center.
* Cast on 35 stitches.
* ROWS 1–10: *K1, P1; repeat from * to last stitch, K1 (seed stitch border).
* ROW 11: (K1, P1) 3 times, K1, K21, (K1, P1) 3 times, K1.
* ROW 12: (K1, P1) 3 times, K1, P21, (K1, P1) 3 times, K1.
* ROWS 13–50: Maintaining the 7-stitch seed stitch borders, follow the chart at right to work the heart motif at the center of the ring pillow.
* ROWS 51–52: Repeat Rows 11 and 12.
* ROWS 53–62: Repeat Rows 1–10.
* Bind off loosely.
* Block by pinning each piece to a firm surface, taking care to square up the corners. Spray lightly with plain water and allow to dry.

Silk Wedding Ring Pillow

☐ knit on RS rows, purl on WS rows

☐• purl on RS rows, knit on WS rows

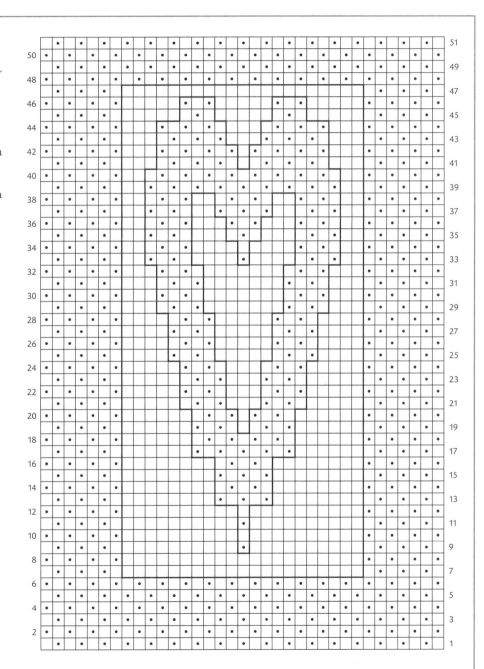

Crocheting the Border

❈ With WS together, pin the pillow front and back pieces together.

❈ ROUND 1: With the front facing you, use single crochet to attach the pieces. Crochet around, working 3 sc stitches at each corner until about 3" (7.5 cm) from the beginning of the round. Do not cut the yarn, but keep the loop active so you can pick it up again.

❈ Loosely stuff the pillow with polyester fiberfill.

❈ Pick up your last loop and continue in the established pattern to the end of the round to close the pillow completely. Slip stitch the last stitch to the first stitch, chain 3.

❈ ROUND 2: Skip 1 stitch, *(1 dc in next stitch, ch 1, skip 1 stitch) to a corner, (dc, ch 2) in each of the 3 corner stitches; repeat from * to end of round. Join the last ch 1 to a dc with a slip stitch and fasten off.

Finishing

❈ Thread the length of white satin ribbon through a tapestry needle and, working from back to front, draw it halfway through at the exact center of the pillow. Remove the needle and thread it with the end remaining at the back. Draw that end through from back to front, inserting the needle close to, but not in, the same stitch just used. Tie the ends of the ribbon in a bow, gently snug, but not so tight that it distorts the motif.

STITCH PATTERNS
knot stitch

ROW 1: Sl 1, *K3, (P3tog, K3tog, P3tog) in next 3 stitches; repeat from * to last stitch, K1.

ROW 2 AND ALL WS ROWS THROUGH 8: Sl 1, purl to end.

ROW 3: Sl 1, knit to end.

ROW 5: Sl 1, *(P3tog, K3tog, P3tog) in next 3 stitches, K3; repeat from * to last stitch, K1.

ROW 7: Knit.

REPEAT ROWS 1–8 FOR PATTERN.

lace edging

CAST ON 9 STITCHES. SLIP ALL STITCHES PURLWISE WITH YARN IN FRONT.

ROW 1: Sl 1, K3, (yo, K2tog) twice, yo, K1.

ROWS 2, 4, 6, 8, AND 10: Knit.

ROW 3: Sl 1, K4, (yo, K2tog) twice, yo, K1.

ROW 5: Sl 1, K5, (yo, K2tog) twice, yo, K1.

ROW 7: Sl 1, K6, (yo, K2tog) twice, yo, K1.

ROW 9: Sl 1, K7, (yo, K2tog) twice, yo, K1.

ROW 11: Sl 1, K8, (yo, K2tog) twice, yo, K1.

ROW 12: Bind off 6, K9.

REPEAT ROWS 1–12 FOR PATTERN.

ALPACA-SILK CHRISTENING BLANKET
DESIGNED BY JUDITH DURANT, *photo on page 19*

White alpaca and silk make this blanket a wonderful gift to commemorate a baby's christening. Knitted in any other color, it would also make a very special receiving or cradle blanket. The body is worked in a simple knot stitch, and the lace edging is attached to the body as it is knitted.

FINISHED MEASUREMENTS	Approximately 24" (61 cm) wide and 36" (91.5 cm) long
YARN	Alpaca with a Twist Fino, 70% baby alpaca/30% silk, 3.5 oz (100 g)/875 yds (800 m), 99 Ivory
NEEDLES	Two US 4 (3.5 mm) circular needles 24" (60 cm) long and two US 3 (3.25mm) double-point needles 5" (12.5 cm) long *or size you need to obtain correct gauge*
GAUGE	29 stitches = 4" (10 cm) in stockinette stitch on larger needle, 30 stitches = 4" (10 cm) in knot stitch pattern on larger needle
OTHER SUPPLIES	Stitch markers, tapestry needle
ABBREVIATIONS	pick up 2+1 pick up 2 stitches by knitting under both loops of 2 ch stitches, pick up 1 more stitch by knitting under only 1 loop of the last ch stitch knitted
	pick up 3+1 pick up 3 stitches by knitting under both loops of 3 ch stitches, pick up 1 more stitch by knitting under only 1 loop of the last ch stitch knitted

Knitting the Body

❄ Using a provisional method (see page 265), cast on 134 stitches. Knit 1 row, purl 1 row, knit 1 row. Work Rows 1–8 of Knot Stitch pattern 33 times, ending with Row 7. Do not break yarn.

Picking Up for Edging

❄ With working yarn still attached and RS facing, place a marker and pick up 194 stitches along edge as follows: (Pick up 3+1) 5 times, (pick up 2+1) 51 times, (pick up 3+1) 5 times, pick up 1. Remove provisional cast-on and place 134 live stitches on second circular needle. Place a marker and pick up 194 stitches along second edge as for first edge. You now have 328 stitches on each needle, 656 stitches total. Break yarn.

ALPACA-SILK CHRISTENING BLANKET *continued*

Knitting the Edging

❀ Note: The lace edging begins on a short end of the blanket, 1 stitch in from the end. It is attached to the blanket by knitting the last stitch of WS rows together with next stitch on blanket needle with WS facing. Bind off 6 stitches loosely on Row 12 as follows: K1, *yo, pass knit stitch over yo, K1, pass yo over knit stitch; repeat from * 5 more times.

❀ Slip the first stitch from first circular needle to second circular needle. Cast 9 stitches onto a double-point needle.

❀ ROW 1 (RS): K4, (yo, K2tog) twice, yo, K1.

❀ ROW 2: K9, K1 together with first stitch on blanket needle.

❀ ROW 3: Sl 1, K4, (yo, K2tog) twice, yo, K1.

❀ ROW 4: K10, K1 together with first stitch on blanket needle.

❀ Continue in this manner with Lace Edging stitch until there is 1 stitch remaining before the corner marker, ending on Row 12 of pattern. Work the corner as follows:

❀ ROW 1: Sl 1, K3, (yo, K2tog) twice, yo, K1.

❀ ROW 2: K9, K1 together with first stitch on blanket needle.

❀ ROW 3: Sl 1, K4, (yo, K2tog) twice, yo, K1.

❀ ROW 4: K10, turn.

❀ ROW 5: Sl 1, K4, (yo, K2tog) twice, yo, K1.

❀ ROW 6: K11, pick up 1 stitch into corner of blanket and knit it together with remaining stitch on edging needle.

❀ ROW 7: Sl 1, K6, (yo, K2tog) twice, yo, K1.

❀ ROW 8: K12, K1 together with picked-up corner stitch as for Row 6.

❀ ROW 9: Sl 1, K7, (yo, K2tog) twice, yo, K1.

❀ ROW 10: K13, turn. Remove corner marker.

❀ ROW 11: Sl 1, K7, (yo, K2tog) twice, yo, K1.

❀ ROW 12: Bind off 6, K8, K1 together with first stitch on blanket needle.

❀ Continue with Lace Edging pattern, working all corners as described above. After last repeat, bind off 9 stitches.

Finishing

❀ Join 9 bind-off stitches with 9 cast-on stitches. Weave in ends. Block to finished measurements.

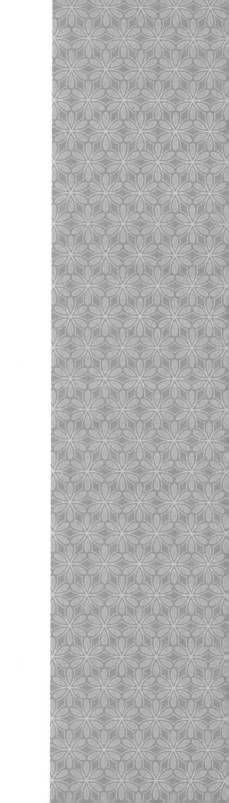

Tiffany Cashmere Socks

DESIGNED BY MELISSA MORGAN-OAKES, *photo on page 14*

If you've ever seen a gift box from Tiffany & Co., you know that these socks are so named for their color. But the socks are also adorned with crystals, making them reminiscent of shiny bright objects that often lurk inside those gift boxes. Knitted with 100% cashmere, they stand up to the name.

SIZES AND FINISHED MEASUREMENTS	To fit adult woman, approximately 7" (18 cm) circumference
YARN	Jade Sapphire Mongolian Cashmere 2-ply, 100% cashmere, 1.9 oz (55 g)/400 yds (366 m), 85 Lichen or Not
NEEDLES	Set of four US 1 (2.25 mm) double-point needles *or size you need to obtain correct gauge*
GAUGE	40 stitches = 4" (10 cm) in stockinette stitch
OTHER SUPPLIES	48 clear 3 mm faceted bicone Swarovski crystals, twisted wire beading needle, cable needle, tapestry needle

Beading Know-how

❈ Begin by threading 24 beads onto your working yarn, using a beading needle. You will need to push the beads down the yarn and out of your way as you work until they are needed. Place beads as indicated on the chart (page 105) by slipping the bead into position on the working yarn and pushing the bead through the stitch you are knitting into.

Knitting the Leg

❈ Cast on 72 stitches and divide evenly onto 3 double-point needles. Join into a round, being careful not to twist the stitches.

Knitting the Picot Edge

❈ **ROUNDS 1–4:** Knit.
❈ **ROUND 5:** *K2, yo, K2tog; repeat from *.
❈ **ROUNDS 6–9:** Knit.
❈ **ROUND 10:** Knit 1 live stitch on needle together with the back loop of the first cast-on stitch. This joins the 2 together and creates a turned hem. Continue in this manner, knitting each successive live stitch together with its cast-on counterpart until the picot edge is completed.
❈ Change to K1, P1 rib and work for 12 rounds.

TIFFANY CASHMERE SOCKS *continued*

WORKING THE CHARTED PATTERN

❈ Begin with Round 1 of chart (page 105); however, on this first round, *do not place beads as indicated.* From this point on, place beads where indicated on chart until all beads have been used. Six repeats of the charted pattern equal one complete round. Continue in charted pattern for 27 rounds total, ending with Round 3. After working 27 rounds of charted pattern, redistribute stitches for working heel flap by slipping stitches as follows: 36 on needle 1, 12 on needle 2, and 24 on needle 3.

Knitting the Heel Flap

❈ Working back and forth on 36 stitches of needle 1 only, work heel flap as follows:

❈ ROW 1: *Slip 1 pwise, K1; repeat from *.

❈ ROW 2: *Slip 1 pwise, purl to end of row.

❈ Repeat Rows 1 and 2 seventeen more times — 36 rows total. Heel flap should measure about 2.25" (5.5 cm). Work Row 1 once more.

Turning the Heel

❈ Continue working in rows on heel flap stitches only.

❈ ROW 1 (WS): P 20, P2tog, P1, turn.

❈ ROW 2: Slip 1 pwise, K5, K2tog tbl, K1, turn.

❈ ROW 3: Slip 1 pwise, P6, P2tog to close gap, P1, turn.

❈ ROW 4: Slip 1 pwise, K7, K2tog tbl to close gap, K1, turn.

❈ Continue as for Rows 3 and 4 above, working 1 more stitch before the decrease until 20 heel stitches remain.

Knitting the Heel Gusset

❈ Using the needle holding the 20 heel stitches (needle 1), pick up and knit (see page 264) 18 stitches down left side of heel flap. Using another needle (needle 2), work 36 instep stitches, following charted pattern beginning with Round 4, ignoring the "place bead" symbol on the chart from this point forward. With another needle (needle 3), pick up and knit 18 stitches up right side of heel flap, then knit 10 stitches from needle 1. You now have 28 heel gusset and sole stitches on needles 1 and 3, and 36 instep stitches on needle 2. Working in rounds, begin heel gusset decreases as follows.

❈ ROUND 1 (DECREASE ROUND):

   ❈ NEEDLE 1: Knit to last 3 stitches, K2tog, K1.

   ❈ NEEDLE 2: Work in charted pattern as established.

   ❈ NEEDLE 3: K1, ssk, knit to end of round.

❊ ROUND 2:

   ❊ NEEDLE 1: Knit.

   ❊ NEEDLE 2: Work in charted pattern as established.

   ❊ NEEDLE 3: Knit.

❊ Repeat these 2 rounds until needles 1 and 3 each have 18 (sole) stitches remaining. This completes the heel gusset decreases.

Knitting the Foot

❊ Continue in stockinette stitch on needles 1 and 3 (sole stitches) and follow charted pattern for needle 2 (instep stitches) until sock measures 1.5" (4 cm) less than desired length from heel to toe.

Shaping the Toe

❊ ROUND 1:

   ❊ NEEDLE 1: Knit to last 3 stitches, K2tog, K1.

   ❊ NEEDLE 2: K1, ssk, knit to last 3 stitches, K2tog, K1.

   ❊ NEEDLE 3: K1, ssk, knit to end of round.

❊ ROUND 2: Knit.

❊ Repeat Rounds 1 and 2 six more times. You now have 44 stitches. Repeat Round 1 only 7 times. You now have 16 stitches.

Finishing

❊ Break yarn, leaving a 10" (25.5 cm) tail. Redistribute stitches onto 2 needles, each containing 8 stitches. Following the instructions on page 262, graft the toe stitches together using kitchener stitch.

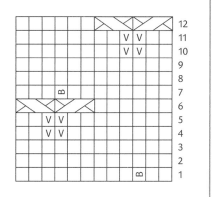

Tiffany Cashmere Socks

☐ knit

V slip 1 pwise wyib

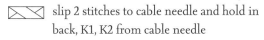 slip 2 stitches to cable needle and hold in back, K1, K2 from cable needle

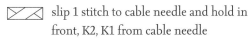 slip 1 stitch to cable needle and hold in front, K2, K1 from cable needle

B knit bead into stitch

Blossom Silk-SeaCell Shawl

DESIGNED BY AMY POLCYN, *photo on page 19*

A perfect first shawl, it uses less than one skein of luxurious Hand Maiden Sea Silk yarn, and uses a quick-to-knit, easy-to-memorize lace pattern. The pattern is mirrored on either side of a center stitch.

FINISHED MEASUREMENTS	Approximately 68" (172.5 cm) wide and 25" (63.5 cm) long, blocked
YARN	Hand Maiden Sea Silk, 70% silk/30% SeaCell, 3.5 oz (100 g)/ 438 yds (400 m), Rose Garden
NEEDLES	US 9 (5.5 mm) circular needle 32" (80 cm) long *or size you need to obtain correct gauge*
GAUGE	18 stitches = 4" (10 cm) in stockinette stitch
OTHER SUPPLIES	Four stitch markers, tapestry needle

Knitting the Shawl

❈ Cast on 7 stitches. Working from either the chart (page 107) or the row-by-row instructions, work lace pattern for 122 rows.

❈ ROW 1 (RS): Knit.

❈ ROW 2: K2, purl to last 2 stitches, K2.

❈ ROW 3: K2, (yo, K1) 3 times, yo, K2. You now have 11 stitches.

❈ ROW 4: Repeat Row 2.

❈ ROW 5: K2, yo, K3, yo, K1, yo, K3, yo, K2. You now have 15 stitches.

❈ ROW 6: Repeat Row 2.

❈ ROW 7: K2, yo, K5, yo, K1, yo, K5, yo, K2. You now have 19 stitches.

❈ ROW 8: Repeat Row 2.

❈ ROW 9: K2, yo, K7, yo, K1, yo, K7, yo, K2. You now have 23 stitches.

❈ ROW 10: Repeat Row 2.

❈ ROW 11: K2, yo, K1, place marker (pm), * (K2tog, yo twice, K2tog) twice **, pm, yo, K1 (center stitch of shawl), yo, pm, work from * to ** once more, pm, K1, yo, K2.

❈ ROW 12: K2, P2, slip marker (sm), K2, P1, K3, P1, K1, sm, purl to next marker, sm, K1, P1, K3, P1, K2, sm, P2, K2.

❈ ROW 13: K2, yo, K2, sm, * K2, K2tog, yo twice, K2tog, K2 **, sm, (K1, yo) twice, K1, sm, repeat from * to ** once more, sm, K2, yo, K2.

❈ ROW 14: K2, P3, sm, K4, P1, K3, sm, purl to next marker, sm, K3, P1, K4, sm, P3, K2.

❈ ROW 15: K2, yo, K3, sm, * (K2tog, yo twice, K2tog) twice **, sm, K2, yo, K1, yo, K2, sm, repeat from * to ** once more, sm, K3, yo, K2.

❈ ROW 16: K2, P4, sm, K2, P1, K3, P1, K1, sm, purl to next marker, sm, K1, P1, K3, P1, K2, sm, P4, K2.

❈ ROW 17: K2, yo, K4, sm, * K2, K2tog, yo twice, K2tog, K2 **, sm, K3, yo, K1, yo, K3, sm, repeat from * to ** once more, sm, K4, yo, K2.

❈ ROW 18: K2, P5, sm, K4, P1, K3, sm, purl to next marker, sm, K3, P1, K4, sm, P5, K2.

❈ After Row 18, the first repeat of the lace pattern is complete. Move the markers at the ends to 3 stitches from edge and the markers in the middle to either side of the center stitch. This adds 8 stitches to each side of the shawl. Repeat rows 11–18, working 2 repeats of the pattern (outlined in bold on the chart) on each side of the center stitch. Once that repeat is complete, move the markers as before and continue (working 3 repeats of the pattern on each side of the center stitch). Continue in pattern as established until there are 14 repeats of the pattern on each side of the center stitch, or 122 rows.

Knitting the Edging

❈ Work 4 rows loosely in garter stitch. Bind off *very* loosely.

Finishing

❈ Weave in ends. Block to specified measurements. Allow to dry completely.

Blossom Silk-SeaCell Shawl

☐ knit on RS rows, purl on WS rows

⊡ purl on RS rows, knit on WS rows

⊙ yarn over

⧄ K2tog

Note: Read the chart from right to left for the right half of the shawl, and from left to right for the left half of the shawl on every row. The leftmost stitch on each row of the chart is the center stitch of the shawl.

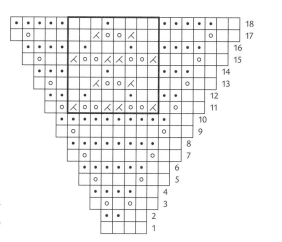

ALPACA ELEPHANT HAT

DESIGNED BY CAROLINE PERISHO, *photo on page 24*

To say this is cute is an understatement at best, and the cuteness is complemented by the softness of pure alpaca wool. Take lots of photos of your toddler in this one!

SIZES AND FINISHED MEASUREMENTS	To fit a toddler, approximately 16" (41 cm) circumference
YARN	Frog Tree Sport Alpaca, 100% alpaca, 1.75 oz (50 g)/130 yds (119 m), 009 Light Gray
NEEDLES	US 5 (3.75 mm) circular needle 16" (40 cm) long and set of four US 5 (3.75 mm) double-point needles *or size you need to obtain correct gauge*
GAUGE	22 stitches = 4" (10 cm) in stockinette stitch
OTHER SUPPLIES	Stitch markers, tapestry needle, scrap yarn for holders, polyester fiberfill, button eyes

Beginning the Hat

❊ Cast on 91 stitches and join into a round, being careful not to twist the stitches, as follows: Slip the last cast-on stitch onto left needle, place marker, knit last cast-on stitch together with first cast-on stitch. You now have 90 stitches. Work stockinette stitch until piece measures 4.5" (11.5 cm).

Decreasing for the Crown

❊ ROUND 1: *K8, K2tog; repeat from *. You now have 81 stitches.

❊ ROUND 2 AND ALL EVEN-NUMBERED ROUNDS: Knit.

❊ ROUND 3: *K7, K2tog; repeat from *. You now have 72 stitches.

❊ ROUND 5: *K6, K2tog; repeat from *. You now have 63 stitches.

❊ Continue in this manner, knitting 1 fewer stitch between the decreases and working 1 round even between decrease rounds, until 18 stitches remain.

❊ NEXT ROUND: *K2tog; repeat from *. You now have 9 stitches.

❊ NEXT ROUND: *K2tog; repeat from * to last stitch, K1. You now have 5 stitches.

❊ Cut yarn, leaving an 8" (20.5 cm) tail. Thread tail onto tapestry needle and draw through remaining stitches twice. Pull up snug and fasten off.

Knitting the Trunk

* Cast on 14 stitches onto double-point needles and work back and forth. Work 6 rows in stockinette stitch.
* NEXT ROW: *K1, ssk; repeat from * to last 3 stitches, K2tog, K1. You now have 12 stitches.
* NEXT ROW: Purl.
* Repeat these 2 rows until 6 stitches remain. Following the instructions on page 262, work 6-stitch I-cord for 5" (12.5 cm).
* NEXT ROW: *K2tog; repeat from *. You now have 3 stitches.
* NEXT ROW: K3tog, cut yarn, leaving a 6" (15 cm) tail, and pull tail through last stitch.

Knitting the Ears
(Make 2)

LEFT FRONT AND RIGHT BACK

* Cast on 8 stitches onto double-point needles and work back and forth.
* ROW 1 (RS): K1, M1, K6, M1, K1. You now have 10 stitches.
* ROW 2: P1, M1, P9. You now have 11 stitches.
* ROW 3: K1, M1, K9, M1, K1. You now have 13 stitches.
* ROW 4: P1, M1, P12. You now have 14 stitches.
* ROW 5: K1, M1, K12, M1, K1. You now have 16 stitches.
* ROW 6: P1, M1, P15. You now have 17 stitches.
* ROW 7: K1, M1, K15, M1, K1. You now have 19 stitches.
* ROW 8: P1, M1, P18. You now have 20 stitches.
* ROW 9: K1, M1, K18, M1, K1. You now have 22 stitches.
* ROW 10: P1, M1, P21. You now have 23 stitches.
* ROW 11: K1, M1, K21, M1, K1. You now have 25 stitches.
* ROW 12: P1, M1, P24. You now have 26 stitches.
* Work 6 rows even in stockinette stitch. Place 26 stitches on holder.

LEFT BACK AND RIGHT FRONT

* Cast on 8 stitches onto double-point needles and work back and forth.
* ROW 1 (WS): P1, M1, P6, M1, P1. You now have 10 stitches.
* ROW 2: K1, M1, K9. You now have 11 stitches.
* ROW 3: P1, M1, P9, M1, P1. You now have 13 stitches.
* ROW 4: K1, M1, K12. You now have 14 stitches.

ALPACA ELEPHANT HAT *continued*

❋ ROW 5: P1, M1, P12, M1, P1. You now have 16 stitches.
❋ ROW 6: K1, M1, K15. You now have 17 stitches.
❋ ROW 7: P1, M1, P15, M1, P1. You now have 19 stitches.
❋ ROW 8: K1, M1, K18. You now have 20 stitches.
❋ ROW 9: P1, M1, P18, M1, P1. You now have 22 stitches.
❋ ROW 10: K1, M1, K21. You now have 23 stitches.
❋ ROW 11: P1, M1, P21, M1, P1. You now have 25 stitches.
❋ ROW 12: K1, M1, K24. You now have 26 stitches.
❋ Work 6 rows even in stockinette stitch. Place 26 stitches on holder.
❋ Pin left back and left front together and seam along the rounded edges, leaving remaining stitches on holders. Lightly stuff the ears with fiberfill, then join the remaining stitches with three-needle bind-off (see page 266). Repeat for right ear.

Finishing

❋ Position the ears along the sides of the hat as shown in photo (see page 24) and sew them in place. Position the base of the trunk centered on the front of the hat between the ears as shown. Lightly stuff the base of the trunk and sew around it, leaving the I-cord free. Tack the end of the I-cord to the side of the face. Weave in ends. Sew on button eyes.

ALPACA GATOR SOCKS

DESIGNED BY CAROLINE PERISHO, *photo on page 24*

Isn't it amazing what two little buttons can do? Here they transform booties into mini alligators for your child's pleasure. Knitted in pure alpaca, they're soft and fun at the same time.

STITCH PATTERNS

woven cable

ROUND 1: *C4F; repeat from *.

ROUND 2: Knit.

ROUND 3: *C4B; repeat from *.

ROUND 4: Knit.

REPEAT ROWS 1–4 FOR PATTERN.

k1, p1 rib

ROUND 1: *K1, P1; repeat from *.

REPEAT ROUND 1 FOR PATTERN.

SIZES AND FINISHED MEASUREMENTS	To fit an infant, approximately 3" (7.5 cm) foot length
YARN	Frog Tree Alpaca, 100% alpaca, 1.75 oz (50 g)/130 yds (119 m), 402 Green
NEEDLES	Set of four US 5 (3.75 mm) double-point needles *or size you need to obtain correct gauge*
GAUGE	28 stitches = 4" (10 cm) in Woven Cable pattern
OTHER SUPPLIES	Stitch marker, cable needle, tapestry needle, four doll eyes
ABBREVIATIONS	**C4F (cable 4 front)** place 2 stitches on cable needle and hold in front, K2, K2 from cable needle **C4B (cable 4 back)** place 2 stitches on cable needle and hold in back, K2, K2 from cable needle

Knitting the Leg

❋ Cast on 41 stitches and distribute onto 3 double-point needles so there are 11 stitches on needle 1, 20 stitches on needle 2, and 10 stitches on needle 3. Join into a round, being careful not to twist the stitches, as follows: Slip the last cast-on stitch onto left needle, place marker, knit the last cast-on stitch together with the first cast-on stitch. You now have 40 stitches.

❋ ROUND 1: Work K1, P1 Rib on needle 1, work Woven Cable pattern on needle 2, work K1, P1 Rib on needle 3.

❋ Continue in this manner until you have completed 6 full repeats of Rounds 1–4 of Woven Cable pattern.

Knitting the Heel Flap

❋ Leave 20 Woven Cable stitches on needle to hold for instep. Knit the 10 rib stitches from needle 1 onto needle 3. Work back and forth on these 20 stitches only as follows:

❋ ROW 1 (WS): Slip 1, purl to end of row.

❋ ROW 2: *Slip 1 pwise, K1; repeat from *.

❋ Repeat Rows 1 and 2 three more times, ending with Row 1.

Turning the Heel

* ❋ ROW 1 (RS): K10, K2tog, K1, turn.
* ❋ ROW 2: P2, P2tog, P1, turn.
* ❋ ROW 3: K3, K2tog, K1, turn.
* ❋ ROW 4: P4, P2tog, P1, turn.
* ❋ ROW 5: K5, P2tog, K1, turn.
* ❋ ROW 6: P6, P2tog, P1, turn.
* ❋ ROW 7: K7, K2tog, K1, turn.
* ❋ ROW 8: P8, P2tog, P1, turn.
* ❋ ROW 9: K9, K2tog, K1, turn.
* ❋ ROW 10: P10, P2tog, turn.

Knitting the Gusset

❋ With needle 1, knit 10 remaining heel stitches and pick up and knit (see page 264) 8 stitches along side of heel. With needle 2, work Woven Cable pattern as established on 20 instep stitches. With needle 3, pick up and knit 8 stitches along other side of heel, knit 5 stitches from needle 1. You now have 13 stitches on needles 1 and 3 and 20 stitches on needle 2.

❋ ROUND 1: Knit to last 3 stitches on needle 1, K2tog, K1; work pattern as established on needle 2; K1, ssk at beginning of needle 3, knit to end of round.

❋ ROUND 2: Knit stitches on needles 1 and 3; continue pattern as established on needle 2.

❋ Repeat Rounds 1 and 2 until 10 stitches remain on needles 1 and 3, then work Round 2 only until 5 repeats of Rounds 1–4 of Woven Cable pattern have been worked from the beginning of heel shaping.

Finishing

❋ Join 10 sole stitches with 10 instep stitches using the three-needle bind-off (see page 266). Weave in ends. Sew doll eyes to front of socks.

Mock Cable Alpaca Tam

DESIGNED BY KATHLEEN TAYLOR, *photo on page 21*

This simple tam is knit with incredibly soft and warm alpaca and merino wool from Decadent Fibers. The mock cable is easy to work, and you don't even need a cable needle!

SIZES AND FINISHED MEASUREMENTS	To fit most adults and youths, approximately 21" (53 cm) circumference after blocking
YARN	Decadent Fibers Marshmallow, 80% alpaca/20% merino wool, 4 oz (113.5 g)/315 yds (288 m), MM Natural
NEEDLES	US 4 (3.5 mm) circular needle 16" (40 cm) long and set of four US 4 (3.5 mm) double-point needles *or size you need to obtain correct gauge*
GAUGE	26 stitches and 32 rounds = 4" (10 cm) in stockinette stitch
OTHER SUPPLIES	Stitch markers, tapestry needle
ABBREVIATIONS	MC mock cable

Getting Started

✻ With circular needle, cast on 176 stitches. Join into a round, being careful not to twist the stitches. Work Rounds 1–4 of Ribbing pattern 3 times, then work Round 1 once more, placing marker after every 22 stitches (8 sections).

Knitting the Crown

✻ Work Rounds 1–4 of Crown pattern 7 times, then work Rounds 1–3 once more. Note: The crown cables will not always line up with a ribbing cable.

Decreasing the Crown

✻ ROUND 1: *P1, K2, P1, P2tog, K14, P2tog; repeat from * 7 times.
✻ ROUND 2: *P1, MC, P2, K14, P1; repeat from * 7 times.
✻ ROUND 3: *P1, K2, P2, K14, P1; repeat from * 7 times.
✻ ROUND 4: *P1, K2, P1, P2tog, K12, P2tog; repeat from * 7 times.
✻ ROUND 5: *P1, K2, P2, K12, P1; repeat from * 7 times.
✻ ROUND 6: *P1, MC, P2, K12, P1; repeat from * 7 times.
✻ ROUND 7: *P1, K2, P1, P2tog, K10, P2tog; repeat from * 7 times.
✻ ROUNDS 8 AND 9: *P1, K2, P2, K10, P1; repeat from * 7 times.
✻ ROUND 10: *P1, MC, P1, P2tog, K8, P2tog; repeat from * 7 times.

STITCH PATTERNS

mock cable (MC)

With right needle, reach past the first stitch on left needle and lift the second stitch up and over the first; knit that stitch, then knit the first stitch.

ribbing

ROUNDS 1, 3, AND 4: *P1, K2, P1; repeat from *.
ROUND 2: *P1, MC, P1; repeat from *.
REPEAT ROUNDS 1–4 FOR PATTERN.

crown

ROUND 1: *P1, MC, P2, K16, P1; repeat from * 7 more times.
ROUNDS 2–4: *P1, K2, P2, K16, P1; repeat from * 7 more times.
REPEAT ROUNDS 1–4 FOR PATTERN.

MOCK CABLE ALPACA TAM *continued*

- ❊ ROUNDS 11 AND 12: *P1, K2, P2, K8, P1; repeat from * 7 times.
- ❊ ROUND 13: *P1, K2, P1, P2tog, K6, P2tog; repeat from * 7 times.
- ❊ ROUND 14: *P1, MC, P2, K6, P1; repeat from * 7 times.
- ❊ ROUND 15: *P1, K2, P2, K6, P1; repeat from * 7 times.
- ❊ ROUND 16: *P1, K2, P1, P2tog, K4, P2tog; repeat from * 7 times.
- ❊ ROUND 17: *P1, K2, P2, K4, P1; repeat from * 7 times.
- ❊ ROUND 18: *P1, MC, P1, P2tog, K2, P2tog; repeat from * 7 times.
- ❊ ROUND 19: *P1, K2, P2, K2, P1; repeat from * 7 times.
- ❊ ROUND 20: *K2tog twice, P2tog twice; repeat from * 7 times.
- ❊ ROUND 21: *K2tog, P2tog; repeat from * 7 times.
- ❊ ROUNDS 22 AND 23: *K2tog; repeat from * to end of round. You now have 4 stitches.

Finishing

- ❊ Slip 4 remaining stitches onto 1 double-point needle and slide to right end of needle. Following instructions for I-cord (see page 262), work 4 rows. Cut yarn, leaving an 8" (20 cm) tail. Thread tail onto tapestry needle and draw through remaining stitches twice. Pull up snug and fasten off. Weave in ends. Wash and block tam on a 10" (25.5 cm) dinner plate.

Silk-Merino Leaf Lace Hat

DESIGNED BY SARAH-HOPE PARMETER, *photo on page 24*

A fingering-weight silk-and-merino blend make this hat perfect for autumn wear. It is knitted in the round with six repeats of a leafy lace pattern.

SIZES AND FINISHED MEASUREMENTS	To fit most adults, approximately 18" (45.5 cm) stretching to 24" (61 cm) circumference
YARN	Curious Creek Fibers Omo, 50% silk/50% merino wool, 1.75 oz (50 g)/205 yds (186 m), Savanna Grasses
NEEDLES	US 3 (3.25 mm) circular needle 16" (40 cm) long and set of four US 3 (3.25 mm) double-point needles *or size you need to obtain correct gauge*
GAUGE	24 stitches = 4" (10 cm) in stockinette stitch, 26 stitches = 4" (10 cm) in pattern
OTHER SUPPLIES	Stitch marker, cable needle, tapestry needle

Knitting the Hat

❊ With circular needle, cast on 114 stitches. Place marker and join into a round, being careful not to twist the stitches. Work 5 rows of K1, P1 Rib (see page 113).

❊ Work Rows 1–6 of chart 1 (see page 118), working the 19-stitch repeat 6 times in each round.

❊ Work Rows 1–20 of chart 2 (see page 119) twice, working the 19-stitch repeat 6 times in each round.

Decreasing for the Crown

❊ Change to double-point needles when there are too few stitches for the circular needle.

❊ Work Rows 1–16 of chart 3 (see page 119). Note: At the beginning of Rounds 5, 7, 9, 11, 13, 15, and 16, remove the marker, slip 1 stitch from left to right needle, replace marker, then work round as charted.

Finishing

❊ Cut yarn, leaving an 8" (20.5 cm) tail. Thread tail onto tapestry needle and draw through remaining stitches twice. Pull up snug and fasten off. Weave in ends.

Silk-Merino Leaf Lace Hat

☐ knit on RS rows, purl on WS rows

⊡ purl on RS rows, knit on WS rows

⊡ yarn over

⊠ ssk

⊠ K2tog

◤ slip 2 stitches to cable needle and hold in front, P1, K2 from cable needle

◣ slip 1 stitch to cable needle and hold in back, K2, P1 from cable needle

⊼ slip 2tog kwise, K2, p2sso

▨ no stitch

CHART 1

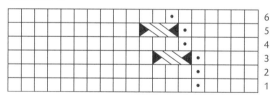

Chart 2

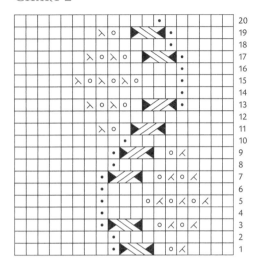

Chart 3

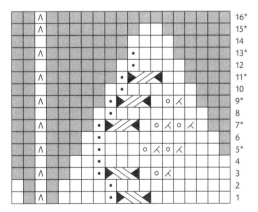

Note: See special instructions for beginning each of these rounds.

Lacy Gray Alpaca Scarf

DESIGNED BY MARY JANE HALL, *photo on page 20*

Light as a feather, this scarf was crocheted in a delicate openwork pattern using a lovely alpaca-and-angora blend, hand spun by Reneé Barnes.

FINISHED MEASUREMENTS	Approximately 4.5" (11.5 cm) wide and 50" (127 cm) long
YARN	Renée Barnes Handspun, 90% alpaca/10% angora, 3.5 oz (100 g)/176 yds (158 m), Gray
CROCHET HOOK	Size G/6 (4 mm) *or size you need to obtain correct gauge*
GAUGE	1 square = 4.5" (11.5 cm)
OTHER SUPPLIES	Tapestry needle
ABBREVIATIONS	**tr cl** triple cluster: [yo twice, insert hook in designated space, yo and draw through (yo and draw through 2 loops on hook) twice] 3 times, yo and draw through last 4 loops on hook

Crocheting the Squares

❊ Ch 6, join with sl st to form a ring.

❊ ROUND 1: Ch 4 (counts as first triple) [yo twice, insert hook in ring, yo and draw through, (yo and draw through 2 loops on hook) twice] 2 times, yo and draw through last 3 loops on hook, *ch 5, [yo twice, insert hook in center of ring, yo and draw through (yo and draw through 2 loops on hook) twice] 3 times, yo and draw through last 4 loops on hook (tr cl made); repeat from * 6 times, ch 5, sl st in top of first cluster. You now have 8 tr cl with ch 5 between each.

❊ ROUND 2: Sl st to center of ch-5 space, ch 1, (sc, ch 3, sc) in same ch-5 space, *ch 5, (sc, ch 3, sc) in next ch-5 space; repeat from * 6 times, ch 5, sl st in first sc. You now have 8 ch-5 spaces.

❊ ROUND 3: Sl st to center of ch-5 space, ch 1, (sc, ch 3, sc) in same ch-5 space, *ch 9 (sc, ch 3, sc) in next ch-5 space; repeat from * 7 times, ch 9, sl st to first sc. You now have 8 ch-9 spaces.

❊ ROUND 4: Sl st to center of ch-9 space, (sc, ch 5, sc) in center ch, *ch 6, (1 tr cl, ch 5) twice in fifth chain of next ch-9, 1 tr cl in same ch, ch 6 (sc, ch 5, sc) in fifth ch of next ch 9; repeat from *, ch 6, join with sl st to first sc. You have 3 tr cl in each corner. Break yarn.

❊ Repeat the ring and Rounds 1–4 ten more times.

Finishing

❊ Weave in ends. With RS together, sew squares together into a strip. Block lightly.

Starfish of Yak

DESIGNED BY DANIEL YUHAS, *photo on page 21*

With five points to grab hold of, your baby will love this toy! The construction is ingenious — no breaking of yarn, no sewing of seams — and the yak-merino yarn keeps things soft.

FINISHED MEASUREMENTS	Approximately 11" (28 cm) from tip to tip
YARN	Karabella Super Yak, 50% yak/50% merino wool, 1.75 oz (50 g)/125 yds (115 m), 10397 Pink
NEEDLES	Set of four US 3 (3.25 mm) double-point needles *or size you need to obtain correct gauge*
GAUGE	22 stitches and 32 rows = 4" (10 cm) in stockinette stitch
OTHER SUPPLIES	Stitch markers, scrap yarn for holders, small amount of polyester fiberfill, tapestry needle
ABBREVIATIONS	**inc L** left lifted increase (see box at left) **inc R** right lifted increase (see box at left)

✳ Note: You'll begin by knitting a pentagon in the round. While knitting the legs back and forth from each side of the pentagon, the first and last stitch of each row are placed on a holder, then joined together with three-needle bind-off (see page 266).

Getting Started

✳ Cut a short piece of scrap yarn from the skein about the same length as one of your needles. Using the backward loop method (see page 261), cast on 10 stitches over the needle and scrap yarn. Divide the stitches so you have 2 stitches on needle 1 and 4 stitches on each of needles 2 and 3. Join into a round, being careful not to twist the stitches.

✳ ROUND 1: K2 on needle 1, (K2, pm, K2) on needles 2 and 3.

✳ ROUND 2: *K1, inc R, K1; repeat from *. You now have 3 stitches on needle 1 and 3 stitches on either side of the markers on needles 2 and 3.

✳ ROUND 3: Knit.

✳ Tie the scrap yarn to tighten the cast-on stitches together.

✳ ROUND 4: *K1, inc L, K1, inc R, K1; repeat from *. You now have 5 stitches on needle 1 and 5 stitches between markers on needles 2 and 3.

✳ ROUND 5: Knit.

increases

LEFT LIFTED INCREASE: Pick up the stitch 2 stitches below the last stitch on the right-hand needle and knit it through the back loop — 1 stitch increased.

RIGHT LIFTED INCREASE: Pick up the stitch below the next stitch on the left-hand needle and knit it — 1 stitch increased.

❊ ROUND 6: *K2, inc L, K1, inc R, K2; repeat from *. You now have 7 stitches on needle 1 and 7 stitches between markers on needles 2 and 3.

❊ ROUND 7: Knit.

❊ ROUND 8: *K3, inc L, K1, inc R, K3; repeat from *. You now have 9 stitches on needle 1 and 9 stitches between markers on needles 2 and 3.

❊ ROUND 9: Knit.

❊ Continue in this manner, working 1 more stitch before the inc L and 1 more stitch after the inc R on the increase rounds and knitting 1 round even between increase rounds until you have 19 stitches on needle 1 and 19 stitches between the markers on needles 2 and 3: 95 stitches total.

Knitting the Legs

❊ Place stitches from needles 2 and 3 onto scrap yarn holders. Working back and forth on remaining 19 stitches, proceed as follows: On every row except on the Set-up Row, slip the first and last stitch of every row onto a holder or extra double-point needle, being careful not to drop any stitches.

❊ SET-UP ROW: K2, inc L, K7, inc L, K1, inc R, K7, inc R, K2. You now have 23 stitches.

❊ ROW 1 (WS): Slip, P21, slip. You now have 21 stitches.

❊ ROW 2: Slip 1, K2, inc L, K7, inc L, K1, inc R, K7, inc R, K2, slip 1. You now have 23 stitches.

❊ ROWS 3 AND 5: Repeat Row 1.

❊ ROWS 4 AND 6: Repeat Row 2.

❊ ROW 7: Repeat Row 1. You now have 21 stitches.

❊ ROW 8: Slip, K2, inc L, K15, inc R, K2, slip.

❊ ROW 9: Slip, P19, slip. You now have 19 stitches.

❊ ROW 10: Slip, K2, inc L, K6, inc L, K1, inc R, K6, inc R, K2, slip. You now have 21 stitches.

❊ ROW 11: Repeat Row 9.

❊ ROW 12: Slip , K2, inc L, K13, inc R, K2, slip.

❊ ROW 13: Slip, P17, slip. You now have 17 stitches.

❊ ROW 14: Slip, K2, inc L, K5, inc L, K1, inc R, K5, inc R, K2, slip. You now have 19 stitches.

❊ ROW 15: Repeat Row 13.

❊ ROW 16: Slip, K2, inc L, K11, inc R, K2, slip. You now have 17 stitches.

❊ ROW 17: Slip, P15, slip. You now have 15 stitches.

❊ ROW 18: Slip, K2, inc L, K4, inc L, K1, inc R, K4, inc R, K2, slip. You now have 17 stitches.

❊ ROW 19: Repeat Row 17.

❋ ROW 20: Slip, K2, inc L, K9, inc R, K2, slip. You now have 15 stitches.

❋ ROW 21: Slip, P13, slip. You now have 13 stitches.

❋ ROW 22: Slip, K2, inc L, K3, inc L, K1, inc R, K3, inc R, K2, slip. You now have 15 stitches.

❋ ROW 23: Repeat Row 21.

❋ ROW 24: Slip, K2, inc L, K7, inc R, K2, slip. You now have 13 stitches.

❋ ROW 25: Slip, P11, slip. You now have 11 stitches.

❋ ROW 26: Slip, K2, inc L, K2, inc L, K1, inc R, K2, inc R, K2, slip. You now have 13 stitches.

❋ ROW 27: Repeat Row 25.

❋ ROW 28: Slip, K2, inc L, K5, inc R, K2, slip. You now have 11 stitches.

❋ ROW 29: Slip, P9, slip. You now have 9 stitches.

❋ ROW 30: Slip, K2, inc L, K1, inc L, K1, inc R, K1, inc R, K2, slip. You now have 11 stitches.

❋ ROW 31: Repeat Row 29.

❋ ROW 32: Slip, K2, inc L, K3, inc R, K2, slip. You now have 9 stitches.

❋ ROW 33: Slip, P7, slip. You now have 7 stitches.

❋ ROW 34: Slip, K2, inc L, K1, inc R, K2, slip. You now have 7 stitches.

❋ ROW 35: Slip, P5, slip. You now have 5 stitches.

❋ ROW 36: Slip, K3, slip. You now have 3 stitches.

❋ ROW 37: Slip, P1, slip. You now have 1 stitch.

SEALING THE LEG

❋ Hold the slipped stitches from both sides of leg with purl sides together. Knit the first 2 stitches from each needle together and slip the last remaining stitch from leg point over the resulting stitch. Join remaining stitches together with the three-needle bind-off (see page 266). You will have 1 remaining stitch at the end of the bind-off. Lightly stuff the leg.

KNITTING THE NEXT LEG

❋ Place the next 19 held stitches on a needle. Knitting the remaining stitch from the first leg together with the first of the 19 stitches, work the Set-up Row: K2tog, K1, inc L, K7, inc L, K1, inc R, K7, inc R, K2. Continue as for first leg. Repeat 3 more times for the other legs.

Finishing

❋ When all legs are stuffed, break the yarn and sew the hole closed. Weave in the end and pull through to the inside.

QIVIUT NECK MUFF

DESIGNED BY JACKIE ERICKSON-SCHWEITZER, *photo on page 21*

Lusciously soft and warm, this lacy neck muff knitted in qiviut is designed to be worn as a yoke or as a cowl. The lace consists of two simple pattern rows that produce a softly scalloped edge.

SIZES AND FINISHED MEASUREMENTS	To fit most adults, approximately 18" (45.5 cm) circumference at neck, 30"(76 cm) circumference at lower edge, and 9" (23 cm) length
YARN	Windy Valley Musk Ox Pure Qiviut, 100% qiviut, 1 oz (28.5 g)/ 218 yds (199 m), Arctic Moss
NEEDLES	US 5 (3.75 mm) circular needle 16" (40 cm) long *or size you need to obtain correct gauge*; circular needle 16" (40 cm) long, 2 sizes larger than gauge needle; and circular needle 16" (40 cm) long, 5 sizes larger than gauge needle
GAUGE	21 stitches = 4" (10 cm) in stockinette stitch, 25 stitches = 4" (10 cm) in pattern on smallest needles
OTHER SUPPLIES	Stitch marker, tapestry needle

Knitting the Muff

❋ With smallest needle, cast on 112 stitches loosely.

❋ EDGE ROW: Slip 1 pwise wyib, knit to end of row.

❋ Place marker and join into a round, being careful not to twist the stitches. Work Rounds 1–20 of Zigzag Ribbed Lace pattern, then work Rounds 1–10 once more.

❋ Change to middle-size needle. Work Rounds 11–20 of pattern.

❋ Change to largest needle. Work Rounds 1–20 of pattern.

❋ Bind off as follows: *P2tog, with yarn in front slip stitch back to left needle; repeat from * until all stitches are bound off. Break yarn and pull through remaining loop.

Finishing

❋ Weave in ends. Steam lightly without touching the fabric. If desired, gently finger block the beginning and end to emphasize the scallops.

BEADED CASHMERE WRISTLETS
DESIGNED BY GRACE MAGGIE COVEY, *photo on page 21*

These wristlets will look lovely peeking out from the sleeves of your favorite coat. They are narrow at the wrist and wider at both ends, so you can wear them either end up.

SIZES AND FINISHED MEASUREMENTS	To fit average woman, approximately 6.5" (16.5 cm) circumference at wrist, 7" (18 cm) long
YARN	JoJoland Cashmere, 100% cashmere, 2 oz (57 g)/200 yds (183 m), CA55 Periwinkle
NEEDLES	Set of four US 3 (3.25 mm) double-point needles *or size you need to obtain correct gauge*
GAUGE	24 stitches = 4" (10 cm) in stockinette stitch, 22 stitches = 4" (10 cm) in pattern
OTHER SUPPLIES	Big-eye beading needle, approximately 882 size 6° seed beads, stitch marker, tapestry needle
ABBREVIATIONS	**S1b** slide bead(s) up next to needle (S2b = slide 2 beads, etc.)

Preparing the Yarn
❁ Thread yarn end onto a big-eye beading needle. Picking up beads with the needle, string 441 beads for one wristlet. Using the knitted-on method (see page 262), cast on 3, S7b, *cast on 5, S7b; repeat from * 5 more times, cast on 2. You now have 7 swags of beads with 5 stitches between each swag, 35 stitches total.

Knitting the Wristlets
❁ Divide the stitches onto 3 needles and join into a round, being careful not to twist the stitches. Place a marker.
❁ ROUND 1: K2, P1, Sb6, P1, *K3, P1, Sb6, P1; repeat from * to last stitch, K1.
❁ ROUND 2: K2, P1, Sb5, P1, *K3, P1, Sb5, P1; repeat from * to last stitch, K1.
❁ ROUND 3: K2, P1, Sb4, P1, *K3, P1, Sb4, P1; repeat from * to last stitch, K1.
❁ ROUND 4: K2, P1, Sb3, P1, *K3, P1, Sb3, P1; repeat from * to last stitch, K1.
❁ ROUND 5: K2, P1, Sb2, P1, *K3, P1, Sb2, P1; repeat from * to last stitch, K1.
❁ ROUND 6: K2, P1, Sb1, P1, *K3, P1, Sb1, P1; repeat from * to last stitch, K1.
❁ ROUND 7: Knit.
❁ Repeat Rounds 6 and 7 twenty-nine times, then work Round 6 once more. You now have 31 single-bead rounds.

❋ Work Round 5, then Round 4.

❋ NEXT ROUND: K2, P1, yo, P1, *K3, P1, yo, P1; repeat from * to last stitch, K1.

❋ Knit 1 round.

❋ Bind off as follows: *P1, move stitch back to left needle, P2tog; repeat from * until all stitches are bound off, pulling yarn tail through last stitch.

Finishing

❋ Weave in ends.

ANGORA PENDANT NECKLACE

DESIGNED BY CATHY CARRON, *photo on page 23*

Here's a new way to show off stone discs. Two styles are shown here, but you may think up more. Knitted in the round, it's nine rounds and you're done!

FINISHED MEASUREMENTS	Approximately 30 " (76 cm) long
YARN	Valeria di Roma Angora, 100% angora, 1.75 oz (50 g)/55 yds (50 m), 8007 Ivory or 8042 Black
NEEDLES	US 5 (3.75 mm) circular needle 24" (60 cm) long *or size you need to obtain correct gauge*
GAUGE	24 stitches = 4" (10 cm) in stockinette stitch
OTHER SUPPLIES	50 mm donut bead, stitch marker, tapestry needle

Knitting Version 1 (Ivory)

❋ Cast on 180 stitches. Slide bead over needle, place marker, and join into a round, being careful not to twist the stitches. Knit 9 rounds, slipping the bead around as necessary. Bind off.

FINISHING

❋ Weave in ends. Tie knot about 2" (5 cm) above bead.

Knitting Version 2 (Black)

❋ Cast on 180 stitches. Place marker and join into a round, being careful not to twist the stitches. Knit 9 rounds. Bind off.

FINISHING

* Weave in ends. Fold the knitted loop in half and push one end through the bead. Slide the bead to center of loop.

ANGORA BRIDAL GARTER

DESIGNED BY CATHY CARRON, *photo on page 22*

The bride will love wearing this angora garter, and the woman who receives it will be delighted! Knitted in the round, it has a lovely pink elastic ribbon woven through the eyelets.

SIZES AND FINISHED MEASUREMENTS	To fit most adults, approximately 14 " (35.5 cm) circumference, stretching to 26" (66 cm)
YARN	Valeria di Roma Angora, 100% angora, 1.75 oz (50 g)/55 yds (50 m), 8007 Ivory
NEEDLES	US 5 (3.75 mm) circular needle 24" (60 cm) long *or size you need to obtain correct gauge*
GAUGE	24 stitches = 4" (10 cm) in stockinette stitch
OTHER SUPPLIES	Stitch marker, tapestry needle, 1.5 yds (137 cm) ³⁄₈" (1 cm) elastic ribbon

Knitting the Garter

* Cast on 171 stitches. Place marker and join into a round, being careful not to twist the stitches.
* ROUNDS 1 AND 2: Knit.
* ROUND 3: *K1, K2tog; repeat from *. You now have 114 stitches.
* ROUND 4: Knit.
* ROUND 5: *Yo, K2tog; repeat from *.
* ROUND 6: Knit.
* ROUND 7: *K2, M1; repeat from *. You now have 171 stitches.
* ROUNDS 8 AND 9: Knit.
* Bind off.

Finishing

* Weave in ends. Weave elastic ribbon through eyelet holes and tie into a bow.

A Pair of Silk Purses

DESIGNED BY JUDITH DURANT, *photo on page 20*

The silk yarn used for these purses is combined with the tiniest bit of polyester and then knitted into a ribbonlike strand. It has beautiful shine and texture and is as light as a feather. The fabric is very accommodating; it took to the frames as if they were made for each other (which, actually, they were).

FINISHED MEASUREMENTS	Approximately 4" (10 cm) tall and 4" (10 cm) wide at widest point
YARN	Lang Yarns Silk, 98% silk/2% polyester, 0.88 oz (25 g)/85 yds (78 m), 727.0023 Blue
NEEDLES	US 5 (3.75 mm) straight needles for square purse, set of five US 5 (3.75 mm) double-point needles for round purse *or size you need to obtain correct gauge*
GAUGE	32 stitches and 40 rows = 4" (10 cm) in stockinette stitch
OTHER SUPPLIES	Tapestry needle, sewing needle and coordinating sewing thread, square or round 2.5" (6.5 cm) purse frame, US D/3 (3.25 mm) crochet hook (for round bag), two jump rings, and chain of desired length (optional)

Knitting the Square-top Purse

GETTING STARTED

❁ Cast on 21 stitches. Purl 1 row. Work Rows 1–8 of Knot Stitch pattern, then work Rows 1 and 2.

BEGIN SHAPING

❁ INCREASE ROW: K1, M1, work in pattern to last stitch, M1, K1.

❁ Continue in pattern as established, working increase row every fourth RS row (knit rows) 5 more times, then purl 1 row. You now have 33 stitches. Work 10 rows even in pattern.

❁ DECREASE ROW: K1, ssk, work in pattern to last 3 stitches, K2tog, K1.

❁ Continue in pattern as established, working decrease row every fourth RS row (knit rows) 5 more times, then purl 1 row. You now have 21 stitches. Work 10 rows even in pattern. Bind off all stitches.

STITCH PATTERN

knot stitch

ROW 1: *K3, (P3tog, K3tog, P3tog in next 3 stitches); repeat from * to last 3 stitches, K3.

ROWS 2 AND ALL WS ROWS THROUGH 8: Purl.

ROWS 3 AND 7: Knit.

ROW 5: K3, *K3 (P3tog, K3tog, P3tog in next 3 stitches); repeat from * to last 6 stitches, K6.

REPEAT ROWS 1–8 FOR PATTERN.

FINISHING

❋ Fold bag in half with WS together and sew side seams with mattress stitch (see page 264) from bottom to end of shaping. Weave in ends. Use sewing needle and thread to sew top of bag to frame. Attach chain with jump rings if desired.

Knitting the Round Purse

GETTING STARTED

❋ Cast on 8 stitches. Place 2 stitches on each of 4 double-point needles and join into a round, being careful not to twist the stitches. Knit 1 round.

❋ Note: If you find it difficult to work this first round, cast on 8 stitches and place 4 stitches on each of 2 needles. With a third needle, knit the stitches from one needle, slide all stitches down to the other end of the needles and, with the empty needle, knit the stitches from the second needle. It should now be easier to distribute the 8 stitches onto 4 needles.

❋ ROUND 1: *Kfb; repeat from *. You now have 16 stitches.

❋ ROUND 2: Knit.

❋ ROUND 3: *K2, M1; repeat from *. You now have 24 stitches.

❋ ROUND 4: Knit.

❋ ROUND 5: *K3, M1; repeat from *. You now have 32 stitches.

❋ ROUND 6: *(P3tog, K3tog, P3tog in next 3 stitches), K1.

❋ ROUND 7: *K4, M1; repeat from *. You now have 40 stitches.

❋ ROUND 8: Knit.

❋ ROUND 9: *K5, M1; repeat from *. You now have 48 stitches.

❋ ROUND 10: Knit.

❋ ROUND 11: *K6, M1; repeat from *. You now have 56 stitches.

❋ ROUND 12: *K2, (P3tog, K3tog, P3tog in next 3 stitches), K2; repeat from *.

❋ ROUND 13: *K7, M1; repeat from *. You now have 64 stitches.

❋ ROUND 14: Knit.

❋ ROUND 15: *K8, M1; repeat from *. You now have 72 stitches.

❋ ROUND 16: Knit.

❋ ROUND 17: *K9, M1; repeat from *. You now have 80 stitches.

❋ ROUND 18: *K4, (P3tog, K3tog, P3tog in next 3 stitches), K3; repeat from *.

❋ ROUND 19: *K10, M1; repeat from *. You now have 88 stitches.

❋ ROUND 20: Knit.

FINISHING THE BOTTOM AND KNITTING THE TOP

* ROW 1: K8, bind off 72, K8, then knit the 8 beginning-of-row stitches again. You now have 16 stitches on 1 needle.
* ROW 2: P16.
* ROW 3: Bind off 2 stitches, K1 (you now have 2 stitches on needle), (P3tog, K3tog, P3tog in next 3 stitches), K2, (P3tog, K3tog, P3tog in next 3 stitches), K4.
* ROW 4: Bind off 2 stitches, purl to end of row.
* ROW 5: Bind off 2 stitches, knit to end of row.
* ROW 6: Bind off 2 stitches, purl to end of row.
* Bind off remaining 8 stitches.
* Repeat for other side of purse.

FINISHING

* With WS together and beginning with the first bound-off stitches, join the front and back together with slip stitch crochet (see page 266). Weave in ends. Use sewing needle and thread to sew top of bag to frame, stretching the knitting as necessary to make a smooth edge. Attach chain with jump rings, if desired.

FRILLY MERINO-ANGORA BOOTIES

DESIGNED BY GWEN STEEGE, *photo on page 22*

Ruffles and pompoms! And what makes them even more appealing is the soft, cozy angora-merino yarn they're knit with. The perfect gift for the newest baby on your block!

FINISHED MEASUREMENTS	Approximately 3.25" (8.5 cm) foot length
YARN	Sublime Angora Merino, 80% extra fine merino/20% angora, 1.75 oz (50 g)/130 yds (119 m), 47 Dusky
NEEDLES	Set of four US 3 (3.25 mm) double-point needles *or size you need to obtain correct gauge*
GAUGE	24 stitches = 4" (10 cm) in stockinette stitch
OTHER SUPPLIES	Stitch holder, tapestry needle

Knitting the Cuff

❋ Cast on 90 stitches, and divide them evenly among 3 needles. Join into a round, being careful not to twist the stitches.

❋ ROUNDS 1 AND 2: Knit.

❋ ROUND 3: * Slip 1, K2tog, psso; repeat from *. You now have 30 stitches.

❋ ROUNDS 4–6: Knit.

❋ ROUND 7: *K3, K2tog; repeat from *. You now have 24 stitches.

❋ ROUND 8: K3, *yo, K4; repeat from * to last stitch, yo, K1. You now have 30 stitches.

❋ ROUNDS 9 AND 10: Purl.

❋ ROUNDS 11–13: * K1, P1; repeat from *.

Working the Heel Flap

❋ SET-UP ROUND: Cut the yarn, leaving a tail to weave in later. Place 7 stitches from needle 1 and 8 stitches from needle 3 onto 1 needle, and attach the yarn to these 15 stitches at the beginning of the RS row: These will be the heel stitches. Place the remaining stitches (instep stitches) on a spare needle or stitch holder and hold aside until the heel is complete. In this section, you will be working back and forth in rows.

❋ ROWS 1, 3, 5, AND 7: *Slip 1 wyib, K1; repeat from *.

❋ ROWS 2, 4, 6, AND 8: Slip 1 wyib, purl to end of row.

❋ Repeat Row 1 once more.

Turning the Heel

❋ ROW 1 (WS): P9, P2tog, P1, turn.

❋ ROW 2: Slip 1, K4, ssk, K1, turn.

❋ ROW 3: Slip 1, P5, P2tog, P1, turn.

❋ ROW 4: Slip 1, K6, ssk, K1, turn.

❋ ROW 5: P8, P2tog, turn.

❋ ROW 6: Knit to end of row. You now have 10 heel stitches.

Forming the Gusset and Instep

❋ SET-UP ROUND: Pick up 8 stitches along the left side of the heel flap. Work the 15 instep stitches that you set aside before working the heel, continuing in the established K1, P1 rib pattern. Use an empty needle to pick up 8 stitches along the right side of the heel flap, then knit the first 5 of the remaining heel stitches again. There are 15 instep stitches on needle 2, and 13 heel stitches each on needles 1 and 3. The middle of the heel is now the beginning of each round.

FRILLY MERINO-ANGORA BOOTIES *continued*

❋ **ROUND 1:**

    ❋ NEEDLE 1: Knit to last 3 stitches, K2tog, K1.

    ❋ NEEDLE 2: * K1, P1; repeat from * to end of row, ending K1.

    ❋ NEEDLE 3: K1, ssk, knit to end of needle.

❋ Repeat Round 1 until 30 stitches remain: 15 instep stitches and 15 stitches total on the other 2 needles (sole stitches). On the last round, you will need to decrease on needle 1 only. You will have 7 stitches on needle 1 and 8 stitches on needle 3.

❋ Work even for 5 more rounds, continuing in the K1, P1 pattern on the instep stitches and plain knit on the heel stitches.

Shaping the Toe

❋ **ROUND 1:**

    ❋ NEEDLE 1: Knit to last 3 stitches, K2tog, K1.

    ❋ NEEDLE 2: K1, ssk, knit to last 3 stitches, K2tog, K1.

    ❋ NEEDLE 3: K1, ssk, knit to end of needle.

❋ Repeat Round 1 until 10 stitches remain: 5 instep stitches and 5 stitches total on the other 2 needles. Move these sole stitches to one needle.

❋ With 5 stitches on each needle, place the needles parallel and use kitchener stitch (see page 262) to weave the toe stitches together.

Finishing

❋ Make ties by working two 2-stitch I-cords (see page 262), each 17" (43 cm) long.

❋ Weave the I-cord ties through the eyelets at the ankles.

❋ Following the instructions on page 264, make 4 pompoms, each about 1" (2.5 cm) in diameter. Leave 2 long tails on the yarn you use to tie the pompoms together at the center. Thread 1 tail through a tapestry needle and draw it through the end of 1 of the I-cords. Use the other tail to tie it very firmly in place. Trim the tails to blend in with the pompom. Repeat for each of the 3 other pompoms.

LACY LINEN TABLE LAYER

DESIGNED BY CHERYL OBERLE, *photo on page 24*

The word "linen" is used for a fiber made of flax and for textiles used in the home. In this case, we have a linen linen! The cloth is started in the center and worked circularly.

FINISHED MEASUREMENTS	Approximately 16" (40.5 cm) square
YARN	Louet Sales Euroflax Sport Weight, 100% linen, 3.5 oz (100 g)/270 yds (247 m), 95 Soapstone
NEEDLES	US 5 (3.75 mm) circular needle 16" (40 cm) long, US 5 (3.75 mm) circular needle 24" (60 cm) long, and set of five US 5 (3.75 mm) double-point needles *or size you need to obtain correct gauge*
GAUGE	18 stitches and 32 rounds = 4" (10 cm) in stockinette stitch
OTHER SUPPLIES	Stitch markers, tapestry needle
ABBREVIATIONS	**p2sso** pass 2 slipped stitches over the last stitch on left needle

Casting On and Setting Up

❋ Note: Bamboo or wooden needles are recommended because they're not as likely to slip as heavy metal ones.

❋ Using a modified circular, start as follows to cast on 8 stitches: Leaving a tail, make a large loop with the yarn, holding the yarn so the crossed area of the loop is on the top and the tail falls off to the left. With 1 double-point needle *reach inside the loop and pull the yarn coming from the ball through to the front to make a stitch, then take the needle over the top of the loop and make a yarn over. Repeat from * until you have the desired number of stitches. Cast on 1 extra stitch (9 stitches on the needle), turn and K2tog, then knit to the end of the row (8 stitches on the needle). Divide the stitches evenly onto 4 double-point needles (2 stitches per needle) and join to begin circular knitting, leaving a large hole in the center. After working several rounds of the pattern, pull on the tail to close up the loop and draw the stitches together into a perfect center.

❋ ROUND 1: K1, yo; repeat from *. You now have 16 stitches.

❋ ROUND 2: Knit.

❋ ROUND 3: [K1 (mark this stitch), yo, K3, yo] 4 times. You now have 24 stitches.

❋ Note: The marked stitches are the corner stitches, and the yarn over increases are worked on either side of these stitches every other round throughout the knitting. Use a distinctly colored stitch marker to indicate the beginning of the round.

LACY LINEN TABLE LAYER *continued*

* **ROUND 4 AND ALL EVEN-NUMBERED ROUNDS:** Knit
* **ROUND 5:** [K1, yo, knit to the next marked stitch, yo] 4 times. You now have 32 stitches: 4 corner stitches and 7 stitches in each section.
* Repeat Rounds 4 and 5 twelve more times. You now have 80 stitches: 4 corner stitches and 19 stitches in each section.

Beginning the Lace Pattern

* **ROUND 1:** [K1 (marked stitch), yo, pm, K1, *yo, ssk, K1, K2tog, yo, K1; repeat from * to next marked corner stitch, pm, yo] 4 times.
* **ROUND 2 AND ALL EVEN-NUMBERED ROUNDS:** Knit.
* **ROUND 3:** [K1 (marked stitch), yo, knit to marker, sm, K2, *yo, sl 2 kwise, K1, p2sso, yo, K3; repeat from * to next marker, sm, knit to next marked stitch, yo] 4 times.
* **ROUND 5:** [K1 (marked stitch), yo, knit to marker, sm, K1, *yo, ssk, K1, K2tog, yo, K1; repeat from * to next marker, sm, knit to next marked stitch, yo] 4 times.
* **ROUND 7:** [K1 (marked stitch), yo, knit to marker, sm, K2, *yo, sl 2 kwise, K1, p2sso, yo, K3; repeat from * to next marker, sm, knit to next marked stitch, yo] 4 times.
* **ROUND 9:** [K1 (marked stitch), yo, knit to marker, sm, K1, *yo, ssk, K1, K2tog, yo, K1; repeat from * to next marker, sm, knit to next marked stitch, yo] 4 times.
* **ROUND 11:** [K1 (marked stitch), yo, knit to marker, sm, K2, *yo, sl 2 kwise, K1, p2sso, yo, K3; repeat from * to next marker, sm, knit to next marked stitch, yo] 4 times.
* **ROUND 12:** Knit, removing markers from needles (these markers will be replaced on next repeat of Round 1). You now have 128 stitches: 4 corner stitches and 31 stitches in each section.)
* **ROUNDS 13–24:** Repeat Rounds 1–12 once more. You now have 176 stitches: 4 corner stitches and 43 stitches in each section.
* **ROUNDS 25–36:** Repeat Rounds 1–12 once more. You now have 224 stitches: 4 corner stitches and 55 stitches in each section.
* **ROUND 37–40:** Repeat Rounds 1–4 once more, removing markers from the needles on Round 4. You now have 240 stitches: 4 corner stitches and 59 stitches in each section.
* **ROUND 41:** [K1, yo, knit to the next marked stitch, yo] 4 times.
* **ROUND 42:** Knit.
* **ROUND 43:** [K1, yo, purl to the next marked stitch, yo] 4 times.
* **ROUND 44:** Knit.
* **LAST ROUND:** Turn and work around on WS, binding off loosely kwise.

Lacy Linen Table Layer

- ☐ knit on RS rows, purl on WS rows
- ⊡ yarn over
- ⊠ ssk
- ⊠ K2tog
- ⋏ slip 2tog kwise, K2, p2sso

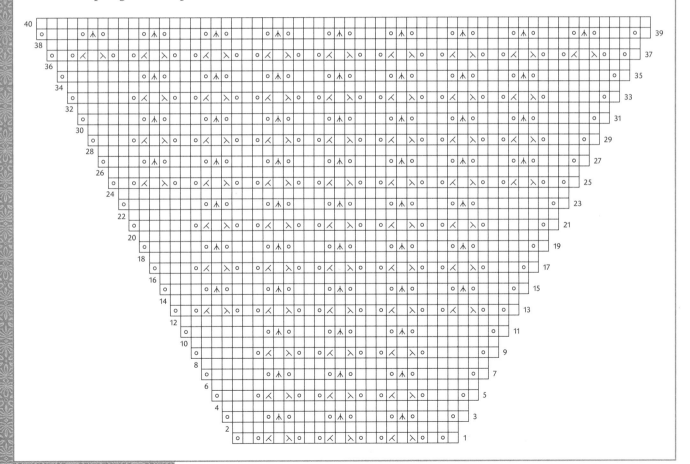

Linen Bag

DESIGNED BY CHERYL OBERLE, *photo on page 23*

Linen fiber, made from the flax plant, is perhaps the oldest natural textile fiber known, and fragments have been found dating back to 8,000 B.C.E. It is cool to the touch and gets softer with washing. For this bag, a sport-weight linen yarn is doubled for a sturdy bag that just may last another 8,000 years! Close this bag by passing the long handle through the short handle.

FINISHED MEASUREMENTS	Body: 7" (18 cm) square, handle: 6.5" (16.5 cm) long
YARN	Louet Sales Euroflax Sport Weight, 100% linen, 3.5 oz (100 g)/ 270 yds (247 m), 04 Soft Coral
NEEDLES	US 3 (3.25 mm) straight needles *or size you need to obtain correct gauge*
GAUGE	18 stitches and 32 rows = 4" (10 cm) in stockinette stitch
OTHER SUPPLIES	Tapestry needle

Preparing the Yarn

❊ Wind the skein into 2 equal balls. For the body of the bag, hold 1 strand from each ball and knit them together.

Knitting the Left Half of the Bag

❊ With 2 strands of yarn held together, cast on 20 stitches. Work in stockinette stitch, creating a pattern by randomly purling on the RS or knitting on the WS. There is no right or wrong way to do this — it all looks good! Continue until piece measures 7" (18 cm).

Knitting the Handle

❊ Cut 1 strand of yarn, leaving a 3" (7.5 cm) tail to be woven in later, and knit the handle with a single strand. Continue in stockinette stitch (no random patterning) for 13" (33 cm).

Knitting the Back

❊ Join a second strand of yarn and work the back as for the front, knitting with 2 strands together and adding a random pattern, until back measures 7" (18 cm). Bind off.

Knitting the Right Half of the Bag

❀ Work as for left half but knit the handle for only 7" (18 cm).

Joining the Halves

❀ For the front, begin at cast-on edge of left front and pick up and knit (see page 264) 30 stitches to top of body (just below the handle). With another needle and beginning at top of right front (just below handle), pick up and knit 30 stitches down to the cast-on edge. With WS together, join 30 stitches of left and right front with three-needle bind-off (see page 266). Join at center back as for front, picking up 30 stitches along each edge and joining with three-needle bind-off.

Finishing

❀ Turn the bag inside out and join side seams with mattress stitch (see page 264). Turn bag right-side out and sew bottom with a backstitch (see page 261). Steam bag lightly.

CASHMERE BABY LEG WARMERS

DESIGNED BY PATTI GHEZZI, *photo on page 33*

If you have trouble wrestling your baby into her tights, these leg warmers provide an easy solution! Knitted in a cashmere-and-merino blend, they're as comfy as they are cute.

SIZES AND FINISHED MEASUREMENTS	To fit infant 0–6 (6–12) months, approximately 7" (9.5") (18 [24] cm) long and 6" (7.5") (15 [19] cm) circumference
YARN	Karabella Boise, 50% cashmere/50% merino wool, 1.75 oz (50 g)/163 yds (149 m), Color 69
NEEDLES	Set of four US 5 (3.75 mm) double-point needles *or size you need to obtain correct gauge*
GAUGE	22 stitches and 28 rows = 4" (10 cm) in stockinette stitch
OTHER SUPPLIES	Stitch marker, tapestry needle

Knitting the Bottom Cuff

❋ Cast on 30 (38) stitches and divide evenly onto 3 double-point needles. Place marker and join into a round, being careful not to twist the stitches. Work K1, P1 rib for 9 (12) rounds.

Knitting the Leg

❋ **INCREASE ROUND:** *K6 (8), Kfb; repeat from * 3 times more, K2. You now have 34 (42) stitches.

❋ Work Rounds 1–12 of Meadow Stitch pattern 2 (3) times.

❋ **DECREASE ROUND:** *K6 (8), K2tog; repeat from * 3 times more, K2. You now have 30 (38) stitches.

Knitting the Top Cuff

❋ Work K1, P1 rib for 9 (12) rounds.

Finishing

❋ Bind off. Weave in ends. Block.

❋ Repeat for the second leg warmer.

STITCH PATTERN
meadow stitch

ROUNDS 1–4, 6–10, AND 12: Knit.

ROUND 5: K3, *(K3tog and leave on needle, knit the first stitch again and drop from needle, knit the second and third stitches together and drop from needle — meadow stitch made), K5; repeat from * to last 7 stitches, make meadow stitch as before, K4.

ROUND 11: K7, *make meadow stitch as before, K5; repeat from * to last 11 stitches, make meadow stitch as before, K8.

REPEAT ROUNDS 1–12 FOR PATTERN.

BOISE CASHMERE SCARF

DESIGNED BY DAWN LEESEMAN, *photo on page 36*

Super-fine merino is one of the softest fibers around, but when you combine it with an equal amount of cashmere, the feel is sublime. Knit it up in this simple Lacy Rib pattern and luxuriate in extreme softness while keeping warm.

FINISHED MEASUREMENTS	Approximately 4" (10 cm) wide and 54" (137 cm) long
YARN	Karabella Boise, 50% cashmere/50% merino wool, 1.75 oz (50 g)/163 yds (149 m), Color 64
NEEDLES	US 10 (6 mm) straight needles *or size you need to obtain correct gauge*
GAUGE	25 stitches = 4" (10 cm) in pattern
OTHER SUPPLIES	Tapestry needle, pins

Knitting the Scarf

✳ Cast on 25 stitches. Work Lacy Rib pattern until piece measures 54" (137 cm) or until you have only 36" (91.5 cm) of yarn remaining for bind off. Bind off in pattern.

Finishing

✳ Weave in ends. Shape and pin the bind-off and cast-on edges to the same width. Spray with water and let dry.

ALPACA BROADWAY GLOVES

DESIGNED BY JAZMINE GREENLAW, *photo on page 32*

Take a simple stockinette stitch glove, add a lovely knot stitch cuff, knit it with pure alpaca, and you end up with an elegant glove that's a delight to wear. The right and left gloves are knit the same.

SIZES AND FINISHED MEASUREMENTS	To fit average woman, approximately 8" (20.5 cm) circumference
YARN	Shibui Knits Baby Alpaca DK, 100% baby alpaca, 3.5 oz (100 g)/255 yds (233 m), 323 Peacock
NEEDLES	Sets of four US 6 (4 mm) and US 4 (3.5mm) double-point needles *or size you need to obtain correct gauge*
GAUGE	24 stitches = 4" (10 cm) in stockinette stitch on larger needle
OTHER SUPPLIES	Stitch markers, scrap yarn for holders, tapestry needle

Knitting the Cuff

❊ With smaller needles, cast on 41 stitches and divide onto 3 double-point needles. Place marker and join into a round, being careful not to twist the stitches.

❊ ROUND 1: *K1, P1; repeat from * to last stitch, K1.

❊ Repeat Round 1 four more times.

❊ Knit 5 rounds. Work Rounds 1 and 2 of Broadway Stitch 1 pattern 2 times. Knit 3 rounds. Work Rounds 1 and 2 of Broadway Stitch 1 pattern twice more. Knit 3 rounds. Work Rounds 1 and 2 of Broadway Stitch 2 pattern 2 times. Knit 1 row, increasing 5 stitches evenly spaced. You now have 46 stitches.

Knitting the Thumb Gusset

❊ ROUND 1: Slip marker, M1, K2, M1, place second marker, knit to end of round.

❊ ROUND 2: Knit.

❊ ROUND 3: Sm, M1, knit to marker, M1, sm, knit to end of round.

❊ ROUND 4: Knit.

❊ Repeat Rounds 3 and 4 until you have 12 stitches between the markers for the thumb gusset.

❊ NEXT ROUND: Place 12 gusset stitches on holder. Cast on 1 stitch, pm, cast on 1 stitch. Join with remaining stitches and knit to end of round. You now have 46 stitches. Continue even in stockinette stitch until piece measures 3.5" (9 cm) above the cuff.

STITCH PATTERNS

broadway stitch 1

ROUND 1: K1, *(P3tog, K3tog, P3tog) in next 3 stitches, K1; repeat from *.

ROUND 2: Knit.

REPEAT ROUNDS 1 AND 2 FOR PATTERN.

broadway stitch 2

ROUND 1: K1, *(P3tog, K3tog, P3tog) in next 3 stitches, K5; repeat from *.

ROUND 2: Knit.

REPEAT ROUNDS 1 AND 2 FOR PATTERN.

Knitting the Little Finger

❋ K17 and place these stitches on a holder. K11, place remaining 18 stitches on second holder. Cast on 1 stitch, K11. Divide these 12 stitches onto 3 double-point needles and work in stockinette stitch until finger measures 2.5" (6.5 cm).

❋ NEXT ROUND: *K2tog; repeat from *. Cut yarn, leaving a 6" (15 cm) tail. Thread tail onto tapestry needle; draw through stitches twice. Pull up snug; fasten off.

Continuing the Hand

❋ Place all held stitches onto double-point needles. Join yarn before the cast-on stitch for little finger and pick up and knit (see page 264) 2 stitches. Place marker between these 2 stitches to mark beginning of round, knit to end of round. You now have 37 stitches. Knit 3 rounds even.

Knitting the Ring Finger

❋ K5, place next 14 stitches on a holder, place following 12 stitches on a second holder, cast on 2 stitches, K6 remaining stitches, cast on 1 stitch. Divide 14 stitches onto double-point needles and work in stockinette stitch until finger measures 3" (7.5 cm). Finish as for little finger.

Knitting the Middle Finger

❋ Place 6 stitches nearest to ring finger from each holder onto needles. Join yarn and pick up and knit 2 stitches from base of ring finger, K6, cast on 2 stitches, K6. Divide 16 stitches onto double-point needles and work in stockinette stitch until finger measures 3.25" (8.5 cm). Finish as for little finger.

Knitting the Index Finger

❋ Place remaining 14 stitches onto needles. Join yarn and pick up and knit 2 stitches from base of middle finger. Divide 16 stitches onto double-point needles and work in stockinette stitch until finger measures 3" (7.5 cm). Finish as for little finger.

Knitting the Thumb

❋ Place 12 held thumb gusset stitches onto needles. Join yarn and pick up and knit 2 stitches from base of stitches cast on for hand at top of thumb gusset. Divide 14 stitches onto double-point needles and work in stockinette stitch until thumb measures 2.5" (6.5 cm). Finish as for little finger.

Finishing

❋ Repeat for second glove. Weave in ends and block.

Beautiful Baby Bamboo-Merino Sweater

DESIGNED BY CAROL J. SORSDAHL, *photo on page 32*

This cute sweater is knitted back and forth from the top down, and the fronts and back are worked together as one. The edging is single crochet.

SIZES AND FINISHED MEASUREMENTS	To fit infant 0–3 months, approximately 20" (51 cm) chest circumference
YARN	Fancy Image Hand-dyed Bamboo Merino, 50% bamboo/50% merino wool, 3.5 oz (99 g)/265 yds (242 m), Coral
NEEDLES	US 6 (4 mm) circular needle 24" (60 cm) long and set of four US 6 (4 mm) double-point needles *or size you need to obtain correct gauge*
GAUGE	22 stitches and 28 rows = 4" (10 cm) in stockinette stitch
OTHER SUPPLIES	Stitch markers, scrap yarn for holders, US E/4 (3.5 mm) crochet hook, tapestry needle, one ¾" (1.9 cm) button, tapestry needle

Knitting the Upper Body

* Cast on 44 stitches.
* SET-UP ROW 1 (RS): K2, pm, K8 (sleeve stitches), pm, K24 (back stitches), pm, K8 (sleeve stitches), pm, K2.
* SET-UP ROW 2: Purl.
* ROW 1 (RS): Knit, and at the same time Kfb in first stitch, Kfb before and after each marker, Kfb in last stitch. You now have 54 stitches.
* ROW 2: Purl.
* Repeat Rows 1 and 2 until you have 12 stitches for each front, 18 stitches for each sleeve, and 34 stitches for the back: 94 stitches total.
* Continue in stockinette stitch and work the increase row (Row 1) every fourth row 5 times. You now have 22 stitches for each front, 28 stitches for each sleeve, and 44 stitches for the back: 144 stitches total. Work even in stockinette stitch until piece measures 4.5" (11.5 cm) from beginning, knitting (not purling) the last WS row.

Dividing the Sleeves from the Body

* Beginning with the left front, slip stitches for each front, sleeve, and the back onto separate holders.

STITCH PATTERNS
moss stitch 1
(WORKED CIRCULARLY)

ROUNDS 1 AND 2: *K2, P2; repeat from *.
ROUNDS 3 AND 4: *P2, K2; repeat from *.
REPEAT ROUNDS 1–4 FOR PATTERN.

moss stitch 2
(WORKED BACK AND FORTH)

ROWS 1 AND 4: *K2, P2; repeat from *.
ROWS 2 AND 3: *P2, K2; repeat from *.
REPEAT ROWS 1–4 FOR PATTERN.

Knitting the Sleeves

❋ Place 28 sleeve stitches onto needle. Change to double-point needles and cast on 5 stitches onto needle 1, then K7 at beginning of sleeve. K5, pm, K4, pm, K5 on needle 2. K7 and cast on 5 stitches onto needle 3. You now have 38 stitches. Join into a round, being careful not to twist the stitches. Place marker for beginning of round and purl 1 round.

Begin Pattern and Sleeve Shaping

❋ Working Moss Stitch I between the markers on needle 2 and knitting all other stitches, work 9 repeats of pattern, decreasing 1 stitch on each side of the beginning-of-round marker every sixteenth round 2 times. You now have 34 stitches.

❋ NEXT ROUND: Knit, decreasing 1 stitch on each side of beginning-of-round marker and on each side of pattern markers, removing markers. You now have 30 stitches. Purl 1 round and bind off loosely. Repeat for other sleeve.

Knitting the Body

❋ Place 88 body stitches onto needle. With RS facing, attach yarn at left front and knit 22 left front stitches, pick up and knit (see page 264) 10 cast-on left underarm stitches, knit 44 back stitches, pick up and knit 10 cast-on right underarm stitches, knit 22 right front stitches. Turn and knit 1 row. You now have 108 stitches.

Begin Moss Pattern

❋ K1 (edge stitch), work Moss Stitch II to last stitch, K1 (edge stitch). Continue until piece measures 4.5" (11.5 cm) from underarm, ending with a WS row. Purl 5 rows and bind off but do not break yarn. Pull remaining yarn through last loop, leaving loop open.

Finishing

❋ Insert crochet hook into last loop and work sc along right front in all purl bumps up to beginning of bodice. Work a second sc in the last bump, then sc in every other row to sleeve. Sc in 2 of every 3 stitches along sleeve top, neck, and second sleeve top. Work sc to bottom of left front as for right front. Ch 1, turn, sc to top of Moss Stitch pattern on left front. Ch 10 (or number to accommodate your button), join with slip stitch to same stitch. Slip stitch around button loop again, then work sc around neck and down to bottom of right front. Optional: Work 1 row of reverse single crochet along entire edge. Weave in all ends. Block. Sew button opposite loop.

Corn Fiber Lace Bath Cloth

DESIGNED BY MYRNA A. I. STAHMAN, *photo on page 31*

Corn is a relatively new fiber for knitting yarn, and it makes a lovely washcloth. This cloth has enough texture to get the job done, but it's soft to the touch. The square is knitted diagonally from corner to corner and uses mirrored increases and decreases.

FINISHED MEASUREMENTS	Approximately 9" (23 cm) square
YARN	South West Trading Company A-Maizing, 100% corn fiber, 1.75 oz (50 g)/142 yds (130 m), 368 Biscotti
NEEDLES	US 5 (3.5 mm) straight needles *or size you need to obtain correct gauge*
GAUGE	24 stitches and 32 rows= 4" (10 cm) in pattern
OTHER SUPPLIES	Tapestry needle

Knitting the Bath Cloth

❄ Cast on **3** stitches and knit 1 row. Follow the chart on the next page to knit the cloth. Note: Only RS rows are charted. All WS rows are plain knit.

Finishing

❄ Cut yarn and pull through last stitch. Weave in ends.

Corn Fiber Lace Bath Cloth

- ☐ knit
- ⊙ yarn over
- ⋎ M1R, make 1 right-leaning increase
- ⋏ M1L, make 1 left-leaning increase
- ⋉ ssk
- ⋌ K2tog
- ⋏ slip 1, K2tog, psso

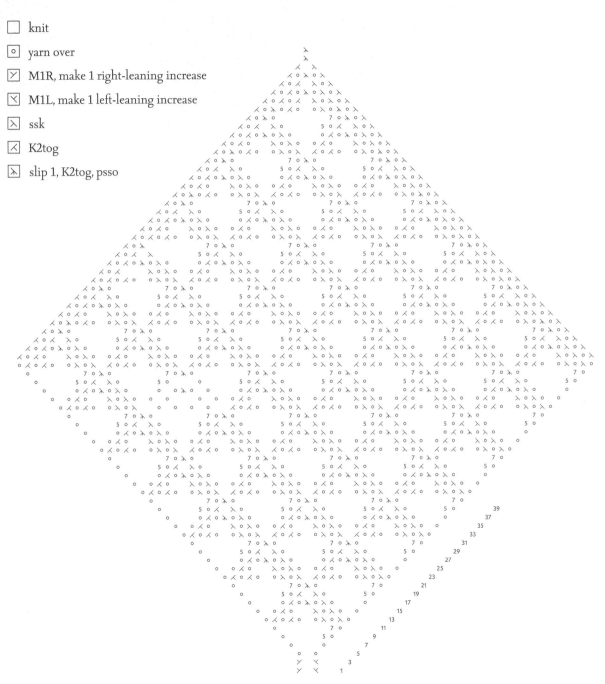

LAOTIAN SILK NECKLACE WITH BEADS

DESIGNED BY ANNI KRISTENSEN, *photo on page 28*

This necklace pays tribute to a custom practiced in Denmark following World War II. Most women had only one dress, in basic black, to wear for all church occasions. The dress was adorned with lacy white crochet collars, from narrow and discreet for funerals to large and flamboyant for joyous occasions. This silk collar is definitely not white, and it is adorned with beads.

FINISHED MEASUREMENTS	Approximately 14.5" (37 cm) circumference and 1.5" (3.8 cm) wide
YARN	Himalaya Yarn Laotian Silk, 100% handspun silk, .88 oz (25 g)/ 54 yds (49 m), Shammy Laker
NEEDLES	US 3 (3.25 mm) circular needle 29" (74 cm) long *or size you need to obtain correct gauge*
GAUGE	18 stitches = 4" (10 cm) in stockinette stitch
OTHER SUPPLIES	Big-eye beading needle, 51 size E beads, tapestry needle, US D/3 (3.25 mm) crochet hook, sewing needle and coordinating sewing thread, hook-and-eye closure

Preparing the Yarn

❊ With big-eye beading needle, slide all beads onto yarn.

Getting Started

❊ *Cast on 5 stitches, slide bead up against needle; repeat from * until all beads are in place, cast on 5 stitches. You will be knitting back and forth on the circular needle on 260 stitches.

❊ ROW 1: Knit.

❊ ROW 2: Purl.

❊ ROW 3: *K2tog, yo; repeat from * to last 2 stitches, K2tog. You now have 259 stitches.

❊ ROW 4: Purl.

❊ ROW 5: *K2tog; repeat from * to last stitch, K1. You now have 130 stitches.

❊ ROW 6: *P2tog, yo; repeat from *.

❊ ROW 7: *K2tog; repeat from *. You now have 65 stitches.

❊ ROW 8: Purl.

❊ ROW 9: Bind off pwise.

Finishing

❊ Weave in loose ends. Work 1 row of single crochet along bind-off edge. With sewing needle and thread, sew hook-and-eye in place at ends of bind-off row.

ANGORA BABY BUNNY CAP

DESIGNED BY RENÉE BARNES, *photo on page 34*

This lovely, bunny-soft angora hat is crocheted beginning at the center of the crown and ending with a lovely ruffle at the bottom. The applied flower is optional, but what's wrong with gilding the lily?

SIZES AND FINISHED MEASUREMENTS	To fit an infant, 14 " (35.5 cm) circumference
YARN	Louisa Harding Kimono Angora, 70% angora/25% wool/ 5% nylon, 0.88 oz (25 g)/125 yds (114 m), 9 Pink
CROCHET HOOK	US E/4 (3.5 mm) *or size you need to obtain correct gauge*
GAUGE	20 dc and 12 rows = 4" (10 cm)
OTHER SUPPLIES	Tapestry needle

Crocheting the Hat

❊ ROUND 1: Ch 4, join with sl st to first ch to form loop.

❊ ROUND 2: Ch 3 (counts as first dc), 15 dc into center of ring. Join with sl st to top of ch 3.

❊ ROUND 3: *Ch 4, skip next 3 dc, sl st in next dc; repeat from * 3 times.

❊ ROUND 4: Sl st into first ch-4 loop, ch 2, 2 dc into ch-4 loop, 1 tr into loop, 2 dc into loop, sc into loop, (sc, 2 dc, tr, 2 dc, sc) into next 3 ch-4 loops.

❊ ROUND 5: Sl st in next 4 st (to next tr), *ch 8, sl st in top of next tr; repeat from * 3 times.

❊ ROUND 6: Sl st in ch-8 loop, ch 3, 11 dc in same ch-8 loop, *12 dc in next ch-8 loop; repeat from * 2 times, join with sl st to top of ch 3.

❊ ROUND 7: *Ch 4, skip next 2 stitches, sl st in next stitch; repeat from * 15 times.

❊ ROUND 8: Sl st in next ch-4 loop, *ch 7, sl st in next ch-4 loop; repeat from * 15 times.

❊ ROUND 9: Sl st in first 3 ch of next ch-7 loop, sl st into ch-7 loop, *ch 5, sl st into next ch-7 loop; repeat from * 15 times.

❊ ROUND 10: Sl st into next 3 ch of ch-5 loop, *ch 4, sl st into next ch-5 loop; repeat from * 15 times.

ANGORA BABY BUNNY CAP *continued*

❋ ROUND 11: Sl st into next ch-4 loop, ch 3 (counts as first dc), 3 dc into ch-4 loop, 4 dc into each ch-4 loop around, sl st to top of ch 3. You now have 64 dc.

❋ ROUND 12: Ch 3 (counts as first dc), dc in each dc around, join with sl st to top of ch 3.

❋ ROUND 13: Ch 3 (counts as first dc), dc in next 13 dc, dec over next 2 dc, *dc in next 14 dc, dec over next 2 dc; repeat from * 2 times, join with sl st to beg ch 3. You now have 60 dc.

❋ ROUND 14: Ch 1, *skip next dc, 5 dc in next dc, skip next dc, ch 1, sl st; repeat from * 14 times.

❋ ROUND 15: Ch 4, *5 dc in third dc of next 5-dc cluster, tr in next sl st; repeat from * 13 times, 5 dc in third dc of next 5-dc cluster, join with sl st to top of beg ch 4.

❋ RND 16: *Ch 3, sl st in top of third dc in next 5-dc cluster, ch 3, sc in next tr; repeat from * 14 times.

❋ ROUND 17: Sl st into next ch-3 loop, ch 3, dc into same ch-3 loop, 2 dc in each ch-3 loop around, join with sl st to top of ch 3.

❋ ROUND 18: Ch 3, dc in each dc around, join with sl st to top of ch 3.

❋ ROUND 19: Ch 2, sc in each dc around, join with sl st to beg ch 2. You now have 60 sc.

❋ ROUND 20: Ch 4, 2 tr in each sc around, sl st to beg ch 4. You now have 120 tr.

❋ ROUND 21: Ch 3, dc in each tr around, join with sl st to beg ch 3, finish off. Weave in ends.

Making the Flower
(optional)

❋ ROUND 1: Ch 4, join with sl st to first ch to form a ring.

❋ ROUND 2: Ch 3 (counts as first dc), 15 dc into center of ring, join with sl st to top of ch 3.

❋ ROUND 3: *Ch 3, skip next dc, sl st in next dc; repeat from * 7 times.

❋ ROUND 4: Sl st into next ch-3 sp, ch 2, (dc, tr, dc, sc) into same ch-3 sp, (sc, dc, tr, dc, sc) into each ch-3 sp around, sl st into first sl st (8 small petals made). Secure yarn and cut, leaving tail to sew on flower.

❋ ROUND 5: Working behind flower, join yarn with sl st around sl st between 2 petals, *ch 4, sl st around sl st between next 2 petals; repeat from * 7 times, sl st into beg sl st.

❋ ROUND 6: Ch 3 (counts as first dc), (2 dc, 3 tr, 3 dc) in next ch-4 sp, (3 dc, 3 tr, 3 dc) into each ch-4 sp around, join with sl st to top of ch 3 (8 large petals made). Secure yarn and cut, leaving tail.

❋ With tapestry needle and using tail, sew flower securely to side of hat. Weave in all ends.

Merino-Silk Shrug for Baby

DESIGNED BY GITTA SCHRADE, *photo on page 30*

Your baby will be the height of fashion in this tiny shrug! It keeps the chill off, yet the openwork stitch keeps it from being too warm. The shrug is knitted from cuff to cuff in a merino-and-silk blend.

SIZES AND FINISHED MEASUREMENTS	To fit infant 0–3 months, approximately 15.75" (40 cm) from cuff to cuff
YARN	Naturally Merino et Soie, 70% merino wool/30% silk, 1.75 oz (50 g)/136 yds (125 m), 226 Red
NEEDLES	US 5 (3.75 mm) and US 3 (3.25 mm) straight needles *or size you need to obtain correct gauge*
GAUGE	22 stitches and 30 rows = 4" (10 cm) in stockinette stitch on larger needle
OTHER SUPPLIES	Tapestry needle, 3 mm crochet hook

Knitting the First Cuff

❀ With smaller needles, cast on 29 stitches. Work K1, P1 Rib for 14 rows.

Beginning the Main Pattern

❀ NEXT ROW: Knit, increasing 9 stitches evenly spaced. You now have 38 stitches.

❀ NEXT ROW: Purl.

❀ Change to larger needles and repeat Rows 1–8 of Eyelet Mesh pattern until piece measures 14.75" (35 cm) from beginning, ending with Row 2 or 6.

❀ NEXT ROW: Change to smaller needles and knit.

❀ NEXT ROW: Purl, decreasing 9 stitches evenly spaced. You now have 29 stitches.

Knitting the Second Cuff

❀ Work K1, P1 Rib for 14 rows. Bind off loosely in pattern.

Finishing

❀ Sew arm seams from edge of cuff to about 1.5" (4 cm) past beginning of Eyelet Mesh pattern. With RS facing and beginning at one of the seams, use the crochet hook to join yarn with slip stitch. *Work 3 sc along edge, ch 4, join with slip stitch to last sc; repeat from * along remaining edge of shrug. Fasten off, weave in ends.

STITCH PATTERNS

k1, p1 rib

(WORKED ON AN ODD NUMBER OF STITCHES)

ROW 1 (RS): *K1, P1; repeat from * to last stitch, K1.

ROW 2 (WS): *P1, K1; repeat from * to last stitch, P1.

REPEAT ROWS 1 AND 2 FOR PATTERN.

eyelet mesh

ROW 1: K1, *K2tog, yo twice, sl 1, k1, psso; repeat from * to last stitch, K1.

ROW 2: P1, *P1, (K1, P1 into double yo), P1; repeat from * to last stitch, P1.

ROW 3: Knit.

ROW 4: Purl.

ROW 5: K1, yo, sl 1, K1, psso, *K2tog, yo twice, sl 1, K1, psso; repeat from * to last 3 stitches, K2tog, yo, K1.

ROW 6: P3, *P1, (K1, P1 into double yo), p1; repeat from * to last 3 stitches, P3.

ROW 7: Knit.

ROW 8: Purl.

REPEAT ROWS 1–8 FOR PATTERN.

SILK-WOOL HORSESHOE LACE SCARF

DESIGNED BY MARCI RICHARDSON, *photo on page 30*

The Horseshoe Lace used for this shawl is a basic Shetland lace pattern with a 10-stitch repeat. The stitch count remains the same from row to row. The lovely silk-and-wool blend yarn was hand painted in New England.

FINISHED MEASUREMENTS	Approximately 13" (33 cm) wide and 78" (198 cm) long after blocking
YARN	Seacoast Handpainted Yarns Silk & Ivory, 50% silk/50% wool, 5.3 oz (150 g)/667 yds (610 m), Chocolate and Caramel
NEEDLES	US 5 (3.75 mm) straight needles *or size you need to obtain correct gauge*
GAUGE	24 stitches and 28 rows = 4" (10 cm) in pattern after blocking
OTHER SUPPLIES	Tapestry needle, size E beads (optional)

Knitting the Stole

❋ Cast on 75 stitches very loosely. Work lace pattern with border as follows:

❋ ROW 1: K3, *yo, K3, sl 1, K2tog, psso, K3, yo, K1; repeat from * to last 2 stitches, K2.

❋ ROW 2 AND ALL WS ROWS THROUGH 8: K2, P to last 2 stitches, K2.

❋ ROW 3: K3, *K1, yo, K2, sl 1, K2tog, psso, K2, yo, K2; repeat from * to last 2 stitches, K2.

❋ ROW 5: K3, *K2, yo, K1, sl 1, K2tog, psso, K1, yo, K3; repeat from * to last 2 stitches, K2.

❋ ROW 7: K3, *K3, yo, sl 1, K2tog, psso, yo, K4; repeat from * to last 2 stitches, K2.

❋ Repeat Rows 1–8 fifty-five more times or until piece measures three-quarters of desired finished length, ending having completed Row 8. Bind off loosely.

Finishing

❋ Weave in all ends. Wet the stole and block to desired measurements. Let dry completely.

❋ Add fringe and beads at end points if desired.

STITCH PATTERN
little fountain

ROUND 1: *Yo, K3, yo, K1; repeat from *.

ROUND 2: Knit.

ROUND 3: K1, sl 1, K2tog, psso, *K3, sl 1, K2tog, psso; repeat from * to last 2 stitches, K2.

ROUND 4: Knit.

REPEAT ROUNDS 1–4 FOR PATTERN.

SILK FOUNTAIN HOOD
DESIGNED BY BETH HOOD, *photo on page 27*

Silk is one of those wonderful fibers that will keep you warm when you need the warmth, but won't overheat you when you don't. Knitted into a lovely hood, this garment may also be worn indoors as a cowl.

SIZES AND FINISHED MEASUREMENTS	To fit most adults, approximately 26" (66 cm) circumference and 12" (30.5 cm) long
YARN	Halcyon Gemstone Soft Twist Silk, 100% silk, 3.5 oz (100 g)/ 315 yds (288 m), 107 Light Blue
NEEDLES	US 6 (4 mm) circular needle 16" (40 cm) long *or size you need to obtain correct gauge*
GAUGE	22 stitches = 4" (10 cm) in stockinette stitch
OTHER SUPPLIES	Stitch marker, tapestry needle

Knitting the Hood

❁ Cast on 104 stitches. Place marker and join into a round, being careful not to twist the stitches. Work 4 rounds in garter stitch. Work Rounds 1–4 of Little Fountain pattern until piece measures 11.25" (29 cm). Note: Stitch count increases to 156 stitches after Round 1 is completed, and returns to 104 stitches after Round 2 is completed.

❁ Work 4 rounds in garter stitch. Bind off loosely.

Finishing

❁ Weave in ends. Block lightly.

Silk-Merino Doll Sweater

DESIGNED BY JEAN AUSTIN, *photo on page 32*

Your 18" (45.5 cm) doll will look even more precious when wearing this picot-edged sweater with three-quarter length sleeves. Made in one piece, this one was knitted with a silk-and-merino blend.

SIZES AND FINISHED MEASUREMENTS	To fit an 18" (45.5 cm) doll, approximately 14.5" (37 cm) chest circumference
YARN	Yarns Northwest Silk & Merino, 70% merino/wool 30% silk, 1.75 oz (50 g)/120 yds (110 m), 11 Blue
NEEDLES	US 6 (4 mm) straight needles and set of four US 6 (4 mm) double-point needles *or size you need to obtain correct gauge*
GAUGE	20 stitches = 4" (10 cm) in stockinette stitch
OTHER SUPPLIES	Scrap yarn for holders, tapestry needle

Knitting the Back

❋ With straight needles, cast on 36 stitches, leaving an 18" (45.5 cm) tail. Knit 1 row, purl 1 row, knit 1 row.

Making the Picot Edge

❋ NEXT ROW (RS): K1, *yo, K2tog; repeat from * to last stitch, K1.

❋ Work even in stockinette stitch until piece measures 3" (7.5 cm) from picot edge.

Shaping the Sleeves

❋ Continue in stockinette stitch and cast on 4 stitches at the beginning of the next 4 rows. Cast on 7 stitches at the beginning of the next 2 rows. You now have 66 stitches. Work even in stockinette stitch until piece measures 2" (5 cm) from last cast-on row.

Shaping the Right Shoulder

❋ ROW 1: K25, turn.

❋ ROW 2: P2tog, purl to end of row.

❋ ROW 3: K22, K2tog, turn.

❋ ROW 4: Repeat Row 2.

❋ ROW 5: K22, turn.

❋ ROW 6: Purl.

- ❈ ROW 7: K21, Kfb, turn.
- ❈ ROW 8: Pfb, purl to end of row.
- ❈ ROW 9: K23, Kfb, turn.
- ❈ ROW 10: Repeat Row 8.
- ❈ Place 26 right back shoulder stitches on a holder.

SHAPING THE LEFT SHOULDER

- ❈ With RS facing, join yarn to beginning of stitches on the needle at right side of neck. K16 and place these stitches on a holder. Continue on 25 left shoulder stitches only.
- ❈ ROW 1: Knit.
- ❈ ROW 2: P23, P2tog.
- ❈ ROW 3: Ssk, knit to end of row.
- ❈ ROW 4: P21, P2tog.
- ❈ ROW 5: Knit.
- ❈ ROW 6: Purl.
- ❈ ROW 7: Kfb, knit to end of row.
- ❈ ROW 8: P22, Pfb.
- ❈ ROW 9: Repeat Row 7.
- ❈ ROW 10: P24, Pfb. You now have 26 stitches.

Knitting the Front

- ❈ Place 26 held right shoulder stitches on the needle and knit; cast on 14 stitches for front neck; knit 26 left shoulder stitches. You now have 66 stitches. Work even in stockinette stitch until piece measures 2" (10 cm) from stitches cast on for front neck.

SHAPING THE SLEEVE

- ❈ Bind off 7 stitches at the beginning of the next two rows. Bind off 4 stitches at the beginning of the next 4 rows. You now have 36 stitches.
- ❈ Work even in stockinette stitch until piece measures same as back to picot edge, ending with a WS row.

MAKING THE PICOT EDGE

- ❈ NEXT ROW (RS): K1, *yo, K2tog; repeat from * to last stitch, K1.
- ❈ Purl 1 row, knit 1 row, purl 1 row. Bind off loosely.

SILK-MERINO DOLL SWEATER *continued*

KNITTING THE NECK EDGE

❋ With double-point needles and RS facing, pick up and knit 6 stitches along left front neck, 14 stitches along front neck, 6 stitches along right front neck, 5 stitches along right back neck, 16 held back stitches, and 5 stitches along left back neck. You now have 52 stitches. Join into a round and knit 3 rounds.

❋ NEXT ROUND: *Yo, K2tog; repeat from *.

❋ Knit 2 rounds. Bind off loosely, leaving a 16" (40.5 cm) tail.

Finishing

❋ Thread tail from neck edge onto tapestry needle. Fold neck to inside along picot edge and stitch in place loosely. Thread tail from cast-on onto tapestry needle. Fold hem to the inside along picot edge and stitch in place loosely. Sew side and sleeve seams. Weave in ends.

AILISH'S ALPACA-MERINO CRUSH HAT

DESIGNED BY TONIA BARRY, *photo on page 35*

Hats with a visor help keep the rain and snow from our eyes, and this one, which includes an optional fleece lining, is cozy and warm as well. The yarn is a blend of alpaca, merino, and silk, and the hat can also be worn comfortably without a lining.

FINISHED MEASUREMENTS	Approximately 19" (48.5 cm) circumference, unstretched
YARN	Sereknity Hand-painted Yarn, 50% alpaca/30% merino wool/20% silk, 3.5 oz (100 g)/230 yds (210 m), Sweet
NEEDLES	US 6 (4 mm) circular needle 16" (40 cm) long and set of four US 6 (4 mm) double-point needles *or size you need to obtain correct gauge*
GAUGE	19 stitches and 28 rows = 4" (10 cm) in pattern
OTHER SUPPLIES	Stitch marker, tapestry needle, 21" x 4" (53.5 cm x 10 cm) piece of coordinating fleece (optional), sewing needle and coordinating sewing thread (optional)

Getting Started

❋ With circular needle, cast on 90 stitches. Place marker and join into a round, being careful not to twist the stitches. Begin Lacy Zigzag pattern and work until piece measures 5.5" (14 cm) from cast-on, ending with a patterned round. Knit 1 round, increasing 1 stitch.

Decreasing for the Crown

❋ ROUND 1: *K2tog, K5; repeat from *. You now have 78 stitches.
❋ ROUNDS 2 AND 3: Knit.
❋ ROUND 4: *K2tog, K4; repeat from *. You now have 65 stitches.
❋ ROUNDS 5 AND 6: Knit.
❋ ROUND 7: *K2tog, K3; repeat from *. You now have 52 stitches.
❋ ROUNDS 8 AND 9: Knit.
❋ ROUND 10: *K2tog, K2; repeat from *. You now have 39 stitches.
❋ ROUNDS 11 AND 12: Knit.
❋ ROUND 13: *K2tog, K1; repeat from *. You now have 26 stitches.
❋ ROUNDS 14 AND 15: Knit.
❋ ROUND 16: *K2tog; repeat from *. You now have 13 stitches.
❋ Cut yarn, leaving an 8" (20.5 cm) tail. Thread tail onto tapestry needle and draw through remaining stitches twice. Pull up snug and fasten off.

Knitting the Visor

❋ With RS facing, pick up and knit (see page 264) 34 stitches along front cast-on edge. The first and last stitches should be about 0.75" (2 cm) in front of the sides when hat is folded in half.

Decreasing for Top of Visor

❋ ROWS 1 AND 3: Purl.
❋ ROW 2: Knit.
❋ ROW 4: K2tog tbl, knit to last 2 stitches, K2tog.
❋ Repeat Rows 1–4 three more times. You now have 26 stitches.

Increasing for Bottom of Visor

❋ ROWS 1 AND 3: Purl.
❋ ROW 2: Knit.
❋ ROW 4: K1, M1, knit to last stitch, M1, K1.
❋ Repeat Rows 1–4 three more times. You now have 34 stitches. Bind off.

STITCH PATTERN
lacy zigzag

ROUNDS 1, 3, AND 5: *Sl1, K1, psso, K2, yo, K2; repeat from *.
ROUND 2 AND ALL EVEN-NUMBERED ROUNDS THROUGH 12: Knit.
ROUNDS 7, 9, AND 11: *K2, yo, K2, K2tog; repeat from *.
NOTE: At the beginning of Round 7, slip the first stitch to the right needle and begin the round with the next stitch. At the beginning of the following Round 1, use the final K2tog from the previous round as the first slip stitch, i.e, knit 1 and pass the K2tog stitch over.
REPEAT ROUNDS 1–12 FOR PATTERN.

Finishing

❋ Fold visor over with WS together and sew side seams. Turn visor right-side out and stitch neatly in place along cast-on edge. Weave in ends.

Adding the Lining (optional)

❋ Sew center back seam of lining with WS together. Insert lining into hat with WS of lining facing inside of hat, and sew lining to cast-on edge with sewing thread and small stitches. Sew top of lining to inside of hat.

SARENA CASHMERE COWL

DESIGNED BY TONIA BARRY, *photo on page 27*

Sarena Cowl is 100% luxurious cashmere, and once you've tried it on, you won't want to take it off. And so what if it isn't subzero weather. Go ahead and tighten up the cord, bringing the cashmere as close as possible to your skin. Lovely.

SIZES AND FINISHED MEASUREMENTS	To fit most adults, approximately 20.5" (52 cm) circumference and 9" (23 cm) length
YARN	Jade Sapphire Mongolian Cashmere 4-Ply, 100% cashmere, 1.9 oz (55 g)/200 yds (183 m), 16 Everglades
NEEDLES	US 6 (4 mm) circular needle 16" (40 cm) long or set of four US 6 (4 mm) double-point needles *or size you need to obtain correct gauge,* and two US 8 (5mm) double-point needles for I-cord
GAUGE	20 stitches and 29 rows = 4" (10 cm) in Snow Shoe pattern on smaller needles
OTHER SUPPLIES	Stitch marker, tapestry needle

Knitting the Cowl

❋ Note: When dropping the stitch in Snow Shoe pattern, gently coax it down to unravel.

❋ With smaller needles, cast on 104 stitches. Place marker and join into a round, being careful not to twist the stitches. Knit 1 round, purl 1 round, knit 1 round.

STITCH PATTERN

snow shoe

ROUND 1: *K1, M1, K1, P2, K2, P2; repeat from *.

ROUNDS 2–7: *K3, P2, K2, P2; repeat from *.

ROUND 8: *K2, drop 1 stitch down 7 rounds, P2, K2, P2; repeat from *.

ROUNDS 9 AND 10: *K2, P2; repeat from *.

ROUND 11: *K2, P2, K1, M1, K1, P2; repeat from *.

ROUNDS 12–17: *K2, P2, K3, P2; repeat from *.

ROUND 18: *K2, P2, K1, drop 1 stitch down 7 rounds, K1, P2; repeat from *.

ROUNDS 19 AND 20: Repeat Rows 9 and 10.

REPEAT ROWS 1–20 FOR PATTERN.

❀ Work Rounds 1–20 of Snow Shoe pattern until piece measures 8" (20.5 cm), ending with Round 20 of pattern. Knit 1 round, purl 1 round, knit 1 round. Bind off loosely.

Knitting the I-cord

❀ With larger double-point needles, follow the instructions on page 262 and knit a 5-stitch I-cord 27" (68.5 cm) long. Following the instructions on page 264, make two 1.5" (4 cm) pompoms.

Finishing

❀ Weave I-cord through the openings in the third pattern repeat from the top. Attach pompoms to the ends of the I-cord. Weave in all ends. Steam to block lightly.

REVERSIBLE CABLE AND EYELET WOOL-SILK SCARF

DESIGNED BY JENI CHASE, *photo on page 35*

T*he very clever cable design shown here is ideal for a scarf — it is completely reversible. And what could be better than two perfect sides of a silky woolen blend? Bet you can't knit just one.*

FINISHED MEASUREMENTS	Approximately 4.5" (11.5 cm) wide and 54" (137 cm) long
YARN	Sheep Shop Yarn Company Sheep 3, 70% wool/30% silk, 3.5 oz (100 g)/325 yds (297 m), F66 Pink
NEEDLES	US 6 (4 mm) straight needles *or size you need to obtain correct gauge*
GAUGE	24 stitches = 4" (10 cm) in stockinette stitch, 36 stitches = 4" (10 cm) in pattern
OTHER SUPPLIES	Cable needle, tapestry needle
ABBREVIATIONS	**C8B (cable 8 back)** slip 4 stitches to cable needle and hold in back, K4, K4 from cable needle

REVERSIBLE CABLE AND EYELET WOOL-SILK SCARF continued

Knitting the Scarf

❋ Note: For a smooth selvedge edge, slip the first stitch of every row knitwise.

❋ Cast on 41 stitches.

Knitting the Set-up Rows

❋ ROW 1: *(K1, P1) 4 times, K1, yo, K2tog; repeat from * to last 8 stitches, (K1, P1) 4 times.

❋ ROW 2: *(K1, P1) 3 times, K1, P4; repeat from * to last 8 stitches, (K1, P1) 4 times.

❋ ROWS 3, 5, AND 7: Repeat Row 1.

❋ ROWS 4 AND 6: Repeat Row 2.

Knitting the Cable Pattern

❋ ROW 1 (RS): *C8B, P3; repeat from * to last 8 stitches, C8B.

❋ ROW 2: *(K1, P1) 4 times, K1, yo, K2tog; repeat from * to last 8 stitches, (K1, P1) 4 times.

❋ ROW 3: *(K1, P1) 3 times, K1, P4; repeat from * to last 8 stitches, (K1, P1) 4 times.

❋ ROWS 4, 6, AND 8: Repeat Row 2.

❋ ROWS 5 AND 7: Repeat Row 3.

❋ Work Rows 1–8 of cable pattern until you have approximately 36" (91 cm) of yarn left, ending with Row 8. Bind off.

Finishing

❋ Weave in ends. Block to finished measurements.

Ocean Wave Merino-Bamboo Vest

DESIGNED BY MARION HALPERN, *photo on page 25*

This lovely vest is knitted in a loose rib and has loads of stretch. Worn close-fitting, there's a size for almost everyone in the three presented here.

FINISHED MEASUREMENTS	Approximately 32"/34" (36"/38", 40"/43") (81.5/86.5 [91.5/96.5, 101.5/109] cm) circumference
YARN	Great Adirondack Yarn Company Lolita, 65% merino wool/ 35% bamboo, 8 oz (227 g)/560 yds (512 m), Nantucket Blue
NEEDLES	US 7 (4.5 mm) straight needles and US 6 (4 mm) circular needle 16" (40 cm) long *or size you need to obtain correct gauge*
GAUGE	27 stitches and 28 rows = 4" (10 cm) in pattern stitch, 22 stitches and 28 rows = 4" (10 cm) in stockinette stitch
OTHER SUPPLIES	Scrap yarn for holders, tapestry needle

STITCH PATTERN
rib stitch

ROW 1 (RS): P3, *K3, P3; repeat from *.

ROW 2 AND ALL WS ROWS THROUGH 8: K3, *P3, K3; repeat from *.

ROW 3: P3, *K2tog, yo, K1, P3; repeat from *.

ROW 5: Repeat Row 1.

ROW 7: P3, *K1, yo, sl 1, k1, psso, P3; repeat from *.

REPEAT ROWS 1–8 FOR PATTERN.

Knitting the Back

❋ With larger needles, cast on 111 (123, 135) stitches. Beginning with Row 1, work Rib Stitch pattern until piece measures 12" (12", 13") (30.5 [30.5, 33] cm) from cast-on, ending with a WS row.

SHAPING THE ARMHOLE

❋ Bind off 6 stitches at the beginning of the next 2 rows, then bind off 3 stitches at the beginning of the next 2 rows. Decrease 1 stitch at the beginning and end of every other row 3 times. You now have 87 (99, 111) stitches. Work even in pattern until piece measures 18" (18", 19") (45.5 [45.5, 48.5] cm) from cast-on, ending with a WS row.

SHAPING THE NECK

❋ NEXT ROW (RS): Work 31 (37, 43) stitches in pattern and place on holder; bind off 25 stitches, work remaining 31 (37, 43) stitches in pattern. Working left side only, bind off 4 stitches at the beginning of the next RS row (neck edge), then bind off 3 stitches at the neck edge 1 (1, 2) times. Decrease 1 stitch at neck edge every other row 3 times. You now have 21 (27, 30) stitches. Work even in pattern until piece measures 20" (20", 21") (51 [51, 53.5] cm) from cast-on. Place stitches on holder. Place held 31 (37, 43) stitches on needle and work as for left side, reversing shaping.

OCEAN WAVE MERINO-BAMBOO VEST *continued*

Knitting the Front

❁ Work as for back until piece measures 16" (16", 17") (40.5 [40.5, 43] cm). Work neck shaping as for back, then work even in pattern until piece measures same as back.

Finishing

❁ Join 21 (27, 30) front and back shoulder stitches with three-needle bind-off (see page 266). Sew side seams. With smaller needle, pick up and knit (see page 264) 130 (130, 142) stitches around neck edge. Knit 6 rows. Bind off loosely and allow fabric to roll. With smaller needle pick up and knit 96 (96, 108) stitches around each armhole. Knit 5 rows. Bind off loosely and allow fabric to roll. Weave in ends.

WISTERIA WAVES
SILK-MERINO BEANIE

DESIGNED BY JANICE BYE, *photo on page 31*

The lace pattern used for this beanie is comprised of a simple sequence of yarn overs and decreases worked over 10 stitches. Every other row is plain knit, so you only have four rows to learn! Knitted in a silk-and-merino blend, this is a good three-season cap.

SIZES AND FINISHED MEASUREMENTS	To fit adult small to medium, approximately 18" (45.5 cm) circumference, unstretched
YARN	Manos del Uruguay Silk Blend, 30% silk/70% extra fine merino wool, 1.75 oz (50 g)/150 yds (137 m), Wisteria
NEEDLES	Set of four US 4 (3.5 mm) double-point needles *or size you need to obtain correct gauge*
GAUGE	24 stitches = 4" (10 cm) in stockinette stitch, 20 stitches = 4" (10 cm) in pattern
OTHER SUPPLIES	Tapestry needle

Knitting the Hat

❁ Cast on 100 stitches. Divide the stitches onto double-point needles so there are 30 stitches on needle 1, 40 stitches on needle 2, and 30 stitches on needle 3. Join into a round, being careful not to twist the stitches. Work 5 rounds of K2, P2 rib.

STITCH PATTERN
lace

ROUND 1: *Yo, K8, K2tog; repeat from *.

ROUND 2 AND ALL EVEN-NUMBERED ROUNDS: Knit.

ROUND 3: *K2, yo, ssk, K3, K2tog, yo, K1; repeat from *.

ROUND 5: *K3, yo, ssk, K1, K2tog, yo, K2; repeat from *.

ROUND 7: *K4, yo, sl 1, K2tog, psso, yo, K3; repeat from *.

REPEAT ROUNDS 1–8 FOR PATTERN.

Knitting the Eyelet Pattern

* ROUND 1: Purl.
* ROUND 2: *Yo, K2tog; repeat from *.
* ROUND 3: Purl.
* ROUND 4: Knit.

Knitting the Lace Pattern

* Work Rounds 1–8 of Lace pattern 5 times.

Decreasing for the Crown

* ROUND 1: *Yo, ssk, K6, K2tog; repeat from *. You now have 90 stitches.
* ROUND 2: Knit.
* ROUND 3: *Yo, ssk, K5, K2tog; repeat from *. You now have 80 stitches.
* ROUND 4: Knit.
* Continue in this manner, knitting 1 fewer stitch between the decreases and working 1 round even between decrease rounds until you have 40 stitches, ending with a plain knit round.
* NEXT ROUND: *Yo, ssk, K2tog; repeat from *. You now have 30 stitches.
* Knit 1 round.
* NEXT ROUND: *K1, K2tog; repeat from *. You now have 20 stitches.
* Knit 1 round.
* NEXT ROUND: *K2tog; repeat from *. You now have 10 stitches.
* Knit 1 round.
* NEXT ROUND: *K2tog; repeat from *. You now have 5 stitches.

Finishing

* Place remaining 5 stitches onto 1 needle. Following the instructions for I-cord on page 262, work 5-stitch I-cord for 5" (12.5 cm). Cut yarn, leaving an 8" (20.5 cm) tail. Thread tail onto tapestry needle and draw through remaining stitches twice. Pull up snug and fasten off. Weave in ends and block.

BAMBOO NAPKIN RINGS

DESIGNED BY ANNE LENZINI, *photo on page 30*

B amboo is a great yarn to use for napkin rings; knitted bamboo will stretch enough to accommodate both your tea and your dinner napkins. Be sure to cast on and bind off loosely.

FINISHED MEASUREMENTS	Approximately 5" (12.5 cm) circumference
YARN	Wisdom Yarns Bamboo Splash, 100% bamboo, 1.75 oz (50 g)/ 87 yds (80 m), 107 Tan/Pink
NEEDLES	Set of five US 6 (4 mm) double-point needles *or size you need to obtain correct gauge*
GAUGE	28 stitches and 32 rows = 4" (10 cm) in pattern
OTHER SUPPLIES	Stitch marker, tapestry needle, .5 yd (46 cm) ⅝" (1.6 cm) satin ribbon (optional)

Knitting the Napkin Ring

❅ Using long-tail cast-on (see page 263), cast on 35 stitches. Distribute stitches over 4 double-point needles and place marker for beginning of round. Join into a round, being careful not to twist the stitches. Work in Reverse Linen Stitch until piece measures 2" (5 cm). Bind off loosely.

Finishing

❅ Weave in ends. If desired, tie ribbon into bows and sew to napkin ring, being careful not to go through both layers.

DIAMOND AND CRYSTAL CASHMERE EVENING BAG

DESIGNED BY CAROL LAMBOS, photo on page 26

This classic evening clutch is knitted in ultraluxurious cashmere, and the silver-lined crystal beads add just the right amount of glamour. Perfect for a night on the town.

FINISHED MEASUREMENTS	Approximately 4.5" (11.5 cm) tall, 7" (18 cm) wide, and 1.5" (4 cm) deep
YARN	Jade Sapphire Mongolian Cashmere 4-ply, 100% cashmere, 1.9 oz (55 g)/200 yds (183 m), 30 La Nuit
NEEDLES	US 4 (3.5 mm) straight needles *or size you need to obtain correct gauge*
GAUGE	30 stitches and 32 rows = 4" (10 cm) in stockinette stitch
OTHER SUPPLIES	1,050 size 6° silver-lined crystal seed beads, cable needle, 12" x 16" (30.5 cm x 40.5 cm) piece of lining fabric, 14.5" x 10" (37 cm x 25 cm) piece of heavy interfacing, fusible web for adhering fabric to interfacing, sewing needle and coordinating sewing thread, one ¾" (2 cm) magnetic purse clasp
ABBREVIATIONS	**C3L** slip 2 stitches to cable needle (cn) and hold in front, K1, slip 1 stitch from cn back to left needle and purl it, K1 from cn **C2L** slip 1 stitch from cn and hold in front, P1, K1 from cn **C2R** slip 1 stitch from cn and hold in back, K1, P1 from cn **SB** slip 1 stitch purlwise with yarn in front, slide bead in front of the slipped stitch, move yarn to back to continue knitting

Preparing the Yarn

❖ Begin by stringing beads onto the yarn as follows. Tie a piece of sewing thread about 4" (10 cm) long securely around the knitting yarn, about 6" (15 cm) from the end. Thread the sewing thread onto a needle. Pick up beads onto sewing needle and push them down the sewing thread and onto the yarn. Do not string all the beads, but rather about one-quarter; you will then cut the yarn and string more after you've used these, as this makes the materials easier to work with and cuts down the wear on the yarn. As you work, push the beads down along the yarn toward the ball, then slide a bead up into position as needed.

DIAMOND AND CRYSTAL CASHMERE EVENING BAG *continued*

Knitting the Purse

❋ Cast on 73 stitches: 49 stitches for the body and 12 stitches for each side. Slipping the first stitch of every row, work Rows 1–16 of chart below 3 times.

❋ Bind off 12 stitches at the beginning of the next 2 rows. Continuing in pattern as established on remaining 49 stitches, work Rows 1–16 of 49 center stitches of chart 6 more times, then work Rows 1–8 once more. Bind off in pattern.

Finishing

❋ Matching the patterns carefully, sew side seams using mattress stitch with half a stitch seam allowance (see page 264).

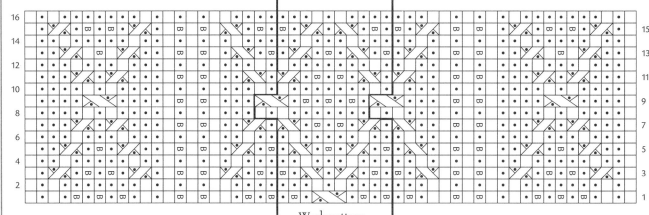

Diamond and Crystal Cashmere Evening Bag

☐ knit on RS rows, purl on WS rows

· purl on RS rows, knit on WS rows

SB

C2L

C2R

C3L

Work pattern repeat 3 times

Lining

❋ Using the illustration below as a guide, cut a piece of heavy interfacing and lining fabric to match the shape of the bag, cutting the fabric 0.5" (1.3 cm) larger
than the interfacing around all edges. Using fusible web and following manufacturer's instructions, adhere interfacing to WS of lining fabric. Fold the lining
over the edges of the interfacing, then fold the entire piece into the shape of
the purse with lining fabric to inside. Secure the edges with fusible web. Place
the assembled lining inside the knitted bag and adjust to fit. Attach the female
side of the clasp to the front of the bag, centering it below the topmost completed diamond. Attach the male side of the clasp to the lining and interfacing
of the flap, 1" (2.5 cm) from the edge. Sew the lining edges to the bag with small
neat stitches.

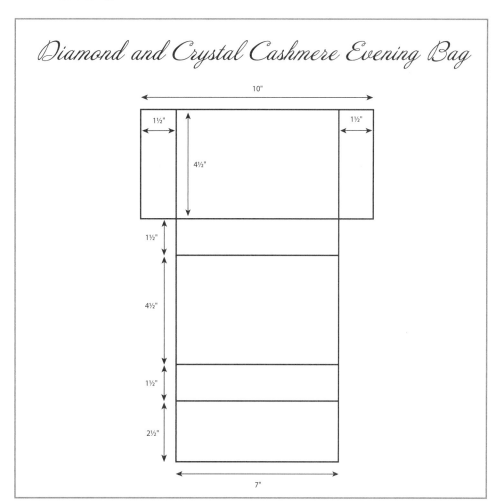

Diamond and Crystal Cashmere Evening Bag

ORGANIC COTTON BUNNIES

DESIGNED BY SUSAN B. ANDERSON, *photo on page 28*

Babies love these soft bunnies knitted with organic cotton, which is grown and harvested without the use of agrochemicals. As the manufacturer says, "From seed to skein, it's a good thing for your needles, for you, and for the environment." One skein of yarn makes several bunnies.

FINISHED MEASUREMENTS	Approximately 5" (12.5 cm) long and 2" (5 cm) tall
YARN	Blue Sky Organic Cotton, 100% organic cotton, 3.5 oz (100 g)/ 150 yds (137 m), 80 Bone, 82 Nut, or 83 Sage
NEEDLES	Set of four US 5 (3.75 mm) double-point needles *or size you need to obtain correct gauge*
GAUGE	22 stitches = 4" (10 cm) in stockinette stitch
OTHER SUPPLIES	Stitch marker, tapestry needle, polyester fiberfill or plastic pellets for stuffing*, pipe cleaner (optional), black embroidery floss *If the gift is for a baby or toddler use fiberfill only. If it's for an older person, you may use pellets and fiberfill for the beanbag feel.

Making the Body

❊ Cast on 9 stitches and place 3 stitches onto each of 3 double-point needles. Place marker and join into a round, being careful not to twist the stitches. Needle 1 is the bottom of the bunny.

❊ ROUND 1: Knit.

❊ ROUND 2: *K1, M1, K1, M1, K1; repeat from * to end of round. You now have 15 stitches.

❊ ROUND 3: Knit.

❊ ROUND 4: *K1 (M1, K1) 3 times, K1; repeat from * on needles 2 and 3. You now have 24 stitches.

❊ ROUND 5: Knit.

❊ ROUND 6: *K1, M1, knit to last stitch, M1, K1; repeat from * on needles 2 and 3. You now have 30 stitches.

❊ ROUND 7: Repeat Round 6. You know have 36 stitches.

❊ ROUNDS 8–19: Knit.

❊ ROUND 20: Knit 20, K2tog twice, ssk twice, knit to end of round. You now have 12 stitches on needle 1 and 10 stitches on needles 2 and 3.

❊ ROUNDS 21–30: Knit.

Stuffing the Body

❈ If using fiberfill only, stuff the body until firm. If using pellets and fiberfill, cover the bottom of the toy and fill about halfway with pellets, then stuff with fiberfill until firm.

Knitting the Neck and Head

❈ ROUND 1: (K2, K2tog) 3 times on needle 1; knit all stitches on needles 2 and 3. You now have 9 stitches on needle 1 and 10 stitches on needles 2 and 3.

❈ ROUND 2: (K1, K2tog) 3 times on needle 1; knit all stitches on needles 2 and 3. You now have 6 stitches on needle 1 and 10 stitches on needles 2 and 3.

❈ ROUND 3: Knit all stitches on needle 1; K1, (K1, K2tog) 3 times on needles 2 and 3. You now have 6 stitches on needle 1 and 7 stitches on needles 2 and 3.

❈ ROUND 4: Knit.

❈ ROUND 5: Knit all stitches on needle 1; (K2, M1) 3 times, K1 on needles 2 and 3. You now have 6 stitches on needle 1 and 10 stitches on needles 2 and 3.

❈ ROUNDS 6–11: Knit.

❈ ROUND 12: (K1, K2tog) twice on needle 1; K1 (K1, K2tog) 3 times on needles 2 and 3. You now have 4 stitches on needle 1 and 7 stitches on needles 2 and 3.

❈ ROUND 13: Knit.

❈ ROUND 14: K2tog twice on needle 1; K1, K2tog 3 times on needles 2 and 3. You now have 2 stitches on needle 1 and 4 stitches on needles 2 and 3.

❈ ROUND 15: Knit.

❈ ROUND 16: K2tog 5 times. You now have 5 stitches.

❈ Stuff the head with fiberfill until it is firm. Cut the yarn, thread onto tapestry needle, and draw through remaining stitches twice. Pull up snug and fasten off. Pull yarn tail through to the inside.

Knitting the Ears

❈ Using double-point needles to knit back and forth, cast on 8 stitches.

❈ ROW 1: *Slip 1 stitch pwise wyib, K1; repeat from *.

❈ Repeat Row 1 until piece measures 1.75" (4.5 cm) from cast-on.

❈ Carefully pull the needle out of the stitches. Squeeze the sides of the ear until they separate and form a tube. Place 4 stitches on one needle and 4 stitches on another needle. Turn the tube inside out so the knit side is now on the outside. With a third needle, bind off all stitches in the round.

❈ OPTIONAL: Cut the pipe cleaner into a 3" (7.5 cm) piece, fold it in half to create a loop and twist the end together. Place the loop inside the ear and sew bottom of ear closed.

ORGANIC COTTON BUNNIES *continued*

Making the Tail

❋ Following the instructions on page 264, make a 1" (2.5 cm) pompom tail with 20 wraps.

Knitting the Front Paws
(Make 2)

❋ Cast on 9 stitches and place 3 stitches onto each of 3 double-point needles. Place marker and join into a round, being careful not to twist the stitches. Knit every round until piece measures 1.25" (3 cm) from cast-on.

❋ NEXT ROUND: *K1, K2tog; repeat from *. You now have 6 stitches.

❋ Cut the yarn, thread onto tapestry needle, and draw through remaining stitches twice. Pull up snug and fasten off. Pull yarn tail through to the inside. Stuff with fiberfill or pellets and stitch the opening closed.

Knitting the Back Paws
(Make 2)

❋ Cast on 12 stitches and place 4 stitches onto each of 3 double-point needles. Place marker and join into a round, being careful not to twist the stitches. Knit every round until piece measures 1.75" (4.5 cm) from cast-on.

❋ NEXT ROUND: *K2, K2tog; repeat from *. You now have 9 stitches.

❋ NEXT ROUND: *K1, K2tog; repeat from *. You now have 6 stitches.

❋ Cut the yarn, thread onto tapestry needle, and draw through remaining stitches twice. Pull up snug and fasten off. Pull yarn tail through to the inside. Stuff with fiberfill or pellets and stitch the opening closed.

Finishing

❋ Sew pompom tail to back of bunny. Sew the ears to the top of the head at neck decrease. Sew paws to underside of bunny, being sure to place shorter paws in front. With black embroidery floss, use small straight stitches to make eyes and nose, as shown in photograph (see page 28).

LACY COTTON-HEMP BLEND VASE

DESIGNED BY JILLIAN MORENO, *photo on page 25*

Yes, you can cover virtually anything with knitted lace. The yarn used for this vase contains modal, a fiber made by spinning reconstituted cellulose from beech trees, putting it in the ecofriendly category.

FINISHED MEASUREMENTS	Approximately 12" (30.5 cm) tall with 11" expanding to 20" (28 to 51 cm) circumference
YARN	Elsebeth Lavold Hempathy, 41% cotton/34% hemp/25% modal, 1.75 oz (50 g)/154 yds (141 m), 009 Cool Blue
NEEDLES	Set of five US 4 (3.5 mm) double-point needles *or size you need to obtain correct gauge*
GAUGE	22 stitches and 28 rows = 4" (10 cm) in stockinette stitch, 24 stitches and 24 rows = 4" (10 cm) in pattern
OTHER SUPPLIES	Stitch markers, 12" (30.5 cm) vase with flute flaring from 11" (28 cm) to 20" (28 cm)*, tapestry needle, small binder clips, industrial strength glue *This is a common sized vase, and the one shown here was purchased at Target.

Knitting the Vase Sleeve

❋ Cast on 66 stitches. Place marker and join into a round, being careful not to twist the stitches. Knit 1 round, purl 1 round. Following chart (page 172), *work lace pattern over 32 stitches, P1, pm; repeat. Continue in pattern as established through Round 7 of lace pattern.

❋ INCREASE ROUND: Continue lace pattern as established and increase 1 stitch before each marker, working increased stitches into a K1, P1 rib pattern.

❋ Repeat the Increase Round every 7 rounds 5 times. You now have 78 stitches.

❋ Repeat the Increase Round every 3 rounds 7 times. You now have 92 stitches.

❋ Repeat the Increase Round every other row 8 times. You now have 108 stitches.

❋ Work even in patterns until piece measures 18.5" (47 cm), ending on Round 12 of chart. Purl 1 round. Bind off.

LACY COTTON-HEMP BLEND VASE continued

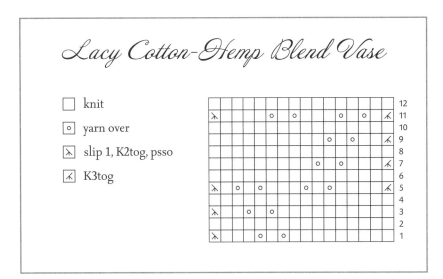

Lacy Cotton-Hemp Blend Vase

- ☐ knit
- ⊡ yarn over
- slip 1, K2tog, psso
- K3tog

Finishing

❋ Weave in ends. Wet block the vase sleeve and shape it over the vase. Use binder clips to hold the sleeve to the top of the vase. When dry, apply small dots of glue to the top of the vase and adhere the sleeve to it. Repeat at bottom if necessary.

SOY BEANIE

DESIGNED BY KATHERINE VAUGHAN, *photo on page 28*

A yarn made from soybeans? You bet! And it knits up into a great lace beanie for warm weather wear. The yarn is so light and drapey that it won't weigh you down, and the lace adds visual interest and breathability.

SIZES AND FINISHED MEASUREMENTS	To fit adult small to medium, approximately 21" (53.5 cm) circumference
YARN	Kollage Yarns Delicious, 100% soybean, 1.6 oz (45 g)/121 yds (111 m), Aruba Blue
NEEDLES	US 5 (3.75 mm) circular needle 16" (40 cm) long and set of five US 5 (3.75 mm) double-point needles *or size you need to obtain correct gauge*
GAUGE	23 stitches and 36 rows = 4" (10 cm) in stockinette stitch, 21 stitches and 40 rows = 4" (10 cm) in lace pattern
OTHER SUPPLIES	Stitch marker, tapestry needle

Knitting the Hat

❋ Cast on 104 stitches. Place marker and join into a round, being careful not to twist the stitches. Work Rounds 1–4 of Lace pattern, then work Rounds 1–16 twice. Work Rounds 1–3 once more.

Decreasing for the Crown

❋ ROUND 1: *P1, P2tog, K2, P3; repeat from *. You now have 91 stitches.

❋ ROUND 2: *P2, K2, P3; repeat from *.

❋ ROUND 3: *P2, K2, P2tog, P1; repeat from *. You now have 78 stitches.

❋ ROUND 4: *P2, K2, P2; repeat from *.

❋ ROUND 5: *P2tog, K2, P2; repeat from *. You now have 65 stitches.

❋ ROUND 6: *P1, K2, P2; repeat from *.

❋ ROUND 7: *P1, K2, P2tog; repeat from *. You now have 52 stitches.

❋ ROUND 8: *P1, K2, P1; repeat from *.

❋ ROUND 9: *K2tog, K1, P1; repeat from *. You now have 39 stitches.

❋ ROUND 10: *K2, P1; repeat from *.

❋ ROUND 11: *K1, ssk; repeat from *. You now have 26 stitches.

❋ ROUND 12: Knit.

SOY BEANIE *continued*

* ROUND 13: *K2tog; repeat from *. You now have 13 stitches.
* ROUND 14: *K1, K2tog; repeat from * to last stitch, K1. You now have 9 stitches.

Finishing

* Cut yarn, leaving an 8" (20.5 cm) tail. Thread tail onto tapestry needle and draw through remaining stitches twice. Pull up snug and fasten off. Weave in ends and block.

MERINO-SILK CABLES FOR BABY
DESIGNED BY ISELA PHELPS, *photo on page 31*

You're sure to spoil your infant with this lovely cabled hat knitted with a merino, silk, and cashmere blend. You'll probably like it so much, you'll want to knit one for yourself — but you'll have to splurge on an extra skein.

SIZES AND FINISHED MEASUREMENTS	To fit an infant 0–6 months, approximately 14" (35.5 cm) circumference, stretched
YARN	Sublime Baby Cashmere Merino Silk, 75% extra fine merino wool/20% silk/5% cashmere, 1.75 oz (50 g)/127 yds (116 m), 49 Pink
NEEDLES	Sets of five US 5 (3.75 mm) and US 4 (3.5 mm) double-point needles *or size you need to obtain correct gauge*
GAUGE	24 stitches and 32 rows = 4" (10 cm) in stockinette stitch on larger needle
OTHER SUPPLIES	Cable needle, tapestry needle
ABBREVIATIONS	**C3B (cable 3 back)** place 1 stitch on cable needle and hold in back, K2, K1 from cable needle

Knitting the Ribbing

* With smaller needles, cast on 80 stitches. Divide evenly onto 4 double-point needles and join into a round, being careful not to twist the stitches.
* ROUND 1: *K2, P2; repeat from *.
* Repeat Round 1 nine more times.

STITCH PATTERN
cable

ROUND 1: *P2, K3, C3B; repeat from *.

ROUNDS 2, 4, 6, AND 8: *P2, K6; repeat from *.

ROUND 3: *P2, K2, C3B, K1; repeat from *.

ROUND 5: *P2, K1, C3B, K2; repeat from *.

ROUND 7: *P2, C3B, K3; repeat from *.

REPEAT ROUNDS 1–8 FOR PATTERN.

Knitting the Hat

✤ Change to larger needles. Work Rounds 1–8 of Cable pattern 3 times, then work Rounds 1–4 once more.

Decreasing for the Crown

✤ **ROUND 1:** *K1, C3B, K2tog, P2; repeat from *.
✤ **ROUND 2:** *K5, P2; repeat from *.
✤ **ROUND 3:** *C3B, K2tog, P2; repeat from *.
✤ **ROUND 4:** *K4, P2; repeat from *.
✤ **ROUND 5:** *K1, C3B, P2tog; repeat from *.
✤ **ROUND 6:** *K1, K2tog, K1, P1; repeat from *.
✤ **ROUND 7:** *K3tog, P1; repeat from *.
✤ **ROUND 8:** *K2tog; repeat from *.
✤ **ROUND 9:** Repeat Round 8. You now have 5 stitches.

Finishing

✤ Cut yarn, leaving an 8" (20.5 cm) tail. Thread tail onto tapestry needle and draw through remaining stitches twice. Pull up snug and fasten off. Weave in ends.

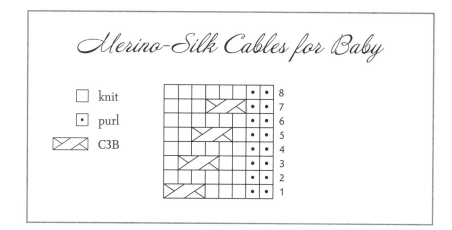

Merino-Silk Cables for Baby

□ knit
⊡ purl
⧖ C3B

ANGORA BEADED HAT

DESIGNED BY BEVERLY VASQUEZ, *photo on page 27*

There's nothing quite like the fluffiness of angora, and the sapphire beads add that certain je ne sais quoi. Be careful when washing angora: It's been known to felt while still on the rabbit!

SIZES AND FINISHED MEASUREMENTS	To fit adult small (medium), approximately 18" (21.5") (46 [54.5] cm) circumference
YARN	Anny Blatt Angora Super, 70% angora, 30% wool 0.88 oz (25 g)/ 116 yds (106 m), 383 Noir
NEEDLES	US 7 (4.5 mm) circular needle 16" (40 cm) long and set of four US 7 (4.5mm) double-point needles *or size you need to obtain correct gauge*
GAUGE	20 stitches = 4" (10 cm) in stockinette stitch
OTHER SUPPLIES	Big-eye beading needle, 104 (120) beads that fit smoothly over yarn, tapestry needle
ABBREVIATIONS	**S1B** slip 1 bead up next to needle

Preparing the Yarn

※ Use a big-eye beading needle to string 80 (96) beads onto yarn.

Getting Started

※ With circular needle, cast on 80 (96) stitches. Place marker and join into a round, being careful not to twist the stitches.

※ ROUND 1: Purl.

※ ROUND 2: Knit.

※ ROUNDS 3 AND 4: Purl.

※ ROUND 5: *P1, S1B; repeat from *.

※ ROUND 6: Knit.

※ ROUND 7: Purl.

※ ROUND 8: Knit.

※ ROUND 9: Purl.

※ ROUND 10: *K8, M1; repeat from *. You now have 90 (108) stitches.

※ Continue even in stockinette stitch for 2.75" (3.25") (7 [8.5] cm).

Decreasing for the Crown

✤ ROUND 1: *K7, K2tog; repeat from *. You now have 80 (96) stitches.

✤ ROUND 2: Knit.

✤ ROUND 3: *K6, K2tog; repeat from *. You now have 70 (84) stitches.

✤ ROUND 4: Knit.

✤ Continue in this manner, working 1 fewer stitch before each decrease and knitting 1 round even between decrease rounds, until you have 20 (24) stitches, changing to double-point needles when there are too few stitches for circular needle.

✤ NEXT ROUND: *K2tog; repeat from *. You now have 10 (12) stitches.

✤ Cut yarn, leaving an 8" (20.5 cm) tail. Thread tail onto tapestry needle and draw through remaining stitches twice. Pull up snug and fasten off.

Knitting the Flower

✤ Using a big-eye beading needle, string 24 beads on yarn. Cast on 47 stitches.

✤ ROUND 1: P1, *yo, P2tog; repeat from *.

✤ ROUND 2: P1, *S1B, yo, P2tog, yo, P2tog; repeat from * to last 2 sts, S1B, yo, P2tog.

✤ ROUND 3: Repeat Round 1.

✤ ROUND 4: Purl.

✤ ROUND 5: K1, *K2tog; repeat from *. You now have 24 stitches.

✤ ROUND 6: *P3tog; repeat from *. You now have 8 stitches.

✤ ROUND 7: K3tog, K2tog, K3tog. You now have 3 stitches.

✤ Slip 3 stitches onto double-point needles. Following the instructions on page 266, work 3-stitch I-cord for 25 rows and at the same time, work every other row as K1, S1B, K2.

✤ Cut yarn and thread tail through remaining 3 stitches. Fasten off.

Finishing

✤ Coil I-cord and tack down to flower center as shown in photo (see page 27). Weave in all ends. Attach flower to hat as desired.

Baby's Cabled Milk-Silk Cap

DESIGNED BY SUSAN BOYE, photo on page 36

The name of this yarn says it all — Cream for Milk. Made with milk fiber, the addition of silk and cashmere bring this yarn into the indulgent "heavy cream" category. Your baby will be happy and warm in this cap, complete with ear flaps.

SIZES AND FINISHED MEASUREMENTS	To fit infant 3–6 months, approximately 13–15" (33–38 cm) circumference
YARN	Rosarios 4 Cream for Milk, 60% milk fiber/30% silk/10% cashmere, 1.75 oz (50 g)/120 yds (110 m), Color 03
NEEDLES	US 6 (4 mm) circular needle 16" (40 cm) long and set of four US 6 (4 mm) double-point needles *or size you need to obtain correct gauge*
GAUGE	24 stitches and 18 rows = 4" (10 cm) in cable pattern
OTHER SUPPLIES	Cable needle, stitch marker, tapestry needle
ABBREVIATIONS	**C4F (cable 4 front)** place next 2 stitches on cable needle and hold in front, K2, K2 from cable needle **C6F (cable 6 front)** place next 3 stitches on cable needle and hold in front, K3, K3 from cable needle

Knitting the Ear Flaps (Make 2)

❋ With 2 double-point needles, cast on 10 stitches.

❋ **ROW 1 (RS):** K1, P1, C6F, P1, K1.

❋ **ROW 2:** K2, P6, K2.

❋ **ROW 3:** K1, M1, P1, K6, P1, M1, K1.

❋ **ROW 4:** K3, P6, K3.

❋ **ROW 5:** K1, M1, P2, K6, P2, M1, K1.

❋ **ROW 6:** K1, P1, K2, P6, K2, P1, K1.

❋ **ROW 7:** K1, M1, K1, P2, K6, P2, K1, M1, K1.

❋ **ROW 8:** K1, P2, K2, P6, K2, P2, K1.

❋ **ROW 9:** K1, M1, K2, P2, K6, P2, K2, M1, K1.

❋ **ROW 10:** K1, P3, K2, P6, K2, P3, K1.

❋ **ROW 11:** K1, M1, K3, P2, C6F, P2, K3, M1, K1.

❋ **ROW 12:** K1, P4, K2, P6, K2, P4, K1.

❋ **ROW 13:** K1, M1, K4, P2, K6, P2, K4, M1, K1.

* ROW 14: K1, P5, K2, P6, K2, P5, K1.
* ROW 15: K1, M1, K5, P2, K6, P2, K5, M1, K1.
* ROW 16: K1, P6, K2, P6, K2, P6, K1.
* ROW 17: K1, M1, K6, P2, K6, P2, K6, M1, K1.
* ROW 18: K2, P6, K2, P6, K2, P6, K2. You now have 26 stitches.
* Cut yarn. Repeat for other flap.

Setting Up for the Cap

* With circular needle, cast on 14 stitches.
* NEXT ROW: K6, P2, K6, knit first ear flap from double-point needle as follows: *P2, K6; repeat from * to last 2 stitches, P2. Cut yarn. With empty double-point needles, cast on 30 stitches and join to stitches on circular needle as follows: *K6, P2; repeat from * to last 6 stitches, K6. Join second ear flap as first. You now have 96 stitches.

Knitting the Cap

* Place marker for beginning of round and join into a round being careful not to twist the stitches.
* ROUND 1: *K6, P2; repeat from *.
* ROUND 2: *C6F, P2; repeat from *.
* ROUNDS 3–11: *K6, P2; repeat from *.
* Repeat Rounds 1–11 once more, then work Rounds 1–3 again. You now have 2 complete cable repeats, not counting ear flaps.

Shaping the Crown

* Change to double-point needles when there are too few stitches to work on circular needle.
* ROUND 1: *K2tog, K2, K2tog, P2; repeat from *. You now have 72 stitches.
* ROUNDS 2–6: *K4, P2; repeat from *.
* ROUND 7: *C4F, P2; repeat from *.
* ROUND 8: *K4, P2; repeat from *.

Decreasing for Top of Crown

* ROUND 1: *K2tog twice, P2; repeat from *. You now have 48 stitches.
* ROUNDS 2–4: *K2, P2; repeat from *.
* ROUND 5: *K2tog, P2tog; repeat from *. You now have 24 stitches.
* ROUNDS 6 AND 7: *K2tog; repeat from *. You now have 6 stitches.

Finishing

❈ Cut yarn, leaving an 8" (20.5 cm) tail. Thread tail onto tapestry needle and draw through remaining stitches twice. Pull up snug and fasten off. Weave in ends, tightening joins at cast-on edges.

SILK-CASHMERE DOMINOES

DESIGNED BY JUDITH DURANT, *photo on page 29*

If you're going to indulge in an afternoon nap, you may as well go all the way and do it on a silk-and-cashmere pillow. This one is made in the technique dubbed Domino Knitting by Vivian Høxbro in her book of the same name (Interweave Press, 2000).

FINISHED MEASUREMENTS	Approximately 12" (30 cm) square
YARN	Art Yarns Ensemble, 75% silk/25% cashmere, 3.5 oz (100 g)/ 256 yds (234 m), Color 250
NEEDLES	US 7 (4.5 mm) straight needles and two US 7 (4.5 mm) double-point needles *or size you need to obtain correct gauge*
GAUGE	22 stitches = 4" (10 cm) in stockinette stitch
OTHER SUPPLIES	Tapestry needle, 12" square (30 cm square) pillow form
ABBREVIATIONS	**p2sso** pass 2 slipped stitches over **sl 1** slip 1 stitch purlwise with yarn in back **sl 2tog** slip 2 stitches together knitwise

Knitting the Pillow Front

❈ Note: You may use regular straight needles for the front, but the knitted strips are small and shorter double-point needles are easier to manipulate.

KNITTING THE FIRST STRIP

❈ Using the knitted-on method (see page 262), cast on 25 stitches. Work Rows 1–24 of Domino pattern and leave last stitch on the needle. *Pick up and knit (see page 264) 12 stitches along the top of the square. The last picked-up stitch should be the last cast-on stitch (see figure 1, page 181). Cast on 12 stitches. You now have 25 stitches. Knit another Domino square and leave the last stitch on the needle. Repeat from * 3 more times for a total of 5 squares, cutting the yarn and pulling it through the last stitch of the last square.

STITCH PATTERN
domino

NOTE: Slip all stitches knitwise.

ROW 1 (WS): Knit.

ROW 2: Sl 1, K10, sl 2tog, K1, p2sso, K10, P1.

ROW 3: Sl 1, purl to end of row.

ROW 4: Sl 1, K9, sl 2tog, K1, p2sso, K9, P1.

ROW 5: Sl 1, knit to last stitch, P1.

ROW 6: Sl 1, K8, sl 2tog, K1, p2sso, K8, P1.

ROW 7: Sl 1, purl to end of row.

ROW 8: Sl 1, K7, sl 2tog, K1, p2sso, K7, P1.

ROW 9: Sl 1, knit to last stitch, P1.

ROW 10: Sl 1, K6, sl 2tog, K1, p2sso, K6, P1.

ROW 11: Sl 1, purl to end of row.

ROW 12: Sl 1, K5, sl 2tog, K1, p2sso, K5, P1.

ROW 13: Sl 1, knit to last stitch, P1.

ROW 14: Sl 1, K4, sl 2tog, K1, p2sso, K4, P1.

ROW 15: Sl 1, purl to end of row.

ROW 16: Sl 1, K3, sl 2tog, K1, p2sso, K3, P1.

ROW 17: Sl 1, knit to last stitch, P1.

ROW 18: Sl 1, K2, sl 2tog, k1, p2sso, K2, P1.

ROW 19: Sl 1, purl to end of row.

ROW 20: Sl 1, K1, sl 2tog, k1, p2sso, K1, P1.

ROW 21: Sl 1, knit to last stitch, P1.

ROW 22: Sl 1, sl 2tog, k1, p2sso, P1.

ROW 23: Sl 1, K1, P1.

ROW 24: Sl 2tog, K1, p2sso.

KNITTING THE SUBSEQUENT STRIPS

❋ Cast on 12 stitches. With RS facing, pick up and knit 13 stitches along right edge of the first square knitted. The first picked-up stitch should be in the cast-on row of the first square (see figure 2 below). Knit a Domino square and leave the last stitch on the needle. *Pick up and knit 11 stitches along the top of the square just knitted, pick up 1 stitch in the corner of the square in the first strip, pick up and knit 12 stitches along the right edge of the next square in the first strip (see figure 3 below). Knit another Domino square and leave the last stitch on the needle. Repeat from * 3 more times for a total of 5 squares, cutting the yarn and pulling it through the last stitch of the last square.

❋ Continue in this manner until you have a block that is 5 squares tall and 5 squares wide. Weave in all ends.

Knitting the Pillow Back

❋ Cast on 60 stitches. Work in stockinette stitch until piece measures about 11" (28 cm). Bind off, leaving a tail about 56" (142 cm) long for sewing the edges together.

Finishing

❋ Thread tail onto tapestry needle. Sew 3 edges together, slip pillow form inside, and sew the last seam. Fasten off the yarn and pull it through to the inside.

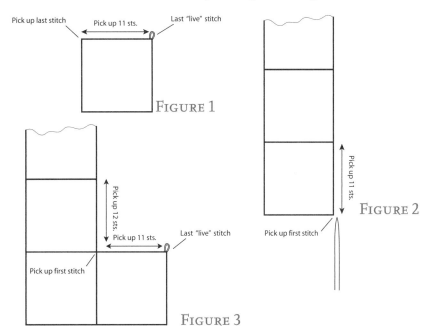

FIGURE 1

FIGURE 2

FIGURE 3

Siostra Mohair-Wool Hat

DESIGNED BY TINA MCELMOYL, *photo on page 28*

Siostra Mohair-Wool Hat features an ingenious little border worked simply by slipping a group of stitches over one stitch. The crown is decreased in three places, forming a lovely swirl pattern.

SIZES AND FINISHED MEASUREMENTS	To fit average woman, approximately 18" (45.5 cm) circumference, unstretched
YARN	Shibui Knits Merino Kid, 55% kid mohair/45% merino wool, 3.5 oz (100 g)/218 yds (200 m), 229 Mulberry
NEEDLES	US 2 (2.75 mm) circular needle 16" (40 cm) long and set of five US 2 (2.75 mm) double-point needles *or size you need to obtain correct gauge*
GAUGE	24 stitches = 4" (10 cm) in pattern stitch
OTHER SUPPLIES	Stitch markers, tapestry needle

STITCH PATTERN

1x1 seed rib

ROUND 1: *K1, P1; repeat from *.

ROUND 2: Knit.

REPEAT ROUNDS 1 AND 2 FOR PATTERN.

Knitting the Bottom Border

❋ With circular needle, cast on 216 stitches. Place marker and join into a round, being careful not to twist the stitches.

❋ ROUND 1: Knit.

❋ ROUND 2: *K1, move stitch back to left needle, pass the next 8 stitches (1 at a time) over the stitch, knit the stitch again, K3; repeat from *. You now have 72 stitches.

❋ ROUND 3: *K2, M1, K1, M1, K1; repeat from *. You now have 108 stitches.

Knitting the Hat

❋ Begin 1x1 Seed Rib and repeat Rounds 1 and 2 until hat measures 4" (10 cm) above border, ending with Round 1.

❋ NEXT ROUND: K36, pm, K36, pm, K36.

Decreasing for the Crown

❋ DECREASE ROUND 1: *K1, P1 to 3 stitches before marker, P3tog; repeat from *

❋ DECREASE ROUND 2: Knit.

❋ Repeat Decrease Rounds 1 and 2 until 12 stitches remain, changing to double-point needles when there are too few stitches for the circular needle.

Finishing

❁ Cut yarn, leaving an 8" (20.5 cm) tail. Thread tail onto tapestry needle and draw through remaining stitches twice. Pull up snug and fasten off. Weave in ends and block.

BIG-KID WOOL-SOY MITTENS

DESIGNED BY AMY GREEMAN, *photo on page 36*

Your young one will feel all grown up with mittens that are not threaded through the sleeves of the jacket or clipped to the cuffs! Knitted in an easy-to-work-with blend of wool and soybean protein, the knitting goes quickly, so you can knit the inevitably needed replacements.

SIZES AND FINISHED MEASUREMENTS	To fit a child, approximately 5.5" (14 cm) circumference
YARN	Rowan Tapestry, 70% wool/30% soybean protein, 1.75 oz (50 g)/131 yds (120 m), 179 Highland
NEEDLES	Set of four US 6 (4 mm) double-point needles *or size you need to obtain correct gauge*
GAUGE	22 stitches = 4" (10 cm) in stockinette stitch
OTHER SUPPLIES	Scrap yarn for holders, tapestry needle

Knitting the Cuff

❁ Cast on 32 stitches and divide onto 3 double-point needles. Join into a round, being careful not to twist the stitches.

❁ ROUNDS 1–15: *K1, P1; repeat from *.

❁ ROUNDS 16–25: Knit.

Knitting the Thumb Gusset

❁ ROUND 26: M1, K3, M1, knit to end of round. You now have 34 stitches.

❁ ROUND 27: M1, K5, M1, knit to end of round. You now have 36 stitches.

❁ ROUND 28: M1, K7, M1, knit to end of round. You now have 38 stitches.

❁ ROUND 29: M1, K9, M1, knit to end of round. You now have 40 stitches.

❁ ROUND 30: M1, K11, M1, knit to end of round. You now have 42 stitches.

❁ ROUND 31: Knit.

❄ ROUND 32: Slip next 13 stitches onto a holder for the thumb. Cast on 3 stitches, knit to end of round. You now have 32 stitches.

Knitting the Hand

❄ Knit 23 rounds even.

Shaping the Top

❄ NEXT ROUND: *K2tog; repeat from *. You now have 16 stitches.

❄ NEXT ROUND: *K2tog; repeat from *. You now have 8 stitches.

❄ Cut yarn, leaving an 8" (20.5 cm) tail. Thread tail onto tapestry needle and draw through remaining stitches twice. Pull up snug and fasten off.

Knitting the Thumb

❄ Divide the 13 held thumb stitches onto needles. Pick up and knit (see page 264) into the 3 cast-on stitches, K13 thumb stitches. You now have 16 stitches.

❄ Knit 14 rounds even.

❄ NEXT ROUND: *K2tog; repeat from *. You now have 8 stitches.

❄ NEXT ROUND: *K2tog; repeat from *. You now have 4 stitches.

❄ Cut yarn, leaving an 8" (20.5 cm) tail. Thread tail onto tapestry needle and draw through remaining stitches twice. Pull up snug and fasten off.

Finishing

❄ Repeat for other mitten. Weave in ends.

SILK OPERA CLUTCH
DESIGNED BY GWEN STEEGE, *photo on page 26*

Seductively silk and plenty large enough to carry your glasses or cell phone, lipstick, comb, and credit card: What more do you need for an evening at the opera? The stitch pattern is taken from Barbara Walker's A Treasury of Knitting Patterns.

FINISHED MEASUREMENTS	Approximately 7.5" (19 cm) wide and 5" (12.5 cm) tall
YARN	Debbie Bliss Pure Silk, 100% silk, 1.75 oz (50 g)/137 yds (125 m), Pale Green
NEEDLES	US 6 (4 mm) straight needles or *size you need to obtain correct gauge*
GAUGE	26 stitches = 4" (10 cm) in stockinette stitch
OTHER SUPPLIES	Tapestry needle, 6" (15 cm) hex-open handbag frame, 0.25 yd (23 cm) lining material, coordinating thread, sewing needle

ROWS 1, 3, 5, 7, AND 9 (RS): K2, *slip 5 wyif, K5; repeat from * to last 7 stitches, slip 5, K2.

ROWS 2, 4, 6, AND 8: Purl.

ROW 10: P4, *(insert right-hand needle down through the 5 loose strands, lift the strands onto the left-hand needle, and purl them together with the first stitch on the left-hand needle), P9; repeat from * to last 4 stitches, P4.

ROWS 11, 13, 15, 17, AND 19: K7, *slip 5 wyif, K5; repeat from * to last 12 stitches, slip 5, K7.

ROWS 12, 14, 16, AND 18: Purl.

ROW 20: P9, *(insert right-hand needle down through the 5 loose strands, lift the strands onto the left-hand needle, and purl them together with the first stitch on the left-hand needle), P9; repeat from *.

Knitting the Front of the Bag
* Cast on 59 stitches.
* Work Rows 1–20 of Butterfly pattern 3 times.

Working the Ribbing
* ROWS 1, 3, 5, 7, AND 9: P3, *K3, P2; repeat from * to last 6 stitches, K3, P3.
* ROWS 2, 4, 6, 8, AND 10: K3, *P3, K2; repeat from * to last 6 stitches, P3, K3.
* Bind off in purl.

Knitting the Back of the Bag
* Work as for front.

Finishing and Assembling
* With RS together, use backstitch (see page 261) to sew bag pieces together at bottom, taking care that the bind-off edges are at the top and matching pattern as closely as possible.
* Fold bag in half with WS together, and use mattress stitch (see page 264) to invisibly stitch side seams together.

SILK OPERA CLUTCH *continued*

❊ To determine lining size, measure assembled bag. Add 1" (2.5 cm) to the width and length, then double the length. Cut a piece of lining fabric to these dimensions, fold the piece in half widthwise, RS together, and stitch the side seams, taking 0.5" (1.3 cm) seam allowances.

❊ Put the hex-open frame together, following package instructions, then fold the top of the lining over the frame, forming a casing. Turn the raw edge under and hemstitch the lining to the frame. (The WS of the lining should face out.)

❊ Slip the knitted bag over the lining and frame. Turn the top edge to the outside about 0.75" (2 cm) to form a decorative cuff; allowing 2 rows of the ribbing to show above the end of the pattern stitch. Blind stitch the top fold of the bag to the top fold of the lining, then blind stitch the cuff in place.

DOWNTOWN LAMB'S WOOL CLUTCH

DESIGNED BY CIRILIA ROSE, *photo on page 26*

This scrumptious yarn knit at a tight gauge makes a simple woven cable along the top and deep ruching in the body stand out in high relief. A neat wrist strap elevates the clutch from cute to functional.

SIZES AND FINISHED MEASUREMENTS	Approximately 12" (31 cm) wide × 4.5" (12 cm) tall
YARN	Manufacturer J. Knits Charming, 80% lambs wool/10% cashmere/10% angora, 3.5 oz (100 g)/280 yds (256 m), Iowa
NEEDLES	US 4 (3.5 mm) straight needles plus 1 extra for bind off *or size you need to obtain correct gauge*
GAUGE	24 stitches = 4" (10 cm) in stockinette stitch
OTHER SUPPLIES	Metal sew-on snaps, cable needle, stitch holder, tapestry needle, two strips of plastic canvas, ¾" (2 cm) × 10" (25 cm)
ABBREVIATIONS	C4F (cable 4 front) Place next 2 stitches on cable needle and hold in front, K2, K2 from cable needle C4B (cable 4 back) Place next 2 stitches on cable needle and hold in back, K2, K2 from cable needle

STITCH PATTERNS
woven cable

ROW 1 (RS): K2, *C4F; repeat from * to last 2 stitches, K2.

ROW 2: Purl.

ROW 3: K4, *C4B; repeat from * to last 4 stitches, K4.

ROW 4: Purl.

REPEAT ROWS 1–4 FOR PATTERN.

Knitting the Sides

❈ Using a provisional method (see page 265), cast on 80 stitches. Knit 2 rows. Work rows 1–4 of Woven Cable pattern 3 times. Purl 1 row.

❈ NEXT ROW: *K1, kfb; repeat from *. You now have 120 stitches. Work even in stockinette stitch for 4.5" (11.5 cm), ending with a WS row.

❈ NEXT ROW (RS): *K1, K2tog; repeat from *. You now have 80 stitches. Place all stitches on holder. Repeat for other side but leave the stitches live and on the needle.

Joining the Sides

❈ Transfer held stitches from side to a needle. With RS of bag sides together, use the spare needle and the three-needle bind off (see page 266) to join the pieces. This is the bottom of the bag.

Knitting the Top Facing

❈ Undo the provisional cast-on from one side of the bag and place the live stitches on a needle. Knit in stockinette stitch until hem facing measures same depth as woven cable section, approximately 1.5" (4 cm). Bind off. Repeat for other side.

❈ Sew the side seams from the three-needle bind-off to the top bound-off edges. Fold the facing to the inside, tucking a strip of plastic canvas under hem for body.

Knitting the Wrist Strap

❈ Cast on 60 stitches and knit 10 rows. Bind off. Fold strap in half and sew the ends together and along the top-border seamline on one side.

Finishing

❈ Weave in ends. Sew snap to center of hem facing. Embellish the bag with a charm (included with Charming skein) if desired.

Stormy Cashmere Purse

DESIGNED BY CECILY GLOWIK, *photo on page 40*

It may be difficult to keep your hands off your purse if you have one like this, knitted from 100% cashmere. Elegant and soft, it makes a statement while holding the goodies.

FINISHED MEASUREMENTS	Approximately 16 " (41 cm) circumference
YARN	Classic Elite Yarns Stormy, 100% cashmere, 1.75 oz (50 g)/ 110 yds (100 m), 10357 Purple
NEEDLES	US 5 (3.75 mm) straight needles *or size you need to obtain correct gauge*
GAUGE	15 stitches and 29 rows = 4" (10 cm) in stockinette stitch
OTHER SUPPLIES	Tapestry needle, two 4.5" (11.5 cm) D-shaped bamboo handles

Getting Started

❋ Cast on 20 stitches. Work even in stockinette stitch until piece measures 2" (5 cm), ending with a WS row.

❋ Continue in stockinette stitch and using the cable cast-on method (see page 261), cast on 10 stitches at the beginning of the next 2 rows. You now have 40 stitches. Work even until piece measures 1" (2.5 cm) from second cast-on row, ending with a WS row.

Shaping the Top

❋ ROW 1(RS): K1, K2tog, K2, *P1, K4; repeat from *.

❋ ROW 2 AND FOLLOWING WS ROWS: Knit the knits and purl the purls (see page 262).

❋ ROW 3: K4, *M1 pwise, P1, M1 pwise, K4; repeat from *.

❋ ROW 5 AND FOLLOWING RS ROWS: K4, *P3, K4; repeat from *.

❋ Continue even in pattern as established until piece measures 3.75" (9.5 cm) from second cast-on row, ending with a WS row.

Increasing for the Body

❋ ROW 1 (RS): K4, *M1 pwise, P3, M1 pwise, K4; repeat from *.

❋ ROW 2 AND FOLLOWING WS ROWS: Knit the knits and purl the purls.

❋ ROW 3 AND FOLLOWING RS ROWS: K4, *P5, K4; repeat from *.

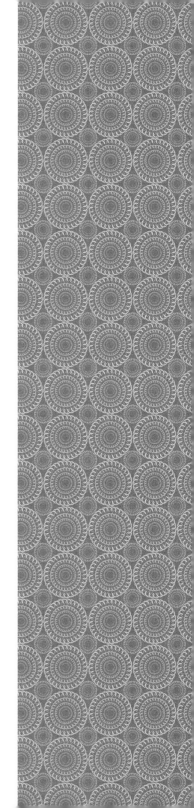

❋ Continue even in pattern as established until piece measures 7" (18 cm) from second cast-on row, ending with a WS row.

Decreasing for the Body

❋ ROW 1 (RS): K4, *P2tog, P1, P2tog; repeat from *.

❋ ROW 2 AND FOLLOWING WS ROWS: Knit the knits and purl the purls.

❋ ROW 3 AND FOLLOWING RS ROWS: K4, *P3, K4; repeat from *.

❋ Continue even in pattern as established until piece measures 9.5" (24 cm) from the second cast-on row, ending with a WS row.

Shaping the Top

❋ ROW 1 (RS): K4, *sl 1, P2tog, psso, K4; repeat from *.

❋ ROW 2 AND FOLLOWING WS ROWS: Knit the knits and purl the purls.

❋ ROW 3: K1, M1, knit to end of row.

❋ Work even in stockinette stitch for 1" (2.5 cm), ending with a RS row.

❋ Bind off 10 stitches at the beginning of the next 2 rows. You now have 20 stitches.

❋ Work even in stockinette stitch until piece measures 2" (5 cm) from bind-off row. Bind off remaining stitches.

Finishing

❋ Fold purse body in half with RS facing out, lining up the 10 cast-on and 10 bound-off stitches on each side. Sew side seams with mattress stitch (see page 264) from where these stitches meet down to the fold. Turn purse inside out and fold front flap over one handle and back flap over other handle and stitch in place.

Ruffle

❋ Cast on 20 stitches.

❋ ROW 1: K1, *Kfb; repeat from * to last stitch, K1. You now have 38 stitches.

❋ Work even in stockinette stitch until piece measures 0.5" (1.25 cm). Bind off. Sew ruffle below handle on front of purse. Weave in ends.

WINTER WINDOWS SILK SCARF
DESIGNED BY MARGARET RADCLIFFE, *photo on page 40*

A ll that glitters is not gold — sometimes it's sequins. Here sequins are combined with a lush and lustrous silk, and the resulting yarn is exquisite. The block stitch pattern accentuates the sheen of the yarn, and the sequins add sparkle.

FINISHED MEASUREMENTS	Approximately 5.5" (14 cm) wide and 57" (119.5 cm) long
YARN	Tilli Tomas Disco Lights, 100% spun silk with sequins, 3.5 oz (100 g)/225 yds (206 m), Natural
NEEDLES	US 5 (3.75 mm) straight needles *or size you need to obtain correct gauge*
GAUGE	24 stitches and 32 rows = 4" (10 cm) in pattern before blocking; 22 stitches and 28 rows = 4" (10 cm) in pattern after blocking
OTHER SUPPLIES	Tapestry needle

Knitting the Scarf

❄ Cast on 30 stitches.

❄ ROW 1: K6, *P6, K6; repeat from *.

❄ ROW 2: P6, *K6, P6; repeat from *.

❄ ROWS 3, 5, AND 7: Repeat Row 1.

❄ ROWS 4, 6, AND 8: Repeat Row 2.

❄ ROWS 9, 11, 13, AND 15: Repeat Row 2.

❄ ROWS 10, 12, 14, AND 16: Repeat Row 1.

❄ ROWS 17, 19, 21, AND 23: K6, *(K1, yo, K2tog) twice, K6; repeat from *.

❄ ROWS 18, 20, 21, AND 24: P6, *(K1, yo, K2tog) twice, P6; repeat from *.

❄ ROWS 25–32: Repeat Rows 9–16.

❄ ROWS 33–40: Repeat Rows 1–8.

❄ ROWS 41, 43, 45, AND 47: P6, K6, (K1, yo, K2tog) twice, K6, P6.

❄ ROWS 42, 44, 46, AND 48: K6, P6, (K1, yo, K2tog) twice, P6, K6.

❄ Repeat Rows 1–48 until scarf is approximately 44" (112 cm) long, ending with Row 39. Bind off in pattern.

Finishing

❄ Wash gently and lay flat to dry, stretching slightly in width to "open the windows."

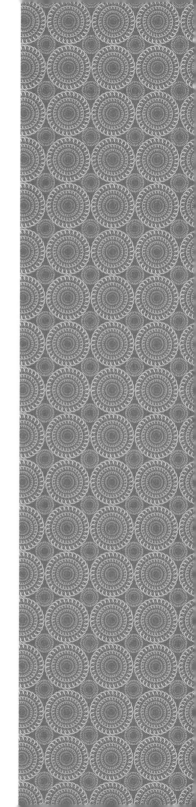

Winter Windows Silk Scarf

- ☐ knit on RS rows, purl on WS rows
- • purl on RS rows, knit on WS rows
- ○ yarn over
- ⋏ K2tog on RS rows
- ◿ K2tog on WS rows

Yak Hat

DESIGNED BY ANNI KRISTENSEN, *photo on page 42*

High in the Himalayas, yak herders comb out the downy soft fibers closest to the animals' skin to spin into luxurious yarn. This yarn comes from a Chinese cooperative that provides a sustainable living to the Tibetan herders.

SIZES AND FINISHED MEASUREMENTS	To fit most adults, approximately 19" (48.5 cm) circumference, unstretched
YARN	Himalaya Yarn Shokay Shambala, 100% yak down, 3.5 oz (100 g)/164 yds (150 m), CN Cerulean
NEEDLES	US 8 (5 mm) circular needle 16" (40 cm) long and set of five US 8 (5 mm) double-point needles *or size you need to obtain correct gauge*
GAUGE	20 stitches = 4" (10 cm) in pattern stitch
OTHER SUPPLIES	Stitch marker, US G/6 (4 mm) crochet hook, tapestry needle

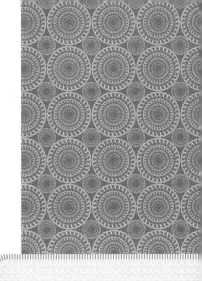

STITCH PATTERN

broken rib

ROUNDS 1–3: *K1, P1; repeat from *.

ROUND 4: *P1, K1; repeat from *.

REPEAT ROUNDS 1–4 FOR PATTERN.

Getting Started

❊ With circular needle, cast on 104 stitches. Place marker and join into a round, being careful not to twist the stitches. Work in Broken Rib pattern until piece measures 6" (15 cm) from cast-on. Purl 1 round.

Decreasing for the Crown

❊ **ROUND 1:** *K6, K2tog; repeat from *. You now have 91 stitches.

❊ **ROUND 2 AND ALL EVEN-NUMBERED ROUNDS:** Knit.

❊ **ROUND 3:** *K5, K2tog; repeat from *. You now have 78 stitches.

❊ Continue in this manner, working 1 fewer stitch before the decreases and knitting 1 round even between decrease rounds, until you have 26 stitches.

❊ **NEXT ROUND:** *K2tog; repeat from *. You now have 13 stitches.

❊ Knit 1 round even.

❊ **NEXT ROUND:** *K2tog; repeat from * to last stitch, K1. You now have 7 stitches.

Finishing

❊ Cut yarn, leaving an 8" (20.5 cm) tail. Thread tail onto tapestry needle and draw through remaining stitches twice. Pull up snug and fasten off. Make two 2" (5 cm) pompoms (see page 264) and attach to top of hat with crochet chain (see page 261). Weave in all ends.

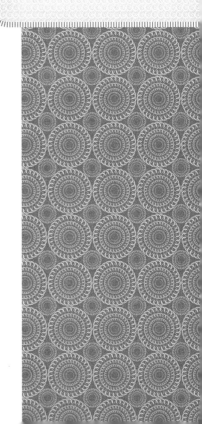

Ruffled Merino-SeaCell Bias Scarf

DESIGNED BY BETTY BALCOMB, *photo on page 42*

Just about anything goes with fibers today. This scarf is knitted with a blend of merino wool and SeaCell, a combination of wood pulp fiber (like Tencel) and seaweed. Used mostly in the commercial clothing industry, SeaCell is an ecofriendly fiber.

FINISHED MEASUREMENTS	Approximately 7" (18 cm) wide and 60" (152.5 cm) long
YARN	Fleece Artist Sea Wool, 70% merino wool/30% SeaCell, 4 oz (115 g)/383 yds (350 m), Angel Fish
NEEDLES	US 8 (5 mm) straight needles *or size you need to obtain correct gauge*
GAUGE	16 stitches and 24 rows = 4" (10 cm) in stockinette stitch, 16 stitches and 32 rows = 4" (10 cm) in pattern
OTHER SUPPLIES	Stitch marker, tapestry needle

Knitting the Bottom Triangle

※ Cast on 2 stitches.
※ ROW 1: Kfb, K1.
※ ROWS 2–6: Kfb, knit to end of row.
※ ROW 7: K1, *yo, K2tog; repeat from * to last stitch, yo, K1.
※ Repeat Rows 2–7 until you have 45 stitches.

Knitting the Body of the Scarf

※ Note: Place a marker on the RS (even rows) to help keep your place.
※ ROWS 1, 3, AND 5: Knit.
※ ROWS 2 AND 4: Kfb, knit to last 2 stitches, K2tog.
※ ROW 6: K1, *yo, K2tog; repeat from *.
※ Repeat Rows 1–6 until scarf measures 50" (127 cm) along longer edge.

Knitting the Top Triangle

※ ROWS 1, 3, AND 5: Knit.
※ ROWS 2 AND 4: K2tog, knit to last 2 stitches, K2tog.

RUFFLED MERINO-SEACELL BIAS SCARF *continued*

❈ ROW 6: K3tog, *yo, K2tog; repeat from *.

❈ Repeat Rows 1–6 until 3 stitches remain. K3tog.

❈ Leave last stitch on needle.

Knitting the Ruffles

❈ With stitch still on needle, pick up and knit (see page 264) 38 more stitches evenly spaced along scarf end.

❈ ROWS 1, 3, AND 5: Knit.

❈ ROW 2: *K1, yo; repeat from * to last stitch, K1. You now have 77 stitches.

❈ ROW 4: K1, *yo, K2tog; repeat from *.

❈ ROW 6: *K2tog, yo; repeat from * to last stitch, K1.

❈ Repeat Rows 3–6 until ruffle is 5" (12.5 cm) long, ending with Row 3 or 5. Bind off loosely.

❈ Pick up 39 stitches along beginning end and repeat ruffle instructions.

Finishing

❈ Weave in ends. Block.

MERINO-AND-GLASS LOVE BAG

DESIGNED BY BOBBE MORRIS, *photo on page 39*

This lovely little bag is perfect for the small things you love — jewelry, potpourri, or other tiny goodies. The Australian merino wool is as soft as alpaca, and the glass beads dress it up.

FINISHED MEASUREMENTS	Approximately 4" (10 cm) wide and 5" (12.5 cm) tall
YARN	Tilli Tomas Flurries, 80% Australian merino wool/20% glass beads, 1.75 oz (50 g)/70 yds (64 m), Natural
NEEDLES	US 6 (5 mm) straight needles *or size you need to obtain correct gauge*
GAUGE	32 stitches = 4" (10 cm) in pattern, unstretched
OTHER SUPPLIES	US D/3 (3.25 mm) crochet hook, tapestry needle
ABBREVIATIONS	**Kfbf** knit into front, back, and front of stitch (2 stitches increased)

Knitting the Bag

❋ Cast on 105 stitches and knit 1 row.

❋ NEXT ROW: *K3tog, p3tog; repeat from * to last 3 stitches, K3tog. You now have 35 stitches.

❋ Knit 1 row.

❋ EYELET ROW: K1, *yo, k2tog; repeat from *.

❋ Begin Rib Stitch pattern and work even for 8" (20.5 cm), ending with Row 2 of pattern.

❋ EYELET ROW: K1, *yo, k2tog; repeat from *.

❋ Knit 1 row.

❋ NEXT ROW: *Kfbf; repeat from*. You now have 105 stitches.

❋ Knit 1 row. Bind off loosely.

Finishing

❋ Fold piece in half and sew side seams. Weave in ends. Make a crochet chain (see page 261) about 44" (112 cm) long. Fold the chain in half, twist the 2 halves together, and knot the ends. Weave the chain through the eyelet holes and tie.

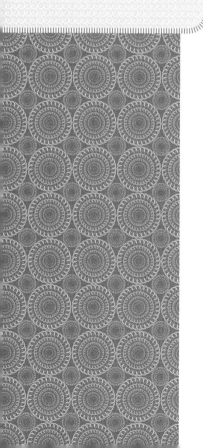

STITCH PATTERN

rib stitch

ROW 1: P1, *K3, P2; repeat from * to last 4 stitches, K3, P1.

ROW 2: K1, *P3, K2; repeat from * to last 4 stitches, P3, K1.

REPEAT ROWS 1 AND 2 FOR PATTERN.

COOL LITTLE LLAMA-SILK MITTENS

DESIGNED BY KELLY BRIDGES, *photo on page 37*

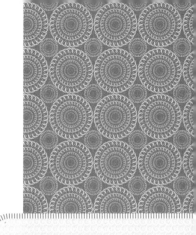

These quick-to-knit mittens are knitted with a llama-and-silk blend. They are such a joy to knit and to wear, you'll want to make them for everyone you know!

SIZES AND FINISHED MEASUREMENTS	To fit most adults, approximately 8" (20.5 cm) circumference
YARN	Plymouth Royal Llama Silk, 60% fine llama/40% silk, 1.75 oz (50 g)/102 yds (93 m), 1844 Green
NEEDLES	Set of four US 8 (5 mm) double-point needles *or size you need to obtain correct gauge*
GAUGE	18 stitches = 4" (10 cm) in stockinette stitch
OTHER SUPPLIES	Stitch markers, scrap yarn for holders, tapestry needle

Knitting the Cuff

(Both Mittens)

❉ Cast on 30 stitches. Divide evenly onto 3 double-point needles and join into a round, being careful not to twist the stitches. Work Rounds 1–4 of Twisted Rib pattern for 2" (5 cm), ending with Round 4.

Knitting the Right Mitten

❉ Note: The rest of the mitten is worked in K1, P1 rib.

❉ ROUND 1: Work 25, pm, M1L, work to end of round.

❉ ROUND 2: Work even in pattern to marker, sm, M1L, work to end of round.

❉ Repeat Round 2, working the new stitches into pattern, until you have 46 stitches total.

❉ NEXT ROUND: Work to marker, place next 14 stitches on holder for thumb, cast on 2 stitches, continue in pattern to end of round.

Knitting the Left Mitten

❉ Note: The rest of the mitten is worked in K1, P1 rib.

❉ ROUND 1: Work 5, M1R, pm, work to end of round.

❉ ROUND 2: Work even in pattern to marker, sm, M1R, work to end of round.

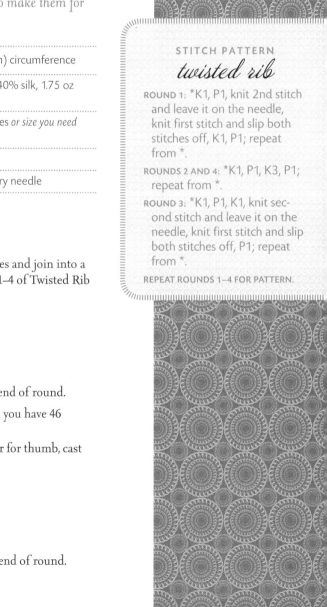

STITCH PATTERN

twisted rib

ROUND 1: *K1, P1, knit 2nd stitch and leave it on the needle, knit first stitch and slip both stitches off, K1, P1; repeat from *.

ROUNDS 2 AND 4: *K1, P1, K3, P1; repeat from *.

ROUND 3: *K1, P1, K1, knit second stitch and leave it on the needle, knit first stitch and slip both stitches off, P1; repeat from *.

REPEAT ROUNDS 1–4 FOR PATTERN.

* Repeat Round 2, working the new stitches into pattern, until you have 46 stitches total.
* NEXT ROUND: Work to marker, place next 14 stitches on holder for thumb, cast on 2 stitches, continue in pattern to end of round.

Finishing the Mitten
(Both Mittens)

* Continue even in pattern as established until mitten measures approximately 7.5" (19 cm) from beginning. Bind off in pattern.

Knitting the Thumb
(Both Mittens)

* Place 14 held thumb stitches onto 2 needles. With empty needle and RS facing, pick up and knit 2 stitches over the gap. Join into a round and knit 5 rounds. Bind off in pattern.

Finishing

* Weave in ends.

ANGORA AND PEARLS FOR SARAH
DESIGNED BY DIANA FOSTER, *photo on page 47*

Your child can go anywhere in her basic pink with pearls! This model was knitted with an angora-and-wool blend. The lacy triangles are knitted individually and joined together to form the bottom of the hat.

SIZES AND FINISHED MEASUREMENTS	To fit a child, approximately 20" (51 cm) circumference
YARN	Classic Elite Lush, 50% angora/50% wool, 1.75 oz (50 g)/ 124 yds (113 m), 4489 Princess Pink
NEEDLES	US 7 (4.5 mm) circular needle 16" (40 cm) long, set of four US 7 (4.5 mm) double-point needles *or size you need to obtain correct gauge,* and two US 1 (2.25 mm) double-point needles
GAUGE	16 stitches = 4" (10 cm) in stockinette stitch on larger needle
OTHER SUPPLIES	Stitch marker, tapestry needle, eleven 7 mm pearls

ANGORA AND PEARLS FOR SARAH *continued*

Knitting the Lace Edging

❊ *With 2 larger double-point needles, cast on 2 stitches, leaving a 6" (15 cm) tail. Work one Lace Edging pattern. Cut the yarn, leaving a tail to be woven in later and transfer the 9 edge stitches onto circular needle with RS facing. Repeat from * 8 more times. You now have 81 stitches on circular needle. Place a marker, join into a round, and work stockinette stitch for 1" (2.5 cm). Knit 1 more round, decreasing 1 stitch.

Knitting the Hat

❊ EYELET ROUND: *Yo, K2tog; repeat from *.

❊ Work stockinette stitch until piece measures 7" (18 cm) from beginning.

Decreasing for the Crown

❊ Change to double-point needles.

❊ ROUND 1: *K2, K2tog; repeat from *. You now have 60 stitches.

❊ ROUND 2: K1, K2tog; repeat from *. You now have 40 stitches.

❊ ROUND 3: *K2tog; repeat from *. You now have 20 stitches.

❊ ROUND 4: Repeat Round 3. You now have 10 stitches.

❊ ROUND 5: Repeat Round 3. You now have 5 stitches.

❊ Cut yarn, leaving an 8" (20.5 cm) tail. Thread tail onto tapestry needle and draw through remaining stitches twice. Pull up snug and fasten off.

Finishing

❊ With smaller double-point needles, cast on 2 stitches. Following the instructions on page 262, knit a 2-stitch I-cord 30" (76 cm) long. Weave I-cord through eyelets. Tie a pearl bead on each end of the I-cord. Tie a bead onto the 6" (15 cm) tails at each lace point. Weave in all ends.

STITCH PATTERN
lace edging

ROW 1 (RS): Knit.
ROW 2: K1, yo, K1.
ROW 3: Knit.
ROW 4: K1, (yo, K1) twice.
ROW 5: Knit.
ROW 6: K1, (yo, K1) 4 times.
ROW 7: Knit.

LYRA WOOL-SOY CABLED BABY BONNET

DESIGNED BY VICKIE HOWELL, *photo on page 43*

Some of us remember this style of hat from our childhood, and we're glad it's back! This one is accented with a wide silk ribbon that ties into a big, luscious bow. Unlike the hats of yesteryear, this one is made with wool and soy fiber, a highly renewable resource.

SIZES AND FINISHED MEASUREMENTS	To fit infant (toddler, child) with approximately 14" (16", 18") (35.5 [41, 45.5] cm) circumference
YARN	South West Trading Company Vickie Howell Collection Vegas, 67% wool/29% Soysilk/4% Lurex, 1.75 oz (50 g) / 110 yds (100 m), 424 Flying Elvis
NEEDLES	US 8 (5 mm) straight needles *or size you need to obtain correct gauge*
GAUGE	20 stitches and 24 rows = 4" (10 cm) in stockinette stitch
OTHER SUPPLIES	Cable needle, tapestry needle, 1 yd (91.5 cm) of 2" (5 cm) wide ribbon
ABBREVIATIONS	**C6F (cable 6 front)** slip 3 stitches to cable needle and hold in front, K3, K3 from cable needle

Knitting the Cable Band

❋ Cast on 10 stitches.

❋ Work Rows 1–8 of Cable Band 9 (10, 11) times. Bind off.

Knitting the Bonnet Body

❋ Pick up and knit 54 (60, 66) stitches along edge of cable band. Work in seed stitch until piece measures 7" (8", 9") (18 [20.5, 23] cm) from the picked up stitches. Bind off in pattern. Fold the bonnet in half with ends of cable band together, and sew a seam up the center back.

Knitting the Bottom Edging

❋ With RS facing, pick up and knit (see page 264) 54 (62, 70) along the bottom of the bonnet (side edges of seed stitch portion and ends of cable band).

❋ ROWS 1–5: Knit.

LYRA WOOL-SOY CABLED BABY BONNET *continued*

- ❀ ROW 6: *K6, yo, K2tog; repeat from * to last 6 stitches, K6. This row creates the eyelet holes for the ribbon.
- ❀ ROWS 7–10: Knit.
- ❀ Bind off using a picot bind-off as follows: K1, *slip stitch from right needle to left needle, cast on 2 stitches, bind off 4 stitches; repeat from *. When you have 1 stitch remaining, cut yarn and pull through the last stitch.

Finishing

- ❀ Weave in ends. Following the instructions on page 264, make a 2" (5 cm) pompom, leaving a 2–3" (5–7.5 cm) tail. Attach the pompom to the top corner of the bonnet with the tail. Weave ribbon through eyelets and tie into a bow.

CASHMERE-SILK NECK CANDY

DESIGNED BY SHELLI WESTCOTT, *photo on page 40*

Yes, this neck warmer feels as good as it looks. It uses a simple stitch pattern and an optional number of buttons, and the finished piece can be worn in a variety of ways. Be creative!

FINISHED MEASUREMENTS	Approximately 22" (56 cm) long and 10" (25 cm) wide
YARN	Tanglewood Fiber Creations Silk/Cashmere, 50% cashmere/50% silk, 4 oz (113 g)/110 yds (101 m), Newport Rocks
NEEDLES	US 10.5 (6.5 mm) straight needles *or size you need to obtain correct gauge*
GAUGE	20 stitches = 4" (10 cm) in stockinette stitch
OTHER SUPPLIES	Tapestry needle, six to twelve ½" (1.3 cm) buttons

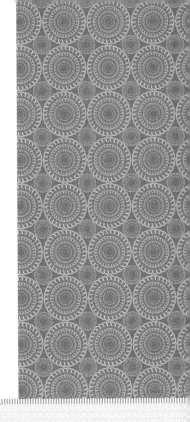

STITCH PATTERN

waves

ROW 1: K2tog 4 times, Kfb 8 times, K2tog 8 times, Kfb 8 times, K2tog 4 times.

ROW 2: Purl.

ROW 3: Knit.

ROW 4: Purl.

REPEAT ROWS 1–4 FOR PATTERN.

Knitting the Neck Warmer

- ❀ Cast on 48 stitches.
- ❀ ROW 1: Purl.
- ❀ ROW 2: Knit.
- ❀ ROW 3: Purl.
- ❀ Note: These 3 rows form the edge where you'll sew on the buttons.
- ❀ Work Rows 1–4 of the Waves pattern until piece measures approximately 22" (56 cm). Bind off.

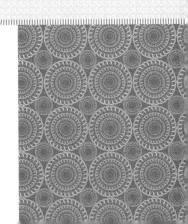

Finishing

❊ Weave in ends. Attach buttons as desired on cast-on edge; they can be pushed through the holes made on the other end by the stitch pattern.

CASHMERE NECK WARMER

DESIGNED BY SARAH KELLER, *photo on page 47*

T his scarf gives luxury hand-painted yarn a whole new look. The woven stitch has lots of texture, and the yarn repeats meld seamlessly down the length of the scarf. All that, and cashmere, too.

FINISHED MEASUREMENTS	Approximately 4.5" (11.5 cm) wide and 22" (56 cm) long
YARN	Artyarns Cashmere 5, 100% cashmere, 1.75 oz (50 g)/102 yds (93 m), 161 Burgundy
NEEDLES	US 8 (5 mm) straight needles *or size you need to obtain correct gauge*
GAUGE	27.5 stitches and 26 rows = 4" (10 cm) in pattern
OTHER SUPPLIES	Tapestry needle, three decorative buttons (optional)

Knitting the Neck Warmer

❊ Cast on 31 stitches.

❊ ROW 1: P1, *yo, slip 1, P2, pass slipped stitch over 2 purl stitches; repeat from *.

❊ ROW 2: K1, *yo, slip 1, K2, pass slipped stitch over 2 knit stitches; repeat from *.

❊ Repeat Rows 1 and 2 until scarf is desired length or you're almost out of yarn (you'll need about 20" [51 cm] for bind-off (1). Bind off loosely.

Finishing

❊ Wet scarf in tepid water and smooth out flat to dry. If desired, sew three buttons diagonally across one scarf end. Buttons will easily pass through the knitted fabric.

Inca-Dincadoo Organic Cotton Baby Cardigan

DESIGNED BY SARAH KELLER, *photo on page 43*

Organic undyed cotton is a very safe fiber for baby's skin, and with this fast-knitting sweater pattern, your baby can have a sweater for every day of the week. The cardigan is knitted in one piece, beginning at the lower back, working up over the shoulders, and then down the front. Sew underarm and side seams, and you're done!

SIZES AND FINISHED MEASUREMENTS	To fit infant 0–3 months, approximately 18" (45.5 cm) chest circumference
YARN	Henry's Attic Inca Organic Cotton, 100% organic cotton, 4 oz (113 g)/155 yds (142 m), Oz
NEEDLES	US 9 (5.5 mm) straight needles *or size you need to obtain correct gauge*
GAUGE	16 stitches = 4" (10 cm) in stockinette stitch
OTHER SUPPLIES	Scrap yarn for holders, tapestry needle, US I/9 (5.5 mm) crochet hook, five ¾" (2 cm) buttons

Knitting the Back

❋ Cast on 32 stitches. Knit 35 rows.

Knitting the Sleeves

❋ Using the backward loop method (see page 261), cast on 4 stitches at the beginning of the next 8 rows. You now have 64 stitches. Knit 17 rows even.

Knitting the Left Sleeve and Left Front

❋ NEXT ROW (RS): K23 and place on holder for right front, bind off 18 stitches for neck, K23 for left front. Knit 7 rows even, ending with WS row.

❋ NEXT ROW (RS): K1, M1, knit to end of row.

❋ Knit 3 rows even.

❋ Repeat these 4 rows 2 more times. You now have 26 stitches.

❋ NEXT ROW: Using the backward loop method, cast on 6 stitches, knit to end of row. You now have 32 stitches.

❋ Knit 2 rows even.

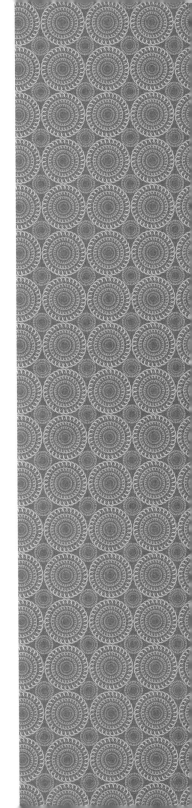

* Bind off 4 stitches at the beginning of the next 4 WS rows. You now have 16 stitches.
* Work even for 36 rows (count 46 rows from the 6 left-front cast-on stitches). Bind off.

Knitting the Right Sleeve and Right Front

* Place 23 held right front stitches on needle. With WS facing, join yarn at neck edge and knit 7 rows, ending with a WS row.
* NEXT ROW (RS): Knit to last stitch, M1, K1.
* Knit 3 rows even.
* Repeat these 4 rows 2 more times. You now have 26 stitches.
* Knit 1 row.
* NEXT ROW (WS): Using the backward loop method, cast on 14 stitches, knit to end. You now have 40 stitches.
* Knit 2 rows even.
* Bind off 4 stitches at the beginning of the next 4 RS rows and at the same time, make buttonholes on the first bind-off row and every following tenth row 4 times as follows: Knit to last 2 stitches, yo, K2tog, K1.
* Work even for 36 rows (count 46 rows from the 6 right-front cast-on stitches). Bind off.

Finishing

* Fold sweater in half at shoulders and sew side and sleeve seams. With RS facing and beginning at lower right front edge, work slip stitch crochet (see page 266) around entire front edge. Weave in ends. Sew buttons opposite buttonholes.

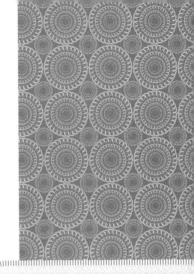

Flirty Merino-Silk Neck Warmer

DESIGNED BY TONIA BARRY, *photo on page 45*

You'll be snuggly and flirty at the same time with this neck warmer. The wonderfully soft blend of alpaca, merino, and silk is hand painted by Sereknity Yarns, and the subtle coloration works beautifully with the openwork and ruffle patterns.

FINISHED MEASUREMENTS	Approximately 6" (15 cm) wide and 29" (73.5 cm) long
YARN	Serenknity Sweet, 50% alpaca/30% merino wool/20% silk, 4 oz (113 g)/230 yds (210 m), Crush
NEEDLES	US 8 (5 mm) and US 6 (4 mm) straight needles *or size you need to obtain correct gauge*
GAUGE	16.5 stitches and 32 rows = 4" (10 cm) in pattern stitch
OTHER SUPPLIES	Tapestry needle, 2" (5 cm) ring buckle

Knitting the Warmer

❊ With larger needles, cast on 121 stitches. Work in Lacy Zigzag pattern until piece measures 4" (10 cm) from cast-on, ending with Row 12 of pattern.

Knitting the Ruffle

❊ Change to smaller needle.
❊ ROW 1: *Kfb; repeat from *. You now have 242 sts.
❊ ROW 2: Purl.
❊ ROW 3: *Pfb; repeat from *. You now have 484 stitches.
❊ Bind off purlwise.

Finishing

❊ Weave in ends. Block, being careful not to flatten the ruffle. Thread tapestry needle with yarn and sew buckle to front of warmer 2" (5 cm) up from top of ruffle and 2" (5 cm) in from edge of warmer.

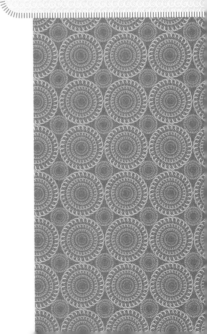

STITCH PATTERN

lacy zigzag

ROWS 1, 3, AND 5 (RS): (Sl 1, k1, psso), K2, yo, K2; repeat from * to last stitch, K1.

ROW 2 AND ALL WS ROWS THROUGH 12: Purl.

ROWS 7, 9, AND 11: K3, *yo, K2, K2tog, K2; repeat from * to last 4 stitches, yo, K2, K2tog.

REPEAT ROWS 1–12 FOR PATTERN.

Crossroads Soy-Wool Hat

DESIGNED BY JENI CHASE, *photo on page 46*

Crossroads is knitted with a blend of soy silk and wool. You can be ecofriendly, warm, and fashionable all at once with this design.

FINISHED MEASUREMENTS	Approximately 20" (51 cm) circumference
YARN	South West Trading Company Karaoke, 50% Soysilk/ 50% wool, 1.75 oz (50 g)/109 yds (100 m), 286 Copper
NEEDLES	Sets of five US 7 (4.5 mm) and US 6 (4 mm) double-point needles *or size you need to obtain correct gauge*
GAUGE	18 stitches and 28 rows = 4" (10 cm) in stockinette stitch on larger needles
OTHER SUPPLIES	Tapestry needle

Knitting the Band

* With smaller needles, cast on 88 stitches and divide evenly onto 4 double-point needles. Join into a round, being careful not to twist the stitches.

* ROUNDS 1, 2, 4, 6, 9, AND 11: Purl.

* ROUNDS 3, 5, AND 10: Knit.

* ROUND 7: *Insert needle into next stitch, wrap yarn around needle 4 times, and knit the stitch, pulling all 4 loops through; repeat from *.

* ROUND 8: *Slip 8 stitches, dropping extra wraps so you have 8 long stitches on right needle. With left needle, skip over the first 4 of these stitches, lift the next 4 together over and onto left needle. Slip the remaining stitches to left needle and K8 stitches in the new order; repeat from *.

Knitting the Crown

* Change to larger needles. Work in stockinette stitch until piece measures 5" (12.5 cm).

DECREASING THE CROWN

* ROUND 1: *Ssk, knit to last 2 stitches on needle, K2tog; repeat from *.

* ROUND 2: Knit.

* Repeat Rounds 1 and 2 until 48 stitches remain.

* Repeat Round 1 five more times. You now have 8 stitches.

CROSSROADS SOY-WOOL HAT *continued*

Finishing

❄ Cut yarn, leaving an 8" (20 cm) tail. Thread tail onto tapestry needle and draw through remaining stitches twice. Pull up snug and fasten off. Weave in ends.

SUEÑO BAMBOO SPA MASK

DESIGNED BY KENDRA NITTA, *photo on page 45*

Inspired by eye pillows used in spas, especially those in the rainforests of the South Pacific where bamboo grows abundantly, Sueño Spa Mask should be stored in the freezer until it is needed to soothe and rejuvenate. Worked in double knitting, your sample swatch also may be filled with dried flowers, making a lovely sachet.

FINISHED MEASUREMENTS	Approximately 4.25" (11 cm) wide and 9.5" (24 cm) long, including edging
YARN	Berroco Bonsai, 97% bamboo/3% nylon, 1.75 oz (50 g)/ 77 yds (71 m), 4101 Tofu
NEEDLES	Three US 4 (3.5 mm) straight needles *or size you need to obtain correct gauge*
GAUGE	18 stitches and 30 rows= 4" (10 cm) in double knitting
OTHER SUPPLIES	¾ cup (168 ml) large-size dried beans, tapestry needle, ¼ cup (56 ml) dried flowers for sachet (optional)
ABBREVIATIONS	inc 1 increase 1 stitch with backward loop method (see page 261)

Knitting the Mask

❄ Using the long-tail method (see page 263), cast on 20 stitches.

BORDER

❄ ROWS 1 AND 2: Knit.

❄ ROWS 3–6: K1, *yo, K2tog; repeat from * to last stitch, K1.

SET-UP FOR DOUBLE KNITTING

❄ NEXT ROW: K1, (yo, K2tog) twice, *inc 1, K1; repeat from * to last 4 stitches, yo, K1, yo, K2tog, K1. You now have 32 stitches.

STITCH PATTERN

double knit with lace edge

ROW 1: K1, (yo, K2tog) twice, *sl 1 wyif, K1; repeat from * to last 3 stitches, yo, K2tog, K1.

ROW 2: Repeat Row 1.

ROW 3: K1, (yo, K2tog) twice, sl 1 wyif, *K1, sl 1 wyif; repeat from * to last 4 stitches, turn.

ROW 4: *K1, sl 1 wyif; repeat from * to last 4 stitches, turn.

ROW 5: * K1, sl 1 wyif; repeat from * to last 4 stitches, K1, yo, K2tog, K1.

ROW 6: Repeat Row 1.

Knitting the Main Body

❧ ROW 1: K1, (yo, K2tog) twice, *sl 1 wyib, K1; repeat from * to last 3 stitches, yo, K2tog, K1.

❧ Work Rows 2–6 of Double Knit with Lace Edge pattern, then work Rows 1–6 4 more times. Piece measures approximately 2.25" (5.5 cm). If added length is needed, work Rows 1–6 once more.

Decreasing to the Center

❧ ROW 1: K1, yo, K2tog, K1, K2tog, *K1, sl 1 wyif; repeat from * to last 6 stitches, K2tog, K1, yo, K2tog, K1. You now have 30 stitches.

❧ ROW 2: K1, (yo, K2tog) twice, *K1, sl 1 wyif; repeat from * to last 5 stitches, K2, yo, K2tog, K1.

❧ ROW 3: K1, (yo, K2tog) twice, *K1, sl 1 wyif; repeat from * to last 5 stitches, turn.

❧ ROW 4: *K1, sl 1 wyif; repeat from * to last 5 stitches, turn.

❧ ROW 5: *K1, sl 1 wyif; repeat from * to last 5 stitches, K2, yo, K2tog, K1.

❧ ROW 6: K1, (yo, K2tog) twice, *K1, sl 1 wyif; repeat from * to last 5 stitches, K2, yo, K2tog, K1.

❧ Repeat Rows 1–6 two more times, but replace Row 1 with the following:

❧ ROW 1 (2ND AND 3RD REPEATS): K1, K2tog, yo, K2tog twice, *K1, sl 1 wyif; repeat from * to last 7 stitches, K2tog twice, yo, K2tog, K1. You now have 22 stitches.

Increasing for Second Half

❧ ROW 1: K1, (yo, K2tog) twice, *K1, sl 1 wyif; repeat from * to last 5 stitches, K2, yo, K2tog, K1.

❧ ROW 2: K1, (yo, K2tog) twice, *K1, sl 1 wyif; repeat from * to last 5 stitches, turn.

❧ ROW 3: *K1, sl 1 wyif; repeat from * to last 5 stitches, turn.

❧ ROW 4: *K1, sl 1 wyif; repeat from * to last 5 stitches, K2, yo, K2tog, K1.

❧ ROW 5: (K1, yo) twice, K2tog, Kfb, *K1, sl 1 wyif; repeat from * to last 5 stitches, Kfb, K1, yo, K2tog, K1. You now have 25 stitches.

❧ ROW 6: Repeat Row 5. You now have 28 stitches.

❧ Repeat Rows 1–6 two more times, but replace Rows 5 and 6 with the following.

❧ ROWS 5 AND 6 (2ND AND 3RD REPEATS): K1, yo, K2tog, K1, Kfb, *K1, sl 1 wyif; repeat from * to last 5 stitches, K2, yo, K2tog, K1. You now have 32 stitches.

Knitting the Second Half

❧ Work Rows 1–6 of Double Knit with Lace Edge pattern 4 times, then work Rows 1–5 once more.

SUEÑO BAMBOO SPA MASK *continued*

FILLING THE MASK

❊ K1, (yo, K2tog) twice, *slip first stitch onto right needle, slip second stitch onto spare needle; repeat from * 3 or 4 more times to create an opening large enough to pour beans through. Fill mask with beans, distributing the beans evenly in both halves. Slip the stitches back to left needle in their original order. Continue with Row 6 of Double Knit with Lace Edge pattern but slip stitches with yarn in back.

KNITTING THE BORDER

❊ SET-UP ROW: K1, yo, K2tog, K1, *K2tog; repeat from * to last 4 stitches, K1, yo, K2tog, K1. You now have 20 stitches.

❊ ROWS 1–4: K1, *yo, K2tog; repeat from * to last stitch, K1.

❊ ROW 5 AND 6: Knit.

Finishing

❊ Bind off as follows: K2, *slip 2 stitches back to left needle, K2tog, K1; repeat from * until all stitches have been worked and 2 stitches remain, K2tog, pull yarn through. Weave in ends, block lace lightly. Put mask in plastic bag and store in freezer.

Knitting the Swatch Sachet
(Optional)

❊ Using the long-tail method (see page 263), cast on 18 stitches. Follow mask instructions through fourth repeat of main body, then work pattern Rows 1–5 once more. Follow instructions for filling the mask, but use dried flowers instead of beans. Finish as for mask.

LLAMA-WOOL SLIPPER SOCKS

DESIGNED BY SONDA J. LEE, *photo on page 44*

These cozy slippers are perfect for padding around the house on winter weekends. Knit with a blend of llama and wool, they are both warm and durable. And at four stitches to the inch, they'll work up quickly.

SIZES AND FINISHED MEASUREMENTS	To fit average woman, approximately 8" (20.5 cm) circumference and 9" (23 cm) foot length
YARN	Cascade Pastaza, 50% llama/50% wool, 3.5 oz (100 g)/ 132 yds (121 m), 017 Purple
NEEDLES	Set of four US 9 (5.5 mm) double-point needles *or size you need to obtain correct gauge*
GAUGE	16 stitches = 4" (10 cm) in stockinette stitch
OTHER SUPPLIES	Tapestry needle

Knitting the Cuff

✳ Cast on 39 stitches. Divide evenly onto 3 double-point needles and join into a round, being careful not to twist the stitches. Knit 1 round, purl 1 round. Work Rounds 1–6 of Scallop pattern 2 times. Knit 1 round, decreasing 3 stitches evenly spaced. You now have 36 stitches, 12 on each needle. Knit 1 round.

Knitting the Heel Flap

✳ K9 from needle 1. Leave remaining 3 stitches on needle 1 and slip 6 stitches from needle 2 onto needle 1. Leave remaining 6 stitches on needle 2 and slip first 3 stitches from needle 3 onto needle 2. You now have 18 instep stitches on 2 needles and 18 heel stitches on needle 1. Work the 18 heel stitches back and forth as follows:

✳ ROW 1: K1, *P1, K1; repeat from * to last stitch, K1.

✳ ROW 2: P2, *K1 P1; repeat from *.

✳ Repeat Rows 1 and 2 five more times.

Turning the Heel

✳ ROW 1: K11, K2tog, K1, turn.

✳ ROW 2: Sl 1, P5, P2tog, P1, turn.

✳ ROW 3: Sl 1, K6, K2tog, K1, turn.

✳ ROW 4: Sl 1, P7, P2tog, P1, turn.

✿ ROW 5: Sl 1, K8, K2tog, K1, turn.

✿ ROW 6: Sl 1, P9, P2tog, P1, turn.

✿ ROW 7: K12.

Knitting the Gussets

✿ With needle holding heel stitches (needle 1), pick up and knit (see page 264) 7 stitches along side of heel flap. With empty needle, knit 18 held instep stitches. With needle 3, pick up and knit 7 stitches along other side of heel flap, K6 from needle 1. You now have 44 stitches: 13 stitches on needle 1, 18 stitches on needle 2, and 13 stitches on needle 3. Knit 1 round.

✿ ROUND 1: Knit to last 3 stitches on needle 1, K2tog, K1; K18 on needle 2; K1, ssk at beginning of needle 3, knit to end of round.

✿ ROUNDS 2 AND 3: Knit.

✿ Repeat Rounds 1–3 three more times. You now have 36 stitches.

Knitting the Foot

✿ Work even in stockinette stitch until foot measures 7" (18 cm) or 2" (5 cm) less than desired finished length.

Shaping the Toe

✿ ROUND 1: Knit to last 3 stitches on needle 1, K2tog, K1; K1, ssk at beginning of needle 2, knit to last 3 stitches, K2tog, k1; K1, ssk at beginning of needle 3, knit to end of round.

✿ ROUND 2: Knit.

✿ Repeat Rounds 1 and 2 four more times. You now have 16 stitches.

✿ Repeat Round 1 two more times. You now have 8 stitches.

Finishing

✿ Knit 2 stitches from needle 1 onto needle 3. Join toe stitches together with kitchener stitch (see page 262). Weave in ends.

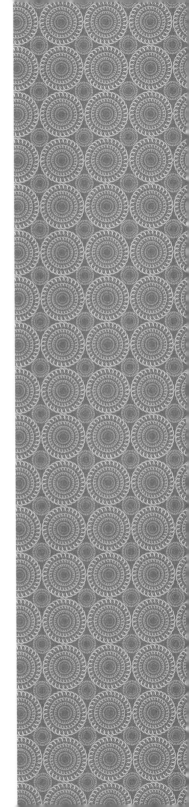

Seaman-Style Cashmere Scarf

DESIGNED BY ERIKA WITHAM, *photo on page 47*

A seaman-style scarf is narrow around the neck for a snug and smooth fit. This one was inspired by Myrna Stahman's book, Stahman's Shawls and Scarves: Lace Faroese-Shaped Shawls from the Neck Down and Seamen's Scarves. The neck is knitted first, then both ends are worked at the same time to get maximum usage from the yarn.

FINISHED MEASUREMENTS	Approximately 2.5" (6 cm) wide at neck, 4.5" (11 cm) wide at ends, and 36" (91.5 cm) long
YARN	Artyarns Cashmere 5, 100% cashmere, 1.75 oz (50 g)/102 yds (93 m), 229 Blue Lagoon
NEEDLES	Two pairs US 8 (5 mm) straight needles *or size you need to obtain correct gauge*
GAUGE	19.5 stitches = 4" (10 cm) in stockinette stitch
OTHER SUPPLIES	US H/8 (5 mm) crochet hook, scrap yarn for cast-on, stitch markers, tapestry needle

Preparing the Yarn

❊ If you want to knit with both panels at the same times (see Increasing for the Panels, page 214), you'll need access to both ends of your ball of yarn, so wind a center-pull ball.

Knitting the Neck

❊ With the crochet hook and scrap yarn, ch 20 stitches (see page 261). Place a stitch marker in the last loop of the chain to ensure it does not unravel. The chain has 1 smooth side and 1 side with a series of bumps. With working yarn, pick up 15 stitches through these "bumps," avoiding the first or last bumps of the chain (see page 265).

❊ ROW 1 (RS): Slip 1, K1, P1, K1, P1, pm, K5, pm, P1, K1, P1, K2.

❊ ROW 2: Slip 1, K1, P1, K1, P1, sm, P5, sm, P1, K1, P1, K2.

❊ Repeat Rows 1 and 2 until piece measures 12.5" (32 cm), ending with Row 2.

SEAMAN-STYLE CASHMERE SCARF *continued*

Picking Up from the Cast-on

❊ Begin by removing the stitch marker at the end of the chain. Slowly unravel the chain until you get to the first live stitch. Using the second pair of needles, pick up this stitch and continue to unravel, picking up 1 stitch at a time until you have 15 stitches. If these stitches are twisted, straighten them now or as you knit them.

Increasing for the Panels

❊ Using both ends of your yarn ball, work both panels at the same time.

❊ ROW 1: Slip 1, K1, P1, K1, P1, sm, *M1, K1 repeat from * to marker, M1, sm, P1, K1, P1, K2. You now have 21 stitches.

❊ ROW 2: Slip 1, K1, P1, K1, P1, sm, P11, sm, P1, K1, P1, K2.

❊ ROW 3: Slip 1, K1, P1, K1, P1, sm, M1, K1, M1, K9, M1, K1, M1, sm, P1, K1, P1, K2. You now have 25 stitches.

❊ ROW 4: Slip 1, K1, P1, K1, P1, sm, P15, sm, P1, K1, P1, K2.

Knitting the Panels

❊ ROW 1 (RS): Slip 1, K1, P1, K1, P1, sm, K15, sm, P1, K1, P1, K2.

❊ ROW 2 (WS): Slip 1, K1, P1, K1, P1, sm, P15, sm, P1, K1, P1, K2.

❊ Working both ends of the scarf at the same time, work until each panel measures 8.75" (22.5 cm) or to desired length, making sure you reserve enough yarn for the borders.

Knitting the Borders

❊ ROWS 1–5: Slip 1, *K1, P1; repeat from * to last 2 stitches, K2.

❊ Bind off.

Finishing

❊ Weave in ends. Block.

FELTED-MERINO TREASURE COZY!

DESIGNED BY LUCY NEATBY, *photo on page 38*

This versatile bag may be easily resized to suit a wide variety of small audio devices, cameras, glasses, or other treasures. It features an adjustable length strap and makes a great introduction to double knitting and felting.

FINISHED MEASUREMENTS	Largest size approximately 6" (15 cm) circumference and 6" (15 cm) length before felting
YARN	Needful Yarns Joy, 100% merino wool, 1.75 oz (50 g)/ 85 yds (78 m), 304 Green or 311 Raspberry
NEEDLES	Set of five US 10 (6 mm) double-point needles *or size you need to obtain correct gauge*
GAUGE	16 stitches and 20 rows = 4" (10 cm) in stockinette stitch, 14 stitches and 16 rows= 4" (10 cm) in pattern (both before felting)
OTHER SUPPLIES	Tapestry needle

Getting Started

❋ Cast on the following number of stitches, depending on desired finished width.

ITEM	FINISHED WIDTH	# OF STITCHES
i-pod Nano	1.75" (4.5 cm)	14 stitches
i-pod video Nano	2" (5 cm)	16 stitches
	2.25" (5.5 cm)	18 stitches
i-pod Touch	2.5" (6.5 cm)	20 stitches
Video i-pod Classic	3" (7.5 cm)	24 stitches

❋ Notes: Begin the cozy by knitting back and forth. Slip all stitches purlwise with yarn forward.

❋ ROW 1: *Slip 1, P1; repeat from *.

❋ ROW 2: Repeat Row 1. The stitches that were slipped on Row 1 are purled, and the stitches that were purled on Row 1 are slipped. Continuing in this manner, you are making a tube — just like knitting in the round.

❋ Work even until bag is desired pre-felted length. The bag should appear to be crazily long, about 40–50% longer than the object to be contained. For a

FELTED-MERINO TREASURE COZY! continued

3" (7.5 cm) long finished bag, knit until the piece measures 4.5" (11.5 cm); for a 4" (10 cm) long bag, knit until the piece measures 5.75" (14.5 cm).

Dividing the Bag

❋ Hold 2 empty needles together and parallel in your right hand with tips pointing left. Hold the work in your left hand with the tip pointing right. Slip the stitches alternately to the 2 empty needles. Slip the first stitch onto the needle farthest from you and slip the next stitch onto the needle in front. Repeat with each pair of stitches.

❋ Now treat these stitches as regular circular knitting, adding more needles as needed. Bind off all stitches purlwise, except the first and last stitches on each side of the bag. See diagram below.

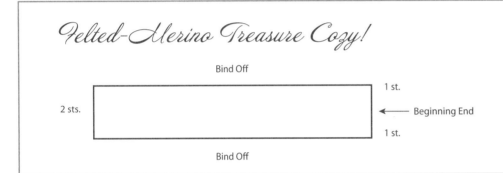

Felted-Merino Treasure Cozy!

Bind Off

1 st.

2 sts. ← Beginning End

1 st.

Bind Off

Knitting the Straps

❋ With the last stitch of the round on your right-hand needle, M1, K1. You now have 3 stitches on this needle. Following the instructions on page 266, knit a 3-stitch I-cord that is approximately 24" (61 cm) long. Cut the yarn, thread tail onto tapestry needle, and draw through the stitches. Pull up snug and fasten off. Repeat on other side of bag for other strap.

Felting and Finishing

❋ Weave in all ends. Immerse the bag in a little hot water, lubricate with a little laundry detergent, then rub, squeeze, knead, and turn the bag inside out and vice versa. Refresh the hot water as it cools and continue. Be sure to work the cords as well as the bag. Continue until bag is desired finished size. Rinse out any remaining soap, squeeze out excess moisture, and stuff the bag with plastic-wrapped cardboard to simulate the shape of your treasure. Allow to dry completely.

ELIZABETH'S WOOL-ANGORA DIAGONAL SCARF

DESIGNED BY ELIZABETH PRUSIEWICZ, *photo on page 41*

This scarf has everything going for it. The merino-and-angora blend is soft to the touch and very warm. The pattern puts the self-forming stripes on the diagonal, and the angora sheds a softening haze over the whole design. Lovely!

FINISHED MEASUREMENTS	Approximately 5.5" (14 cm) wide and 65" (165 cm) long
YARN	Tanglewood Fiber Creations, 80% merino wool/20% angora, 4 oz (113 g)/210 yds (192 m), Newport Rocks
NEEDLES	US 10 (6 mm) straight needles *or size you need to obtain correct gauge*
GAUGE	18 stitches and 28 rows= 4" (10 cm) in stockinette stitch
OTHER SUPPLIES	Tapestry needle

Knitting the Scarf

✳ Cast on 5 stitches.

✳ ROW 1(WS): Knit.

✳ ROW 2 (RS): P2, yo, K1, yo, P2.

✳ ROW 3: K3, P1, K3.

✳ ROW 4: P2, yo, K3, yo, P2.

✳ ROW 5: K3, P3, K3.

✳ ROW 6: P2, yo, K5, yo, P2.

✳ ROW 7: K3, P5, K3.

✳ ROW 8: P2, yo, K7, yo, P2.

✳ ROW 9: K3, P7, K3.

✳ ROW 10: P2, yo, K9, yo, P2.

✳ Continue in this manner, increasing 2 stitches every other row, until you have 31 stitches.

✳ NEXT ROW (WS): K3, P25, K3.

✳ NEXT ROW (RS): P1, P2tog, yo, K2tog, K24, yo, P2.

✳ Repeat these 2 rows until scarf is 63" (160 cm) or desired length from cast-on, ending with a WS row.

ELIZABETH'S WOOL-ANGORA DIAGONAL SCARF *continued*

Decreasing for the Scarf End

❈ **ROW 1 (RS):** P1, P2tog, yo, K2tog, K22, K2tog, yo, P2.

❈ **ROW 2:** K3, P2tog, P22, K3.

❈ **ROW 3:** P1, P2tog, yo, K2tog, K20, K2tog, yo, P2.

❈ **ROW 4:** K3, P2tog, P20, K3.

❈ **ROW 5:** P1, P2tog, yo, K2tog, K18, K2tog, yo, P2.

❈ **ROW 6:** K3, P2tog, P18, K3.

❈ Continue in this manner, decreasing 1 stitch per row, until you have 5 stitches.

Finishing

❈ Bind off. Weave in ends.

SILK DELIGHT SCARF

DESIGNED BY CAROL SCOTT, *photo on* **page 46**

This lovely hand-painted silk is exploited in the most positive way with the "modular" or "domino" style of knitting. The scarf is lovely to look at and feels like a dream.

FINISHED MEASUREMENTS	Approximately 3.5" (9 cm) wide and 38" (96.5 cm) long
YARN	Alchemy Silk Purse, 100% silk, 1.75 oz (50 g)/163 yds (149 m), Clear H2O
NEEDLES	US 7 (4.5 mm) straight needles *or size you need to obtain correct gauge*
GAUGE	20 stitches = 4" (10 cm) in pattern
OTHER SUPPLIES	Tapestry needle

Knitting the First Ruffle

❈ Cast on 76 stitches.

❈ **ROWS 1–5:** Knit.

❈ **ROW 6:** *K2tog; repeat from *. You now have 38 stitches.

❈ **ROW 7:** Repeat Row 6. You now have 19 stitches.

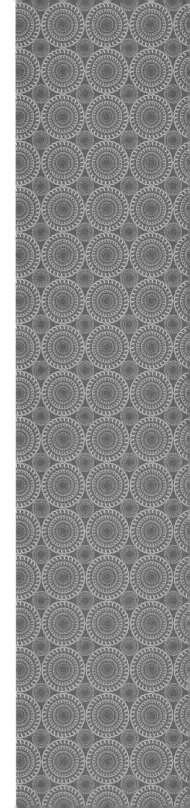

Knitting the Rectangles

❋ ROW 1 (RS): Cast on 18 stitches at beginning of row, K19. You now have 37 stitches.

❋ ROW 2: K18, P1, K18.

❋ ROW 3: K17, sl 2, K1, psso, K17.

❋ ROW 4: K1, purl to last stitch, K1.

❋ ROW 5: K16, sl 2, K1, psso, K16.

❋ ROW 6: Repeat Row 4.

❋ Continue in this manner, working 1 fewer stitch before the decrease on RS rows, until you have 1 stitch.

❋ With RS facing and 1 stitch still on needle, pick up and knit (see page 264) 18 stitches along top of the rectangle. Cast on 18 stitches. You now have 37 stitches.

❋ Beginning with Row 2, proceed as for the first rectangle. Continue until you have a strip of 7 rectangles.

Knitting the Second Ruffle

❋ With RS facing and 1 stitch still on needle, pick up and knit (see page 264) 18 stitches along top of the last rectangle. You now have 19 stitches.

❋ ROW 1: *Kfb; repeat from *. You now have 38 stitches.

❋ ROW 2: Repeat Row 1. You now have 76 stitches.

❋ ROWS 3–7: Knit.

❋ Bind off.

Finishing

❋ Weave in ends. Steam block.

Lacy Leaf Alpaca-Angora Hat

DESIGNED BY BONNIE EVANS, *photo on page 42*

As lovely to knit as it is to wear, this lacy hat was knitted with an alpaca-and-angora blend. Heavenly.

SIZES AND FINISHED MEASUREMENTS	To fit average woman's head, approximately 19" (48.5 cm) circumference, unstretched
YARN	Cascade Yarns Indulgence, 70% superfine alpaca/30% angora, 1.75 oz (50 g)/123 yds (112m), 519 Green
NEEDLES	US 4 (3.5 mm) circular needle 16" (40 cm) long and set of five US 4 (3.5 mm) double-point needles *or size you need to obtain correct gauge*
GAUGE	18 stitches = 4" (10 cm) in pattern
OTHER SUPPLIES	Stitch markers

Knitting the Hat

❃ With circular needle, cast on 85 stitches loosely. Place marker and join into a round, being careful not to twist the stitches.

❃ ROUND 1: Purl.

❃ ROUND 2: Knit.

❃ ROUND 3: Purl, placing a marker every 17 stitches.

❃ Work Rounds 1–10 of Lacy Leaf chart (page 221) between the markers 4 times total.

Decreasing for the Crown

❃ Work Rounds 1–19 of Crown Decrease chart (page 221) between the markers, changing to double-point needles when there are too few stitches for the circular needle. When Round 19 is complete, you will have 5 stitches.

Finishing

❃ Cut yarn, leaving an 8" (20.5 cm) tail. Thread tail onto tapestry needle and draw through remaining stitches twice. Pull up snug and fasten off. Block lightly with a steam iron.

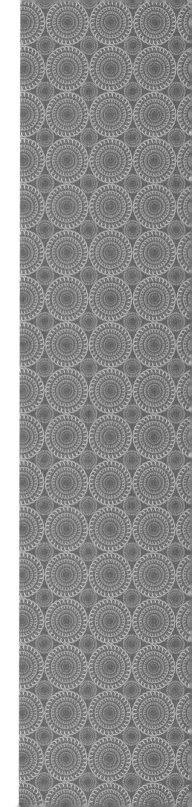

Lacy Leaf Alpaca-Angora Hat

- ☐ knit
- ⊡ purl
- ⊙ yarn over
- ⊠ ssk
- ⊠ K2tog
- ⊠ slip 1, K2tog, psso
- ▨ no stitch

CROWN DECREASES

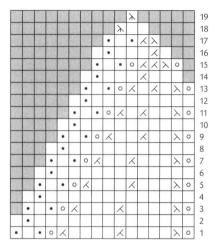

LACE

Baby's Wool-Tencel Booties

DESIGNED BY LINDA BURT, *photo on page 39*

These booties are knit with a blend of merino and Tencel. Tencel is a trade name for lyocell, which is a fiber made from wood pulp. The processing produces little by-product, putting the fiber in the ecofriendly category.

SIZES AND FINISHED MEASUREMENTS	To fit infant 0–6 months, approximately 3" (7.5 cm) foot length
YARN	Valley Yarns Colrain, 50% merino wool/50% Tencel, 1.75 oz (50 g)/109 yds (100 m), Natural
NEEDLES	US 7 (4.5 mm) straight needles *or size you need to obtain correct gauge*
GAUGE	18 stitches = 4" (10 cm) in stockinette stitch
OTHER SUPPLIES	1 yd (1 m) ⅜" (1 cm) ribbon

Knitting the Cuff

❉ Cast on 37 stitches.

❉ ROW 1: K1, yo, *K5, pass second, third, fourth, and fifth stitches over first stitch, yo; repeat from * to last stitch, K1. You now have 17 stitches.

❉ ROW 2: P1, *(P1, yo, K1 tbl) in next stitch, P1; repeat from *. You now have 33 stitches.

❉ ROW 3: *K4, K2tog; repeat from * to last 3 stitches, K3. You now have 28 stitches.

❉ ROW 4: Purl.

❉ ROW 5: Knit.

❉ ROW 6: Purl.

❉ ROW 7: K1, *yo, K2tog; repeat from * to last stitch, K1.

❉ ROWS 8–10: Repeat Rows 4–6.

Setting Up for the Foot

❉ K19, turn, P10. Working on these 10 center stitches only, work stockinette stitch for 9 rows. Cut yarn and slip all stitches to left-hand needle.

❉ With RS facing, K9, pick up and knit (see page 264) 6 along first side, K10 center stitches, pick up and knit 6 along second side, K9. You now have 40 stitches. Work in stockinette stitch for 3 rows.

Knitting the Foot

❅ ROW 1 (RS): K1, K2tog, K12, K2tog, K6, ssk, K12, ssk, K1. You now have 36 stitches.
❅ ROW 2: P14, P2tog tbl, P4, P2tog, P14. You now have 34 stitches.
❅ ROW 3: K1, K2tog, K11, K2tog, K2, ssk, K11, ssk, K1. You now have 30 stitches.
❅ ROW 4: P13, P2tog tbl, P2tog, P13. You now have 28 stitches.
❅ ROW 5: Knit.

Finishing

❅ Cut yarn, leaving an 18" (45.5 cm) tail. Divide stitches evenly onto 2 needles. Using the yarn tail, join sole together with kitchener stitch (see page 262). Sew back seam. Weave in ends. Cut ribbon in half, thread through eyelets, and tie into a bow.

SEED STITCH WOOL-SOY HAT

DESIGNED BY MARCI BLANK, *photo on page 43*

This simple seed stitch cap is a great design for sampling all kinds of yarn. The one shown here is knitted in a wool-and-soy blend, and the color makes it an all-round down-to-earth project.

SIZES AND FINISHED MEASUREMENTS	To fit most adults, approximately 22" (56 cm) circumference, unstretched
YARN	Patons SWS Soy Wool Stripes, 70% wool, 30% soy, 2.8 oz (80 g)/110 yds (100 m), 70013 Natural Earth
NEEDLES	US 7 (4.5 mm) circular needle 16" (40 cm) long and set of four US 7 (4.5 mm) double-point needles *or size you need to obtain correct gauge*
GAUGE	16 stitches and 20 rows= 4" (10 cm) in stockinette stitch
OTHER SUPPLIES	Stitch marker, tapestry needle

Knitting the Brim

❅ Cast on 80 stitches. Place marker and join into a round, being careful not to twist the stitches. Knit 3 rounds. Work 25 rounds in seed stitch. Purl 2 rounds, decreasing 1 stitch on last round. You now have 79 stitches.

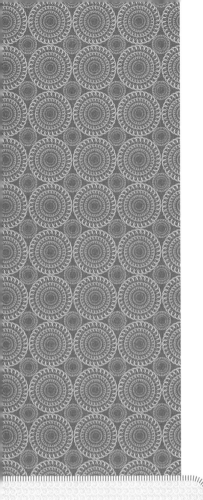

STITCH PATTERN
seed stitch
(WORKED CIRCULARLY ON AN EVEN NUMBER OF STITCHES)

ROUND 1: *K1, P1; repeat from *.
ROUND 2: *P1, K1; repeat from *.
REPEAT ROUNDS 1 AND 2 FOR PATTERN.

SEED STITCH WOOL-SOY HAT *continued*

Decreasing for the Crown

❊ ROUND 1: *K8, K2tog; repeat from * to last 9 stitches, K9.

❊ ROUNDS 2 AND 3: Knit.

❊ ROUND 4: *K7, K2tog; repeat from *.

❊ ROUNDS 5 AND 6: Knit.

❊ ROUND 7: *K6, K2tog; repeat from *.

❊ ROUNDS 8 AND 9: Knit.

❊ Continue in this manner, knitting 1 fewer stitch before the decrease on each decrease round and knitting only 1 round between decrease rounds until you have 16 stitches.

❊ NEXT ROUND: *K2tog; repeat from *. You now have 8 stitches.

❊ Cut yarn, leaving an 8" (20.5 cm) tail. Thread tail onto tapestry needle and draw through remaining stitches twice. Pull up snug and fasten off. Weave in ends.

RECLAIMED CASHMERE LACY SCARF

DESIGNED BY BEVERLY VASQUEZ, *photo on page 38*

This scarf is loaded with TLC. It began its life as yards of cashmere from cast-off sweaters. That cashmere was "reclaimed" and hand spun with other such yardage to produce a wonderful skein of 100% cashmere yarn. That skein was knitted into this lovely lace scarf. Really special.

FINISHED MEASUREMENTS	Approximately 6" (15 cm) wide and 50" (127 cm) long
YARN	Ellie's Reclaimed Cashmere, 100% cashmere, 2.2 oz (62.5 g)/ 230 yds (210 m), Blue
NEEDLES	US 8 (5 mm) straight needles *or size you need to obtain correct gauge*
GAUGE	20 stitches = 4" (10 cm) in stockinette stitch
OTHER SUPPLIES	Tapestry needle

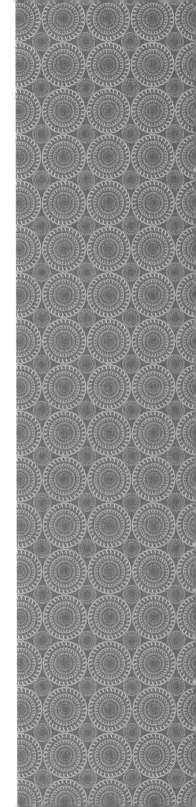

Knitting the Scarf

* Cast on 35 stitches with the knitted-on cast-on (see page 262).
* Knit 4 rows.
* ROW 1: (K1, P1) twice, *K3, P1; repeat from * to last 3 stitches, K1, P1, K1.
* ROW 2: (P1, K1) twice, *P3, K1; repeat from * to last 3 stitches, P1, K1, P1.
* ROW 3: (K1, P1) twice, *yo, sl 1, K2tog, psso, yo, P1; repeat from * to last 3 stitches, K1, P1, K1.
* ROW 4: Repeat Row 2.
* ROW 5: Repeat Row 1.
* ROW 6: Repeat Row 2.
* Repeat Rows 1–6 until piece measures approximately 40" (101.5 cm), ending with Row 5 of pattern.
* Knit 4 rows.
* Bind off loosely.

Finishing

* Weave in ends. Block to finished size.

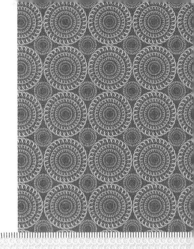

ARACHNE'S ALPACA LACE RING

DESIGNED BY CHERYL OBERLE, *photo on page 37*

Wonderfully soft alpaca shrouds your head and neck with warmth and elegance when wearing this lace wimple. This particular lace is a little tricky to knit in the round, so instructions are given for knitting flat and seaming up the back.

FINISHED MEASUREMENTS	Approximately 26" (66 cm) circumference and 18" (45.5 cm) long
YARN	Henry's Attic Prime Alpaca, 100% alpaca, 8 oz (227 g)/ 650 yds (594 m), Natural Black
NEEDLES	US 7 (4.5 mm) straight needles *or size you need to obtain correct gauge*
GAUGE	17 stitches and 27 rows = 4" (10 cm) in lace pattern, blocked
OTHER SUPPLIES	Tapestry needle
ABBREVIATIONS	**p2sso** pass 2 slipped stitches over **sl 2tog** slip 2 stitches together knitwise

Getting Started

Cast on 109 stitches. Work in garter stitch for 7 rows, ending with a RS row. Work Rows 1–12 of Lace pattern 9 times. Work in garter stitch for 7 rows. Bind off loosely (use a larger needle if necessary for the bind off).

Finishing

Wet block, stretching lace out to finished measurements. When dry, sew ends together. Weave in ends. Steam the seam lightly.

STITCH PATTERN

lace

ROW 1 AND ALL ODD-NUMBERED (WS) ROWS: Purl.

ROWS 2, 4, AND 6: K1, *yo, ssk, K1, K2tog, yo, K1; repeat from *.

ROW 8: K1, *K1, yo, sl 2tog, K1, p2sso, yo, K2; repeat from *.

ROW 10: K1, *K2tog, yo, K1, yo, ssk, K1; repeat from *.

ROW 12: K2tog, *yo, K3, yo, sl 2tog, K1, p2sso; repeat from * to last 5 stitches, yo, K3, yo, ssk.

REPEAT ROWS 1–12 FOR PATTERN.

Arachne's Alpaca Lace Ring

- ☐ knit
- ⊙ yarn over
- ⟍ ssk
- ⟋ K2tog
- ⋏ slip 2tog kwise, K2, p2sso

⟍	o				o	⋏	o				o	⋏	o			o	⟍	12
	⟍	o		o	⟋		⟍	o		o	⟋		⟍	o		o	⟋	10
		o	⋏	o				o	⋏	o				o	⋏	o		8
o	⟍		⟋	o		o	⟍		⟋	o		o	⟍		⟋	o		6
o	⟍		⟋	o		o	⟍		⟋	o		o	⟍		⟋	o		4
o	⟍		⟋	o		o	⟍		⟋	o		o	⟍		⟋	o		2

Note: Only RS (even-numbered) rows are charted. Purl all WS rows.

Mojito Alpaca Necktie

DESIGNED BY MARTHA TOWNSEND, *photo on page 44*

An alpaca tie is great for winter wear, and this one in cool blues will look good at the office or the theater. It is knitted in seed stitch, which stabilizes the perfectly tapered shaping.

FINISHED MEASUREMENTS	Approximately 4" (10 cm) at widest point and 56" (142 cm) long
YARN	Alpaca with a Twist Mojito, 100% baby alpaca, 3.5 oz (100 g)/ 145 yds (133 m), Winter Blues
NEEDLES	US 7 (4.5 mm) straight needles *or size you need to obtain correct gauge*
GAUGE	19 stitches and 27 rows = 4" (10 cm) in seed stitch
OTHER SUPPLIES	Safety pin, tapestry needle
ABBREVIATIONS	**seed 2tog** work 2 stitches together as to knit or purl to maintain seed stitch pattern

Knitting the Tie

❊ Cast on 3 stitches.

❊ ROW 1: K1, P1, K1.

❊ ROW 2: Kfb, P1, Kfb. You now have 5 stitches.

❊ ROW 3: P1, Kfb, P1, Kfb, P1. You now have 7 stitches.

❊ ROW 4: P1, Kfb, K1, P1, K1, Kfb, P1. You now have 9 stitches.

❊ ROW 5: P1, Kfb, *P1, K1; repeat from * to last 3 stitches; P1, Kfb, P1. You now have 11 stitches.

❊ ROW 6: P1, Kfb, K1, *P1, K1; repeat from * to last 2 stitches, Kfb, P1. You now have 13 stitches.

❊ ROW 7: Repeat Row 5. You now have 15 stitches.

❊ ROW 8: Repeat Row 6. You now have 17 stitches.

❊ ROW 9: Repeat Row 5. You now have 19 stitches.

❊ Continue even in pattern as established until piece measures approximately 6" (15 cm) from cast-on.

STITCH PATTERNS

seed stitch

(OVER AN ODD NUMBER OF STITCHES)

ROW 1: *K1, P1; repeat from * to last stitch, K1.

REPEAT ROW 1 FOR PATTERN.

seed stitch

(OVER AN EVEN NUMBER OF STITCHES)

ROW 1: *K1, P1; repeat from *.
ROW 2: *P1, K1; repeat from *.

REPEAT ROWS 1 AND 2 FOR PATTERN.

NOTE: When increasing or decreasing in seed stitch, be sure to knit the stitches that look like purls and purl the stitches that look like knits.

Decreasing

❋ Note: Be sure to work loosely on decrease rows to create a smoothly tapered edge.

❋ DECREASE ROW 1: P1, K2tog, work in pattern as established to last 3 stitches, K2tog, P1. You now have 17 stitches.

❋ Continue even in pattern as established for 1.5" (4 cm), then work decrease row again.

❋ Continue in this manner, decreasing every 1.5" (4 cm) until you have 13 stitches and tie measures approximately 10.75" (27 cm).

❋ From this point on, decreases will be worked at the beginning of a row only, alternating from 1 side to the other every 1.5" (4 cm) as follows:

❋ P1, K2tog, work in pattern as established to end of row. Place a safety pin at the beginning of the row where you worked the decrease. Work even in pattern as established for 1.5" (4 cm) and decrease at the beginning of the row on the opposite side from the safety pin. Move the safety pin to mark the decrease.

❋ Continue in this manner until 7 stitches remain. Work even on these 7 stitches until tie measures 55" (139.5 cm) from cast-on.

❋ NEXT ROW: Seed 2tog, work in pattern as established to last 2 stitches, seed 2tog.

❋ Work 1 row even in pattern.

❋ Repeat these 2 rows once more.

❋ NEXT ROW: K3tog. Cut yarn and pull through loop to secure.

Finishing

❋ Weave in ends and block.

SILK BERRY JEWELRY BAG

DESIGNED BY GWEN STEEGE, *photo on page 39*

Whether you travel often or just like to keep your favorite earrings out of harm's way in the bureau drawer, this silk-lined jewelry bag with a traditional berry motif is a pleasure to use. The triangular flap ends in a chain stitch loop so you can fasten it down over the topmost "berry."

FINISHED MEASUREMENTS	Approximately 5" (12.5 cm) wide, exclusive of crocheted edging, and 6" (15 cm) tall
YARN	Artyarn Regal Silk, 100% hand-painted silk, 1.75 oz (50 g)/ 163 yds (149 m), 110 Pink
NEEDLES	US 4 (3.5 mm) straight needles *or size you need to obtain correct gauge*
GAUGE	32 stitches = 4" (10 cm) in stockinette stitch
OTHER SUPPLIES	US D/3 (3.25 mm) crochet hook, tapestry needle ⅛ yard (11 cm) lining fabric, sewing needle and coordinating sewing thread, straight pins

Knitting the Flap

❄ Note: You begin knitting at the tip of the triangular flap, increasing to its top, then working even down the back and up the front, all in one piece.

❄ Make a slip knot and place it on 1 needle to begin.

❄ ROW 1: Kfb. You now have 2 stitches.

❄ ROWS 2–5: Kfb, knit to end of row. At the end of Row 5 you have 6 stitches.

❄ ROW 6: K3, yo, knit to the end of the row. You now have 7 stitches.

❄ Repeat Row 6, knitting each yo from each previous row, until you have 34 stitches.

❄ NEXT 4 ROWS: Knit.

Knitting the Body

❄ ROW 1: (P1, K1) 4 times, K1, P7, K2, P7, K1, (P1, K1) 4 times.

❄ ROW 2: (K1, P1) 4 times, P1, K7, P2, K7, P1, (K1, P1) 4 times.

❄ Repeat Rows 1 and 2 until piece measures 9.25" (23.5 cm) from tip of flap.

❄ Work the berry design by following the chart (page 231), beginning at the bottom right of the chart and maintaining the seed stitch border on both sides of the bag.

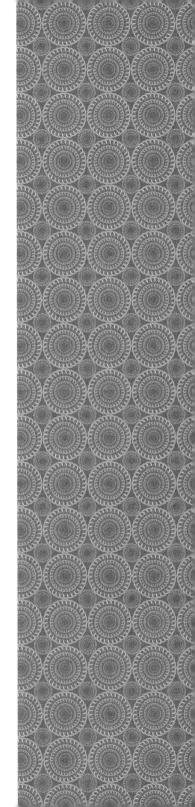

* When you have completed the chart, continue working as established until the piece measures 15" (38 cm) from the tip of the flap.
* Bind off loosely in pattern.

Finishing

* Fold the front up, WS together, so that the top edge is even with the end of the flap. (When you fold the flap down over the front, the tip should just touch the top berry.)
* Pin the edges in place and, working with the front facing you, use single crochet (see page 266) to attach the front and back at the side edges.

Silk Berry Jewelry Bag

☐   knit on RS rows, purl on WS rows

▪   purl on RS rows, knit on WS rows

◹   slip 1 stitch to cable needle and hold in back, K1, P1 from cable needle

◺   slip 1 stitch to cable needle and hold in front, P1, K1 from cable needle

5   knit into front, back, front, back, and front of stitch (turn and P5, turn and K5) twice. Pull second, third, fourth, and fifth stitches over first

◿   K2tog

▨   no stitch

SILK BERRY JEWELRY BAG *continued*

❋ Work a 6- to 8-stitch ch at the tip of the flap, then slip stitch the end to the first ch to form a loop. Weave in ends.

❋ Pin the purse flat, taking care to square up the corners and leaving the flap open. Spray lightly with water and allow to dry.

Making the Lining

❋ To get the measurements for the lining, measure the bag, add 1" (2.5 cm) to both the length and width for hem and seam allowances, then double the length measurement. The measurements will be about 6" (15 cm) wide × 13" (33 cm) long.

❋ Fold the lining piece in half widthwise, and stitch both long edges, leaving 0.5" (1.25 cm) for seam allowances. Leave the lining inside out, with RS together, and turn back the upper edge over the wrong side about 1" (2.5 cm).

❋ Tuck the lining into the jewelry bag and pin it in place along the top edge. Use a blind stitch to fasten the top edge to the bag.

PAMPER-YOURSELF SILK-LINEN SPA SET
DESIGNED BY GWEN STEEGE, *photo on page 44*

A silk-and-linen combo knitted up in a textured geometric pattern provides just the right luxurious feel for this trim bath set. Tuck a bar of a favorite delicately scented soap into the bag!

FINISHED MEASUREMENTS	Facecloth: approximately 8.5" (21.5 cm) square; soap bag: approximately 4" (10 cm) wide and 7" (18 cm) tall
YARN	Tahki Yarns Sierra, 62% silk/30% linen/8% nylon, 1.75 oz (50 g)/135 yds (125 m), Blue Blush
NEEDLES	US 6 (4 mm) straight needles *or size you need to obtain correct gauge*
GAUGE	18 stitches = 4" (10 cm) in stockinette stitch
OTHER SUPPLIES	Tapestry needle

Knitting the Facecloth

❋ Cast on 46 stitches.

STITCH PATTERN
geometrics

ROW 1 (RS): K2, *P8, K2; repeat from *.

ROW 2: P2, *K8, P2; repeat from *.

ROWS 3, 5, AND 7: K2, *P2, K4, P2, K2; repeat from *.

ROWS 4, 6, AND 8: P2, *K2, P4, K2, P2; repeat from *.

ROW 9: Repeat Row 1.

ROW 10: Repeat Row 2.

✴ Note: The first 2 rows set up a seed stitch pattern, which borders the facecloth all the way around, including the first and last 2 stitches of the pattern rows.

✴ BORDER ROW: *K1, P1; repeat from *.

✴ NEXT BORDER ROW: P1, *K1, P1; repeat from * to last stitch, K1.

✴ ROW 1: K1, P1, work Row 1of pattern to last 2 stitches, K1, P1.

✴ ROW 2: P1, K1, work Row 2 of pattern to last 2 stitches, P1, K1.

✴ NEXT ROWS: Continue working pattern as established, keeping 2 stitches in seed stitch at the beginning and ends of rows and alternating with 2 seed stitch rows above and below the pattern rows until you have repeated the pattern and seed stitch rows 5 times. Bind off. Weave in ends.

Knitting the Soap Bag

✴ Note: Work bag in 1 piece, then fold in half widthwise to stitch the edges.

✴ Cast on 20 stitches.

✴ BORDER ROW: *K1, P1; repeat from * to end of row.

✴ NEXT BORDER ROW: P1, *K1, P1; repeat from * to last stitch, K1.

✴ ROW 1: (K1, P1) twice, K2, P8, K2, (K1, P1) twice.

✴ ROW 2: (P1, K1) twice, P2, K8, P2, (P1, K1) twice.

✴ ROWS 3, 5, AND 7: (K1, P1) twice, K2, P2, K4, P2, K2, (K1, P1) twice.

✴ ROWS 4, 6, AND 8: (P1, K1) twice, P2, K2, P4, K2, P2, (P1, K1) twice.

✴ ROW 9: Repeat Row 1.

✴ ROW 10: Repeat Row 2.

✴ ROW 11: *K1, P1; repeat from * to end of row.

✴ ROW 12: P1, *K1, P1; repeat from * to last stitch, K1.

✴ Repeat Rows 1–12 until you have completed 4 motifs.

✴ NEXT ROWS: Repeat Rows 11 and 12 three more times.

✴ NEXT ROWS: Repeat Rows 1–12 four times.

✴ Bind off on the RS in knit stitch.

Finishing

✴ Fold piece in half with WS together and top edges even. Use mattress stitch (see page 264) to sew the edges together.

✴ Work a 2-stitch I-cord (see page 262) that measures 28" (51 cm). Bind off.

✴ Thread the I-cord through a tapestry needle and draw it through the knitted fabric about 1" (2.5 cm) from the top edge to form a drawstring tie. Use the stitch pattern as your guide.

RECLAIMED CASHMERE MITTENS

DESIGNED BY CHERYL OBERLE, *photo on page 37*

A simple mitten becomes the height of luxury and sustainability when knitted in 100% reclaimed cashmere. The yarn is "reclaimed" from gently used cashmere sweaters. The sweaters are washed (with natural soap, of course) and then carefully unraveled. The yarn is then wound into skeins and washed again. And it is delicious to work with!

SIZES AND FINISHED MEASUREMENTS	To fit adult small (medium, large), approximately 7" (7.5", 8") (18, 19, 20.5 cm) circumference
YARN	Ellie's Reclaimed Cashmere, 100% cashmere, 2.5 oz (71 g)/ 238 yds (218 m), Brown Tweed
NEEDLES	Set of four US 7 (4.5 mm) and set of four US 4 (3.5mm) double-point needles *or size you need to obtain correct gauge*
GAUGE	20 stitches = 4" (10 cm) in stockinette stitch on larger needle
OTHER SUPPLIES	Stitch markers, scrap yarn for holders, tapestry needle
ABBREVIATIONS	**inc 1** increase 1 stitch with M1 (see page 263) or backward loop (see page 261)

Knitting the Cuffs

❈ With smaller double-point needles, cast on 36 (40, 44) stitches. Join into a round, being careful not to twist the stitches. Work K2, P2 rib until piece measures 3" (7.5 cm).

Knitting the Thumb Gusset

❈ Change to larger needles.

❈ ROUND 1: K2, pm, P1, inc 1, P1, pm, knit to end of round.

❈ You now have purl stitches on each side of the thumb gusset. Purl these 2 stitches on all thumb gusset rounds.

❈ ROUNDS 2–4: K2, sm, P1, K1, P1, sm, knit to end of round.

❈ ROUND 5 (INCREASE ROUND): K2, sm, P1, inc 1, knit to 1 stitch before second marker, inc 1, P1, sm, knit to end of round.

❈ Repeat Rounds 2–5 until you have 11 (11, 13) stitches between the markers, ending with Round 4.

❈ NEXT ROUND: K2, place the next 11 (11, 13) gusset stitches (including the purl stitches) on a holder. Using backward loop method (see page 261), cast on

4 stitches onto right needle. Join again by knitting next stitch on left needle, knit to end of round. You now have 38 (42, 46) stitches.

Knitting the Hand

❋ Continue even in stockinette stitch until hand measures 3.5" (3.5", 4") (9 [9, 10] cm) from the top of the thumb gusset, or until it reaches the top of the little finger when tried on.

Shaping the Top

❋ DECREASE ROUND 1: *K2, k2tog; repeat from * to last 2 stitches, K2. You now have 29 (32, 35) stitches.

❋ Knit 4 rounds.

❋ DECREASE ROUND 2: *K1, K2tog; repeat from * to last 2 stitches, K2. You now have 20 (22, 24) stitches.

❋ Knit 3 (3, 4) rounds.

❋ DECREASE ROUND 3: *K2tog; repeat from *. You now have 10 (11, 12) stitches.

❋ Cut yarn, leaving an 8" (20.5 cm) tail. Thread tail onto tapestry needle and draw through remaining stitches twice. Pull up snug and fasten off.

Knitting the Thumb

❋ K11 (11, 13) thumb stitches from holder, pick up and knit (see page 264) 6 (6, 7) stitches (1 stitch before cast-on stitches, 4 [4, 5] cast-on stitches, 1 stitch after cast-on stitches). You now have 17 (17, 20) stitches.

❋ Divide stitches onto 3 needles, join into a round and knit even for 2.25" (2.25", 2.5") (5.5 [5.5, 6.5] cm) or until thumb reaches top of thumb nail when tried on.

Shaping the Thumb

❋ DECREASE ROUND 1: *K1, K2tog; repeat from * to last 2 stitches, K2.

❋ Knit 2 rounds.

❋ DECREASE ROUND 2: *K2tog; repeat from *.

❋ Cut yarn, leaving an 8" (20.5 cm) tail. Thread tail onto tapestry needle and draw through remaining stitches twice. Pull up snug and fasten off.

Finishing

❋ Weave in ends. Make the mate and enjoy!

BUTTON-DOWN ALPACA-WOOL HAT

DESIGNED BY CHERYL OBERLE, photo on page 45

This classically styled hat looks good on just about anyone. Directions are given for three sizes, so it's sure to fit anyone, too! This one is knitted in an alpaca-and-wool blend and embellished, if desired, with your favorite buttons.

FINISHED MEASUREMENTS	Approximately 16" (18", 20") (40.5 [45.5, 51 cm]) circumference and 7.5" (8", 8.5") (19 [20.5, 21.5 cm]) depth
YARN	Berroco Ultra Alpaca, 50% super fine alpaca/50% Peruvian highland wool, 3.5 oz (100 g)/215 yds (197 m), 6259 Beetroot
NEEDLES	US 6 (4 mm) circular needle 16" (40 cm) long and US 6 (4 mm) straight needles for bind-off *or size you need to obtain correct gauge*
GAUGE	20 stitches and 28 rows = 4" (10 cm) in stockinette stitch
OTHER SUPPLIES	Stitch marker, two decorative buttons (optional), tapestry needle

Knitting the Hat

✤ Cast on 80 (90, 100) stitches. Place a marker and join into a round, being careful not to twist the stitches. Work even in stockinette stitch for 10.5" (11", 11.5") (26.5 [28, 29] cm). The bottom 2.5" (6.5 cm) will roll toward the RS to form the border.

✤ Divide stitches evenly onto 2 straight needles with the join centered on 1 needle. With WS together, use the circular needle to join the 2 halves with the 3-needle bind-off (see page 266). Steam hat lightly, avoiding rolled edge.

Finishing

✤ Fold corners of top down to the side with points 3" (3", 3.5") (75. [7.5, 9 cm]) from the bottom of the rolled edge. Tack corners down and sew on buttons, if desired.

Yak Neck Cuff

DESIGNED BY CHERYL OBERLE, *photo on page 40*

This simple cuff can be worn either around the neck as a cowl or pulled up onto your head to protect you from the wind. The yak-and-merino blend is bulky, but light, soft, and warm.

FINISHED MEASUREMENTS	Approximately 18" (45.5 cm) circumference and 8" (20.5 cm) long
YARN	Karabella Yarns Superyak, 50% yak/50% merino wool, 1.75 oz (50 g)/125 yds (114 m), 10398 Rust
NEEDLES	US 8 (5 mm) straight needles *or size you need to obtain correct gauge*
GAUGE	17 stitches and 26 rows = 4" (10 cm) in stockinette stitch
OTHER SUPPLIES	Tapestry needle.

Knitting the Cuff

❉ Cast on 75 stitches.

❉ ROW 1: *K2, P2; repeat from * to last 3 stitches, K2, P1.

❉ Repeat Row 1 until piece measures 8" (20.5 cm). Bind off in pattern.

Finishing

❉ Sew center back seam to form a ring. Weave in ends.

Bulky
Weight

MERMAID ORGANIC BLEND NECK WARMER

DESIGNED BY ANNE KUO LUKITO, *photo on page 48*

Somewhat resembling a mermaid's tail, this neck warmer is luxurious and soft. The cables form an elegant scalloped edge, and the ends feature a drop-stitch detail.

FINISHED MEASUREMENTS	Approximately 3.25" (8 cm) wide and 25" (63.5 cm) long
YARN	The Fibre Company Savannah Bulky, 50% merino wool/ 20% organic cotton/15% linen/15% soy fiber, 1.75 oz (50 g)/65 yds (51 m), Lime
NEEDLES	US 10 (6 mm) straight needles *or size you need to obtain correct gauge*
GAUGE	14 stitches = 4" (10 cm) in stockinette stitch
OTHER SUPPLIES	Scrap yarn for cast-on and holders, cable needle, tapestry needle, one 1" (2.5 cm) button, sewing needle, and coordinating sewing thread
ABBREVIATIONS	C6B slip 3 stitches onto cable needle and hold in back, K3, K3 from cable needle C6F slip 3 stitches onto cable needle and hole in front, K3, K3 from cable needle

STITCH PATTERN
cable stitch
ROWS 1, 3, 5, AND 7 (WS): Purl.
ROWS 2, 6, AND 8: Knit.
ROW 4: C6B, K2, C6F.
REPEAT ROWS 1–8 FOR PATTERN.

Knitting the First Half

❋ Using a provisional method (see page 265), cast on 14 stitches.

❋ Work Rows 1–8 of Cable Stitch pattern 5 times.

❋ NEXT ROW (WS): Purl.

❋ NEXT ROW: (K3, yo) twice, K2, (yo, K3) twice. You now have 18 stitches.

❋ NEXT ROW: Purl.

❋ Work 10 rows of stockinette stitch, ending with a purl row.

❋ NEXT ROW: (K3, drop 1 stitch and unravel, cast on 2 stitches with backward loop method [see page 261]) twice, K2, (cast on 2 stitches, drop 1 stitch and unravel, K3) twice. You now have 20 stitches.

❋ Bind off loosely.

Knitting the Second Half

❖ With WS facing, pick up stitches from provisional cast-on from left to right. Work Rows 1–8 of Cable Stitch pattern 4 times, then work Rows 1–4 once more.

❖ ROW 5: P7, place next 7 stitches on holder.

❖ ROWS 6–9: Work even in stockinette stitch. Place stitches on second holder.

❖ With WS facing, transfer stitches from first holder onto needle from left to right. Begin with a purl row and work 5 rows of stockinette stitch.

❖ NEXT ROW: (K3, yo) twice, K1, join to stitches from second holder and K1, (yo, K3) twice. You now have 18 stitches.

❖ Finish as for first half.

Finishing

❖ Weave in ends. Sew button centered between last cable and beginning of dropped stitches. Block.

CROPPED ECOFRIENDLY VEST

DESIGNED BY ANNE RYAN, *photo on page 48*

This yarn offers an ecofriendly alternative to chemically processed wool. A standard worsted-weight wool in lovely natural colors, Ecological Wool comes in huge hanks for your knitting pleasure. This vest has an asymmetrical front opening and is meant to be worn very close-fitting.

FINISHED MEASUREMENTS	Approximately 30" (32", 34") (76 [81.5, 86.5 cm]) chest circumference
YARN	Cascade Ecological Wool, 100% natural Peruvian wool, 8.8 oz (250 g)/478 yds (437 m), 9012 Brown
NEEDLES	US 10.5 (6.5 mm) circular needle 24" (60 cm) long and US 10.5 (6.5 mm) circular needle 16" (40 cm) long or US 10.5 (6.5 mm) double-point needles for armholes *or size you need to obtain correct gauge*
GAUGE	12 stitches and 21 rows = 4" (10 cm) in stockinette stitch
OTHER SUPPLIES	Scrap yarn for holders, tapestry needle, five 7/8" (2.2 cm) buttons

CROPPED ECOFRIENDLY VEST *continued*

Knitting the Lower Body

❀ Cast on 115 (121, 129) stitches. Note: Slip all stitches purlwise with yarn in back. Work back and forth in rows as follows:

❀ ROW 1: Sl 1, *K1, P1; repeat from *.

❀ ROW 2: Sl 1, *P1, K1; repeat from *.

❀ Repeat Rows 1 and 2 once more, then work Row 1 only.

Knitting the Body

❀ ROW 1 (RS): Sl 1, (P1, K1) 3 times, knit to last 7 stitches, (K1, P1) 3 times, K1.

❀ ROW 2 (WS): Sl 1, (K1, P1) 3 times, knit to last 7 stitches, (P1, K1) 3 times, P1.

❀ Repeat Rows 1 and 2 until piece measures 6" (15 cm), ending with Row 2.

Divide for Underarms and Fronts

❀ NEXT ROW: Sl 1, (P1, K1) 3 times, K35 (37, 39) and place stitches on holder, bind off 3 (4, 5) for right underarm, K43 (44, 47) for back and place on holder, bind off 3 (4, 5) for left underarm, K17 (18, 19) for left front, (K1, P1) 3 times, K1.

Knitting the Left Front

❀ With 24 (25, 26) stitches on needle, work the left front as follows:

❀ ROW 1 (WS): Sl 1, (K1, P1) 3 times, purl to end of row.

❀ ROW 2: Sl 1, knit to last 7 stitches, (K1, P1) 3 times, K1.

❀ ROW 3: Repeat Row 1.

❀ ROW 4 (DECREASE ROW): Sl 1, K1, ssk, knit to last 7 stitches, (K1, P1) 3 times, K1.

❀ ROW 5: Repeat Row 1.

❀ ROW 6: Repeat Row 4. You now have 22 (23, 24) stitches.

❀ Continue even in pattern until piece measures 12.5" (13.25", 14") (32 [33.5, 35.5] cm) from cast-on, ending with a WS row. Place the 7 left front border stitches on a holder.

SHAPING THE LEFT NECK

❀ ROW 1 (RS): Sl 1, knit to last 3 stitches, K2tog, K1.

❀ ROW 2: Sl 1, purl to end of row.

❀ Repeat Rows 1 and 2 two more times. You now have 12 (13, 14) stitches.

❀ Continue even (slipping the first stitch of every row, knitting the RS rows, and purling the WS rows) until piece measures 14" (14.75", 15.5") (35.5 [37.5, 39.5] cm) from cast-on, ending with a RS row. Cut yarn, leaving an 8" (20 cm) tail, place stitches on holder.

Knitting the Right Front

❖ Place 42 (44, 46) held right front stitches on needle.
❖ ROW 1 (WS): Attach yarn, sl 1, purl to last 7 stitches, (P1, K1) 3 times, P1.
❖ ROW 2: Sl 1, (P1, K1) 3 times, knit to end of row.
❖ ROW 3: Sl 1, purl to last 7 stitches, (P1, K1) 3 times, P1.
❖ ROW 4 (DECREASE ROW): Sl 1, (P1, K1) 3 times, knit to last 4 stitches, K2tog, K2.
❖ ROW 5: Repeat Row 3.
❖ ROW 6: Repeat Row 4. You now have 40 (42, 44) stitches.
❖ Continue even in pattern until piece measures 12.5" (13.25", 14") (32 [33.5, 35.5] cm) from cast-on, ending with a WS row.

SHAPING THE RIGHT NECK

❖ ROW 1 (RS): Sl 1, (P1, K1) 3 times, K14 (15, 16), place the 21 (22, 23) stitches just worked on a holder, K1, ssk, knit to end of row.
❖ ROW 2: Sl 1, purl to last 3 stitches, ssp, K1.
❖ ROW 3: Sl 1, ssk, knit to end of row.
❖ Repeat Rows 2 and 3 twice more. You now have 12 (13, 14) stitches.
❖ Continue even (slipping the first stitch of every row, knitting the RS rows, and purling the WS rows) until piece measures 14" (14.75", 15.5") (35.5 [37.5, 39.5] cm) from cast-on, ending with a RS row. Cut yarn, leaving an 8" (20 cm) tail, place stitches on holder.

Knitting the Back

❖ Place 43 (44, 47) held back stitches on needle.
❖ ROW 1 (WS): Attach yarn, sl 1, purl to end of row.
❖ ROW 2: Sl 1, knit to end of row.
❖ ROW 3: Sl 1, purl to end of row.
❖ ROW 4: Sl 1, K1, ssk, knit to last 4 stitches, K2tog, K2.
❖ ROW 5: Repeat Row 3.
❖ ROW 6: Repeat Row 4. You now have 39 (40, 43) stitches.
❖ Continue even in pattern until piece measures 14" (14.75", 15.5") (35.5 [37.5, 39.5] cm) from cast-on, ending with a WS row.

SHAPING THE NECK

❖ ROW 1 (RS): Sl 1, K11 (12, 13), place next 15 (14, 15) stitches on holder for back neck, place remaining 12 (13, 14) stitches on separate holder for left shoulder.

* Working 12 (13, 14) right shoulder stitches only, continue in pattern for 3 more rows. Place stitches on holder.
* Place left shoulder stitches on needles and beginning with a RS row, work in pattern for 4 rows.

Joining the Shoulders

* Graft right and left front and back shoulders together with kitchener stitch (see page 262).

Knitting the Collar

* With RS facing, work 21 (22, 23) held right front stitches in pattern, pick up and knit (see page 264) 13 stitches along shaped right front neck edge, K15 (14, 15) held back stitches on needle, pick up and knit 13 stitches along shaped left front neck edge, work 7 held left front stitches in pattern. You now have 69 (69, 71) stitches.
* ROW 1 (WS): Sl 1, *K1 tbl, P1; repeat from *.
* ROW 2: Sl 1, *P1 tbl, K1; repeat from *.
* Repeat Rows 1 and 2 until collar measures 2.5" (6.5 cm), ending with a WS row.
* NEXT ROW (RS): Sl 1, *P1, K1; repeat from *.
* NEXT ROW (WS): Sl 1, *K1, P1; repeat from *.
* Repeat these 2 rows until collar measures 5" (12.5 cm). Bind off loosely.

Knitting the Armhole Ribbing

* With 16" (40 cm) circular needle or double-point needles, pick up and knit 52 (58, 64) stitches around each armhole. Work K1, P1 rib for 4 rounds. Bind off loosely in pattern.

Finishing

* Weave in all ends. Block. Make 5 buttonholes as shown in photograph (page 48), the lowest about 1" (2.5 cm) above the cast-on edge, the highest 1" (2.5 cm) above collar pick-up row, and the remaining 3 evenly spaced in between, as follows: Stretch out a stitch in buttonhole position to about the size of your button. Stitch around each stretched opening using the buttonhole stitch (see page 261).

HEIRLOOM MERINO-ALPACA BABY HAT

DESIGNED BY KATHY ELKINS, *photo on page 48*

Here's a quick knit that is made extra special because of the yarn. Knitted with a blend of alpaca, merino, and soy, this baby hat is soft, soft, soft. The optional tassel is threaded with seed beads.

SIZES AND FINISHED MEASUREMENTS	To fit newborn, approximately 16" (41 cm) circumference
YARN	The Fibre Company Pemaquid, 60% merino/30% baby alpaca/10% soy fiber, 1.75 oz (50 g)/60 yds (55 m), Crème Fraîche
NEEDLES	Set of five US 10 (6 mm) double-point needles *or size you need to obtain correct gauge*
GAUGE	12 stitches and 24 rows = 4" (10 cm) in stockinette stitch
OTHER SUPPLIES	Stitch markers, tapestry needle, big-eye beading needle (optional), fifteen size E seed beads (optional)

Knitting the Hat

❋ With circular needle, cast on 48 stitches and divide evenly onto 4 double-point needles. Place marker and join into a round, being careful not to twist the stitches.

❋ **ROUND 1 AND 2:** Knit.

❋ **ROUNDS 3–6:** Purl.

❋ **ROUNDS 7–9:** Knit.

❋ **ROUND 10:** Purl.

❋ **ROUNDS 11–14:** *K3, P1; repeat from *.

❋ **ROUND 15:** Purl.

❋ **ROUNDS 16–19:** Repeat Rounds 11–14.

❋ **ROUND 20:** Purl, placing markers after every sixth stitch.

Shaping the Crown

❋ **ROUND 1:** *Knit to 2 stitches before marker, K2tog; repeat from *.

❋ **ROUND 2:** Knit.

❋ Repeat Rounds 1 and 2 three more times. You now have 16 stitches.

❋ **NEXT ROUND:** *K2tog; repeat from *. You now have 8 stitches.

HEIRLOOM MERINO-ALPACA BABY HAT *continued*

Finishing

* Cut yarn, leaving an 8" (20.5 cm) tail. Thread tail onto tapestry needle and draw through remaining stitches twice. Pull up snug and fasten off. Weave in ends.

Adding the Tassel (Optional)

* Cut a piece of yarn 10" (25 cm) long and thread onto big-eye needle. Knot the end of the yarn and thread 5 beads. Use the tapestry needle to sew tassel to top of hat. Repeat as desired.

LEAF BAND ALPACA-MERINO HAT

DESIGNED BY JUDITH L. SWARTZ, *photo on page 48*

Here's a lovely lacy hat knitted at a bulky gauge with two strands of yarn held together. If you've always wanted to try lace but didn't want to get in over your head, try this project with six repeats of a narrow lacy band. Then put that lacy band on your head!

SIZES AND FINISHED MEASUREMENTS	To fit most adults, approximately 21" (53 cm) circumference
YARN	Aslan Trends Guanaco, (60% alpaca/40% merino) 3.5 oz (100g)/145 yds (133 m), Color 172 *Note:* Yarn is used doubled throughout.
NEEDLES	US 13 (9 mm) straight and set of five US 13 (9 mm) double-point needles *or size you need to obtain correct gauge*
GAUGE	10 stitches and 13 rows = 4" (10 cm) in stockinette stitch with two strands held together
OTHER SUPPLIES	Stitch marker, tapestry needle, three ½" (12 mm) buttons, sewing needle, and coordinating sewing thread

Knitting the Band

* With 2 strands held together and straight needles, cast on 10 stitches. Work Rows 1–12 of Veined Leaf pattern 6 times. Note: Stitch count will vary from row to row.

* Knit 4 rows and bind off.

STITCH PATTERN
veined leaf

ROW 1 (RS): P3, (K1, yo) twice, K1, P2, K2.

ROW 2: K4, P5, K3.

ROW 3: P3, K2, yo, K1, yo, K2, P2, K2.

ROW 4: K4, P7, K3.

ROW 5: P3, ssk, K1, (yo, K1) twice, K2tog, P2, K2.

ROW 6: Repeat Row 4.

ROW 7: P3, ssk, K3, K2tog, P2, K2.

ROW 8: Repeat Row 2.

ROW 9: P3, ssk, K1, K2tog, P2, K2.

ROW 10: K4, P3, K3.

ROW 11: P3, yo, sl 2tog, K1, p2sso, yo, P2, K2.

ROW 12: Repeat Row 10.

REPEAT ROWS 1–12 FOR PATTERN.

Knitting the Crown

❅ With double-point needles and RS facing, begin at cast-on end of leaf band and pick up and knit (see page 264) 54 stitches evenly spaced along upper edge (the edge without the garter trim), excluding the 4 knit rows at the end. Place marker and join into a round, being careful not to twist the stitches. Knit 2 rounds.

Decreasing the Crown

❅ ROUND 1: *K4, K2tog; repeat from *. You now have 45 stitches.

❅ ROUND 2 AND ALL EVEN-NUMBERED ROUNDS: Knit.

❅ ROUND 3: *K3, K2tog; repeat from *. You now have 36 stitches.

❅ ROUND 5: *K2, K2tog; repeat from *. You now have 27 stitches.

❅ ROUND 7: *K1, K2tog; repeat from *. You now have 18 stitches.

❅ ROUND 9: *K2tog; repeat from *. You now have 9 stitches.

❅ ROUND 11: *K1, K2tog; repeat from *. You now have 6 stitches.

❅ Knit 1 more round even. Cut yarn, leaving an 8" (20.5 cm) tail. Thread tail onto tapestry needle and draw through remaining stitches twice. Pull up snug and fasten off.

Finishing

❅ Lap short garter edge of band over cast-on end and stitch in place invisibly. Sew buttons evenly placed as shown in photograph (page 48).

Appendix

About the Designers

Susan B. Anderson

Susan has been knitting for almost 25 years. She is the author of Itty-Bitty Hats and Itty-Bitty Nursery and an upcoming knitted toy book for release in 2009. She blogs at: http://susanbanderson.blogspot.com.

Andra Asars

With the encouragement of a co-worker and the disbelief of her family, Andra took the plunge from a nuclear engineering career to become a manufacturer's representative in the knitting industry. She traded atoms for string — really great string. It's been more than 16 years, and she hasn't looked back yet. When not driving or showing new yarns, Andra knits, grows tasty organic greens and veggies, drinks gallons of soy lattes, smiles when the days are rough, and always keeps an emergency supply of dark chocolate in her handbag.

Jean Austin

Although Jean's real passion in life is knitting, by day she is a mom/wife/voice teacher/opera singer/church musician. She can be found on Saturdays at Never Enough Knitting in Wheaton, Illinois. Her favorite place on the planet is the Highlands of Scotland, and she would one day like to meet Alice Starmore.

Betty Balcomb

Following the publication of 101 Designer One-Skein Wonders, Betty held several workshops at Knitty City in New York City to promote "her book" (see pages 6 and 81). Knitty City's loyal clientele eagerly embraced the workshops and the book. Betty is delighted to appear in book three, Luxury Yarn One-Skein Wonders, and can't wait to do the workshops again.

Reneé Barnes

Reneé designs from her cabin in the Arkansas Ozarks. She also spins her own yarn. Find out what she's up to at www.crochetrenee.com.

Tonia Barry

After years in the corporate world, Tonia decided to turn her passion for knitting and designing into her next career. In 2004, she founded Tonia Barry Original Designs (www.toniabarryoriginaldesigns.com). Her creations range from accessories to coats and are designed to be timeless wardrobe staples. She enjoys various fibers and textures and this is reflected in her design work. Tonia has also designed for several yarn companies and knitting publications such as Knitscene, Knit Simple, Cast-On, and Creative Knitting, with more to come. Ravelry name: ToniaBarry.

Marci Blank

Knitting since she was in the third grade, Marci has turned her love of the craft into a full-time career. As owner of Th' Red Head, she designs, knits, and markets garments for art fairs, galleries, and shops. She also dyes and spins yarns that she sells or makes into fabulous one-of-a-kind garments. Memberships include Association of Knitwear Designers, The Knitting Guild Association, Kansas City Weaver's Guild, Fiber Guild of Greater Kansas City, Lawrence (KS) Art Guild.

Susan Boye

Sue has been knitting for more than 25 years and designing for more than 20. She has sold her patterns through retail outlets, and has designed and knit many private commissions. Sue resides with her family in the Greater Toronto area.

Kelly Bridges

Kelly is the manager of the Elegant Ewe yarn and fiber shop (71 South Main Street, Concord, NH 03301; www.elegantewe.com), where she also designs patterns and teaches classes for all fiber sorts. Her love of handwork started when her beautiful grandmother taught her to knit in high school.

Linda Burt

As customer service manager for WEBS — America's Yarn store (see address under Kathy Elkins, page 251), Linda gets inspiration from all the wonderful and ever-changing yarns at her fingertips.

MELISSA BURT

Melissa is the Knit Picks art director and designs fabric for the quilting division, Connecting Threads. She lives in Vancouver, Washington, with her husband and their menagerie of pets.

JANICE BYE

Janice has a bachelor of mathematics and is a Canadian master knitter. She has taught knitting classes and worked for the distributor of Manos Yarns for many years. Janice continues to knit and edit patterns for yarn companies and designers.

CATHY CARRON

Knitwear designer and author Cathy left behind a corporate career in marketing once her daughters, Emma and Lydia, were born. Ever since, her focus has been on handknitting, first as a small business owner and importer of children's sweaters, next as a writer and researcher on handknitting for the military during wartime, and most recently, as the author of two books on handknitting technique: Hip Knit Hats (2005), now in its sixth printing, and Knitting Sweaters from the Top-Down (2007). This year, her design work can also be seen in Vogue Knitting, Interweave Knits, Knit Simple, Knit.1, Vogue Knits-on-the-Go (Gifts, Bags Book II), Rowan International Vol. #42, Vogue's The Ultimate Sock Book, and 101 Designer One-Skein Wonders.

JENI CHASE

Jeni is a Silicon Valley-based knitwear designer whose first design was published last year in Knittery.com. More of her work can be found on her Web site, www.theknitist.com.

GRACE MAGGIE COVEY

Maggie has loved creating with fibers since the age of five. She weaves, quilts, sews, does cross stitch, and spins her own yarn, but knitting is her first love. She enjoys charity knitting for the Dayton Knitting Guild and My Brother's Keeper. Between knitting for family, three children, 10 grandchildren and special friends, Maggie teaches knitting classes at Fiberworks in Beavercreek, Ohio (www.fiberworks_Dayton.blogspot.com). Tuesdays and Sundays find her with Knit and Nibble friends at Fiberworks.

MARLAINE DESCHAMPS

Marlaine lives in upstate New York where she enjoys playing with all types of fiber arts, her family, and her two dogs. Family, friends, and natural surroundings have always been, and continue to be, the inspiration for her projects.

JUDITH DURANT

Judith is author of Never Knit Your Man a Sweater* (*unless you've got the ring!) and editor of Luxury Yarn One-Skein Wonders, 101 Designer One-Skein Wonders, and One-Skein Wonders: 101 Yarn Shop Favorites. She also authored Ready, Set, Bead and coauthored Beadwork Inspired by Art: Art Nouveau Jewelry and Accessories, Beadwork Inspired by Art: Impressionist Jewelry and Accessories, and The Beader's Companion. Judith is a freelance editor who currently knits and beads in Lowell, Massachusetts.

EDIE ECKMAN

A former yarn shop owner, Edie has her hands in many aspects of the fiber arts — teaching, writing, designing, and editing. Her knit and crochet designs have appeared in many magazines, yarn company publications, pattern leaflets, and books. Edie also travels extensively, teaching at conventions, shops, and guilds. She is the author of The Crochet Answer Book (2005) and Beyond-the-Square Crochet Motifs (2008).

KATHY ELKINS

Kathy, along with her husband Steve, is the owner of WEBS — America's Yarn Store (75 Service Center Road, Northampton, MA 01060). She holds an MBA in marketing and has extensive experience in corporate marketing and branding. Her love of modern design elements, coupled with her belief that items should be "knittable, wearable, and usable," provide a solid foundation for her designs. You can catch up with Kathy at WEBS, on her blog websyarnstore.blogspot.com, or on the weekly podcast, Ready, Set, Knit!, that she and her husband host.

Jackie Erickson-Schweitzer

Jackie is a long-time knitting enthusiast who shares her love of knitting through designing, publishing, and teaching. The structure of handknitted lace has infinite variations, creating excitement in Jackie's artistic discoveries and challenging her to intriguing possibilities. With a background in music and mathematics, she enjoys the process of capturing the melody of lacy light and shadow, and harmonizing it with the style and function of the intended article. The process of design and experimentation evolves, sometimes through much iteration, to arrive at a coherent whole before she is satisfied. Her growing roster of Heart Strings patterns is available through an ever-increasing network of retailers and can be seen at *www.heartstringsfiberarts.com*.

Bonnie Evans

Bonnie has been knitting for 35 years. She is currently a full-time professional sports clothing designer/manufacturer, but knitting and knitwear design remain her true passion. She teaches knitting technique classes locally, where she resides in central Mississippi, and helps teach new knitters on several online knitting lists. Her designs are available on various pattern sites on the Internet, as well as Ravelry, and in some publications such as *Knit It!* and *Knitting Fun for Everyone*. She also makes and sells bags and needle organizers for knitters on Etsy under seller name Sewbizgirl Originals. On Ravelry, she is Sewbizgirl.

Diana Foster

Diana is owner and designer for Lowellmountain Wools (194 Mitchell Road, Lowell, VT; 802-744-6440), a farm shop in the Green Mountains of Vermont's "Northeast Kingdom," where she offers classes, along with knitting and spinning fibers, organic herbs, and wool from her sheep. She is a member of The Knitting Guild of America.

Bev Galeskas

Bev, owner of Fiber Trends Pattern Company and author of *Felted Knits* (Interweave Press, 2003), has been designing handknit patterns for her company since 1994. Three years ago, she added yarn to the Fiber Trends' line as the U.S. distributor for Naturally New Zealand Yarns. She has been a guest on both *Knitty Gritty* and *Shay Pendray's Needle Art Studio* and has taught at many knitting conferences and yarn stores across the country.

Patti Ghezzi

Patti is an Atlanta-based knitter and writer. This book includes her second published pattern.

Anne Carroll Gilmour

Almost every day, Anne does at least a little knitting, spinning, and/or weaving in her home studio in Park City, Utah. Once a week, she works at the Black Sheep Wool Company in Salt Lake City, and her patterns are available through the Wooly West catalog and through her Web site: *www.wildwestwoolies.com*.

Cecily Glowik

After receiving her BFA with a concentration in painting, Cecily decided to move to New York in 1999. Upon realizing that the cramped living of her Brooklyn apartment did not mix well with oil painting, she took up knitting as a creative outlet. What began as a hobby soon became a passion, quickly leading her into designing her own handknitting patterns. Since moving back to Massachusetts, Cecily has had numerous designs featured in books, magazines, and in the Classic Elite Yarns collections and Web letters.

Amy Greeman

Amy is a latecomer to knitting, but like most converts, she is passionate about wool. She lives (and knits) in Northampton, Massachusetts.

JAZMINE GREENLAW

Jazmine is a designer in Hatfield, Massachusetts.

MARY JANE HALL

Professional designer of crochet garments and accessories for three years, Mary Jane has authored two books: *Positively Crochet!* (August 2007) and *Crochet that Fits* (due out November 2008). This new book has patterns for fitted and flattering garments and accessories with no increases or decreases. She also has many other designs in various books and magazines.

MARION HALPERN

Marion has been knitting for more than 50 years, and she works at WEBS (see address under Kathy Elkins) where she enjoys meeting knitters from all over. Marion believes that all knitters are designers; we have to decide what yarn to use, select the color or colors, and sometimes (more often than not) alter the given pattern to fit the situation. Now that is creativity! She most enjoys designing dresses for her six-year-old granddaughter, Roley.

BETH HOOD

Beth was a timid knitter until she went to work at Halcyon Yarn (12 School Street, Bath, ME, 04530; *www.halcyonyarn.com*). Amid such inspiration, she's ventured into unexplored fibers and projects and done some basic designing. Beth enjoys working on projects displaying some of the lesser-known yarns and accessories.

AMY O'NEILL HOUCK

Amy is a crochet and knit designer living and working in Cordova, Alaska. She blogs at *www.thehookandi.com*.

VICKIE HOWELL

Vickie is the host of television's *Knitty Gritty*, co-host of Lifetime's Webseries *Crafted*, columnist for *Kiwi* and *Knit.1* magazines, and author of books including *Knit Aid*. For more info, visit *www.craftrocklove.com*.

SARAH KELLER

Sarah has an amazing husband and two beautiful daughters, and is "livin' the dream" as a yarn shop owner in the scenic Columbia River Gorge. Her shop, Knot Another Hat, can be found in the heart of downtown Hood River, Oregon, or online at *www.knotanotherhat.com*.

ANNI KRISTENSEN

Anni feels fortunate to be doing exactly what she loves to do. She works with wonderful people, she works with wonderful colors, and she gets to play with yarn whenever she wants to! Working with beautiful natural fiber yarns that come to her at Himalaya Yarn from around the world, Anni has a deep sense of belonging to the natural environment and a connectedness across cultures. For more info, visit *www.himalayayarn.com*.

CAROL LAMBOS

Carol is an attorney who practices in New York City. Her love affair with cashmere started the day she met her first skein of Jade Sapphire. She has created numerous designs using Jade Sapphire Yarns.

SONDA J. LEE

Sonda designs, teaches, and inspires knitting at Stitch 'N Hook Yarn Shop in Shorewood, Illinois (*www.stitchnhook.com*). Knitting has been her passion ever since she picked up knitting needles and made her first pair of socks. Sonda says there's always something new to knit and learn.

DAWN LEESEMAN

Dawn has been knitting for more than 25 years and is a freelance designer in Northern California. Many of her designs have appeared in *Vogue*, *Interweave Knits*, *Pampered Pooches* by Edie Eckman, and *Crystal Palace Yarns*. In addition, she has coauthored a book with Faina Goberstein, *Casual, Elegant Knits* (Martingale Publishing).

ANNE LENZINI

Anne, a former clothing designer, started Blue Daisy Knitting (www.bluedaisyknitting.com) to fill a void for the very inexperienced knitter. Blue Daisy Knitting features easy-to-read patterns with additional teaching instructions. Kits are also geared toward the new knitter.

ANNE KUO LUKITO

Anne has been crafty and creative since she was a young child and is self-taught in her crafty endeavors and hobbies. She focuses her creative energies as co-owner of Handicraft Café (www.handicraftcafe.com). Anne's designs have been published in books and magazines and by yarn companies.

ANN MCCLURE

Ann has been crocheting since she was little and knitting since 2001. She is a professional writer and editor who lives in Connecticut with her husband and their two golden retrievers. She blogs about her crafts and days at travelingann.blogspot.com.

TINA MCELMOYL

Tina lives in Northampton, Massachusetts, with her husband and two Jack Russell terriers. She works in her local yarn store, WEBS (see address under Kathy Elkins), and as a consultant for a nonprofit teen sexual health education program. Having never found much to love about math, her friends are amazed at the calculations she is willing to do for knitting. (See also www.measuredwithspoons.etsy.com.)

MARY MCGURN

Mary is co-owner of Colorful Stitches (48 Main Street, Lenox, MA 01240) and the online store, www.colorful-stitches.com. Her store was recognized by Vogue Knitting International in Fall 2007 as the "most inspirational yarn store in the nation."

JILLIAN MORENO

Jillian lives in Michigan and is a knitwear designer living her dream with jobs as catalyst for the largest free web-only knitting magazine, Knitty.com, and as editor for Knitty's little sister, Knittyspin.com.

MELISSA MORGAN-OAKES

Melissa learned to crochet, tat, and sew without the use of commercial patterns. She later taught herself to knit and spin. She is author the book 2-at-a-time Socks, publishes a line of patterns under the name Melissaknits, and teaches a wide range of knitting and fiber related classes.

BOBBE MORRIS

Bobbe works and designs for Haus of Yarn in Nashville, Tennessee, which opened in 2003. She loves the shop and describes it as cozy, comfortable, and full of wonderful, beautiful yarns — a great place to work. Bobbe has designs in all of the One-Skein Wonders books. She also had her shawl design used in an ad for Tilli Tomas Yarns in Interweave Knits (Spring 2008). She at one time owned Bandywood Knit Shop, where she specialized in custom-written patterns for her customers. She has participated in the Tennessee Association of Craft Artists Show, where she has shown and sold her work. Bobbe is very passionate about her knitting and believes it should be relaxing and fun. She thinks of knitting as magical and spiritual, with a little whimsy thrown in for good measure.

LUCY NEATBY

Once a British Merchant Navy navigating officer, Lucy now sails under the Tradewind Knitwear Designs flag while teaching knitting around the world. She creates her superb knitting patterns, books, and instructional DVDs in Dartmouth, Nova Scotia, Canada. (See also www.lucyneatby.com.)

LAURA NELKIN

Laura is the design director at Schaefer Yarn Company, a small hand-dyed yarn company in upstate New York. She is lucky to be surrounded by yarn every day!

KENDRA NITTA

Kendra was taught to knit in 2005 by her 10-year-old cousin, Madeleine Vilas. Since then, Kendra has become an avid knitter, freelance knitwear designer, and sample knitter. Her work has appeared here in *Luxury Yarn One-Skein Wonders* and in *Knitty*.

CHERYL OBERLE

Cheryl lives in Denver, Colorado, where she designs garments for hand knitting and dyes her own line of yarns. (Cheryl Oberle Designs, 3315 Newton Street, Denver, CO 80211; www.cheryloberle. com.)

SARAH-HOPE PARMETER

Sarah-Hope teaches writing at the University of California, Santa Cruz, and knits whenever she can. You can find more of her patterns and read about her adventures in knitting at her blog "What If Knits," at www.whatifknits.com.

CAROLINE PERISHO

Caroline began her fiber art design work with quilts. Progressing from quilting to knitting, Caroline bought Wild & Wooly in 2001 and transformed it into a popular Northwest knitting store with her artistic flare for presentation and design. She then began designing knitwear; each piece reflects her creative vision of knitting. Her knitting patterns are sold by Fiber Trends and T & C Imports/Frog Tree Yarns; or you may visit her Web site: *www. wildandwooly.com.*

ISELA G. PHELPS

Isela resides in Cache Valley, Utah. In her spare time, she enjoys knitting and listening to a good book. When she is not knitting, she can be found out on her bike, running, or swimming. She blogs at www.isela.typepad.com.

AMY POLCYN

Amy is a regular contributor to a variety of knitting magazines and yarn company pattern collections. She blogs about knitting and more at http://frottez.blogspot.com.

ELIZABETH PRUSIEWICZ

Elizabeth likes to knit to her dreams and imagination. She does knit swatches (a must), she does slip the first stitch (always), she does not knit socks, she does not use patterns. She may be one of the fastest knitters in this country.

MARGARET RADCLIFFE

Margaret is the author of *The Knitting Answer Book* (2005) and *The Essential Guide to Color Knitting Techniques* (2008). She publishes the Maggie's Rags line of knitting patterns. Learn more at www.maggiesrags.com.

MARCI RICHARDSON

Marci is the owner of a very successful yarn shop, The Elegant Ewe (71 South Main Street, Concord, NH 03301), which is now in its 11th year of operation. Featured in 2000 in *Knitter's Stash* and as an editor's choice "must visit" shop in the *Yankee Magazine Travel Guide to New England*, the shop has become a destination for knitters around the world.

CIRILIA ROSE

Cirilia lives in Western Massachusetts and is pursuing a career in knitwear design. She loves translating woven fabric effects in knitted garments and prefers "kitchen sink" yarns that combine many disparate fibers.

HÉLÈNE RUSH

Hélène is currently owner of Knit One, Crochet Too, Inc. She sold her first design in 1979 and has designed hundreds of projects since. She's past editor of *McCall's Needlework & Crafts* and *Cast On* magazines and author of five knitting books.

ANNE K. RYAN

Anne graduated from Rhode Island School of Design in 2006. She works in the design industry.

GITTA SCHRADE

Gitta is a designer and pattern writer.

CAROL SCOTT

A professor of fashion design and merchandising for 26 years, Carol recently retired to pursue her passion for knitting and sewing. She began knitting and sewing at an early age when she decided that creating unique garments and looking different were good things. Carol continues to teach knitting and sewing, as well as designing knit garments under her own label, TruThreads.

CAROL J. SORSDAHL

Carol learned to knit while living in Ketchikan, Alaska, 40 years ago. Knitting brought Carol through the tough times in her life — caring for her son Clint, who battled brain tumors. She blogged the final months of his life and continues blogging "The Next Season of my Life," at http://junebugknits.bravejournal. com. Since the loss of her son in 2004, Carol has knit hundreds of hats and other items for charity in memory of Clint. She has also expanded into quilting and machine embroidery, and plays keyboard with the music team at her church.

Carol got her first knitting machine in 1974 and through the years, she sold her children's knits in gift shops, children's boutiques, and online. She has designed for Coats & Clark and translated Japanese patterns for a yarn company. Her patterns have appeared in several machine- and handknitting publications, including *Creative Knitting*.

MYRNA A. I. STAHMAN

One of Myrna's first knitting memories is as a fourth-grader in 1954, knitting a long scarf, which, she realized many years later, was feather-and-fan lace. Is it any wonder that she is a lace lover? Myrna has worked as a social worker, Peace Corps volunteer, elementary school teacher, and director of a day activity center for developmentally challenged adults. In 2000, she founded Rocking Chair Press, publishing *Stahman's Shawls and Scarves: Lace Faroese Shaped Shawls from the Neck Down and Seamen's Scarves*. In 2004 Myrna retired from the practice of law after 30 interesting years. During most of her legal career, she represented the state in the criminal appellate arena, including one case heard by the United States Supreme Court.

Myrna's knitting-related activities have taken her to places she could not even have dreamed of as a fourth-grader in rural Minnesota. She has taught knitting classes throughout the United States and in New Zealand, Australia, and Orkney. Myrna now devotes much of her time designing, writing, publishing, teaching lace knitting, and sponsoring an annual lace knitting retreat. She is currently at work on several books — stay tuned.

GWEN STEEGE

A confirmed knitter since childhood, Gwen has edited more than two dozen knitting and crochet books, and has contributed designs to several of them. She has her own sheep, and spins and dyes their wool for her woven and knitted projects. She lives in Williamstown, Massachusetts.

JUDITH L. SWARTZ

Judith has an MS in textile design from the University of Wisconsin. Author of *Dogs in Knits, Hip to Knit, Hip to Crochet, Getting Started Crochet* (all Interweave Press publications), she is also co-owner of Nina's Department & Variety Store in Spring Green, Wisconsin (family-owned since 1916).

KATHLEEN TAYLOR

Kathleen is a South Dakota wife, mother, grandmother, spinner, knitter, writer, and blogger. She has written 51-plus Tory Bauer mysteries and three knitting books (*Knit One, Felt Too; Yarns to Dye For; I Heart Felt*); her fourth, a sock knitting book, will be published by The Taunton Press in September 2009. Check out her blog, "Kathleen Taylor's Dakota Dreams," for blather about books, music, yarn, wool, and TV, at *http://Kathleen-dakotadreams. blogspot.com.*

MARTHA TOWNSEND

As a Vidal Sassoon Academy graduate, Martha wields her skills as a colorist/stylist in Louisville, Kentucky. Her creative passions include gourmet cooking, gardening, a lifetime of quilting, and over nine years of knitting.

JoLENE TREACE

JoLene is an independent knitwear designer from the Midwest. She has been published in books and magazines and has a line of pattern leaflets through her business, Kristmen's Design Studio. She is a professional member of the Association of Knitwear Designers.

BEVERLY VASQUEZ

Beverly has been owner of Ewe'll Love It! in Nashua, New Hampshire, for six years, knitting for 50 years, designing for 20 years, and loving every minute.

KATHERINE VAUGHAN

Katherine spends her days as an academic librarian in North Carolina, and her nights and weekends designing warm-weather garments and accessories for adults and children. She offers free and for-sale patterns and commentary on her blog at *http://knitwithkt.blogspot.com.*

RENÉ E. WELLS

René was taught to knit and crochet as a young child by her Grandma Kay. Together, they designed and sold to boutiques under the name Granny an' Me. She loves to teach the art of the hands and heart.

SHELLI WESTCOTT

Owner and designer of Knitterly in Petaluma, California, Shelli has a true love for texture and color. A former landscape designer with her own company, she loves creating things with beautiful hand-dyed and luxury fibers. It's like creating a wearable small garden for everyone to see and feel. The yarn used for her pattern was hand-dyed and handspun by Trish Andersen of Tanglewood Fibers. We call this our drug of choice! The buttons on Neck Candy were hand made by Shella Ernst, who also makes fine blown glass circular knitting needles. Fabulous! (See *www. knitterly.net*)

ERIKA WITHAM

Erika is a relatively new knitter with almost three years under her belt. Her LYS is Knot Another Hat and she is on *Ravelry.com* — StickErika.

DANIEL YUHAS

Daniel lives in Brooklyn, but has his eye on a solar powered hover-castle. You can see more of his knitting creations at *www. moltingyeti.com.*

SIZING GUIDELINES

Finding the measurements of the recipient of your knitted luxury wonder is the best way to insure a proper fit. If those measurements are not available, however, here are some general guidelines to help. Sizes are approximate.

HEAD CIRCUMFERENCE [1]

	Premie	Baby	Toddler	Child	Woman	Man
		Infant/Child			Adult	
in.	12	14	16	18	20	22
cm	30.5	35.5	40.5	45.5	50.5	56

For an accurate head measure, place a tape measure across the forehead and measure around the full circumference of the head. Keep the tape snug for accurate results.

GARMENTS [1]

Babies	3 mo.	6 mo.	12 mo.	18 mo.	24 mo.
Chest	16" (40.5 cm)	17" (43 cm)	18" (45.5 cm)	19" (20.5 cm)	20" (50.5 cm)
Center Back Neck-to-Cuff	10.5" (26.5 cm)	11.5" (29 cm)	12.5" (31.5 cm)	14" (35.5 cm)	18" (45.5 cm)
Back Waist Length	6" (15.5 cm)	7" (17.5 cm)	7.5" (19 cm)	8" (20.5 cm)	8.5" (21.5 cm)
Cross Back (Shoulder to Shoulder)	7.25" (18.5 cm)	7.75" (19.5 cm)	8.25" (21 cm)	8.5" (21.5 cm)	8.75" (22 cm)
Sleeve Length to Underarm	6" (15.5 cm)	6.5" (16.5 cm)	7.5" (19 cm)	8" (20.5 cm)	8.5" (21.5 cm)
Children	2	4	6	8	10
Chest	21" (53 cm)	23" (58.5 cm)	25" (63.5 cm)	26.5" (67 cm)	28" (71 cm)
Center Back Neck-to-Cuff	18" (45.5 cm)	19.5" (49.5 cm)	20.5" (52 cm)	22" (56 cm)	24" (61 cm)
Back Waist Length	8.5" (21.5 cm)	9.5" (24 cm)	10.5" (26.5 cm)	12.5" (31.5 cm)	14" (35.5 cm)
Cross Back (Shoulder to Shoulder)	9.25" (23.5 cm)	9.75" (25 cm)	10.25" (26 cm)	10.75" (27 cm)	11.25" (28.5 cm)
Sleeve Length to Underarm	8.5" (21.5 cm)	10.5" (26.5 cm)	11.5" (29 cm)	12.5" (31.5 cm)	13.5" (34.5 cm)

SOCKS

Children	2–4 years	4–8 years	8–small adult
Foot circumference	5.5" (14 cm)	6.5" (16.5 cm)	7.5" (19 cm)
Total foot length	6" (15 cm)	7" (18 cm)	7.5" (19 cm)
Women	Small	Medium	Large
Foot circumference	7.5" (19 cm)	8" (20.5 cm)	8.5" (21.5 cm)
Total foot length	8.5" (20.25 cm)	9.5" (23.75 cm)	10" (25 cm)
Men	Small	Medium	Large
Foot circumference	9" (23 cm)	9.5" (24 cm)	10" (15 cm)
Total foot length	10" (25.5 cm)	11" (28 cm)	11.5" (29 cm)

[1] Reprinted from *Standards & Guidelines for Crochet and Knitting*, (April 2003), with permission of the Craft Yarn Council of America.

MITTENS

Children	2–4 years	4–6 years	6–8 years	8–small adult
Hand circumference	5.5" (14 cm)	6" (15 cm)	6.5" (16.5 cm)	7" (18 cm)
Cuff length	2" (5 cm)	2" (5 cm)	2.5" (6.5 cm)	2.5" (6.5 cm)
Length from cuff to top shaping*	3" (7.5 cm)	3.5" (9 cm)	4" (10 cm)	4.5" (11.5 cm)
Length of thumb (after gusset)	1.5" (4 cm)	1.5" (4 cm)	2" (5 cm)	2" (5 cm)
Women	Small	Medium	Large	
Hand circumference	7" (18 cm)	7.5" (19 cm)	8" (20.5 cm)	
Cuff length	2.5" (6.5 cm)	2.5" (6.5 cm)	3" (7.5 cm)	
Length from cuff to top shaping*	4.5" (11.5 cm)	5" (12.5 cm)	5.5" (14 cm)	
Length of thumb (after gusset)	2" (5 cm)	2" (5 cm)	2.5" (6.5 cm)	
Men	Small	Medium	Large	
Hand circumference	8" (20.5 cm)	8.5" (21.5 cm)	9" (23 cm)	
Cuff length	3" (7.5 cm)	3" (7.5 cm)	3" (7.5 cm)	
Length from cuff to top shaping*	5.5" (14 cm)	6" (15 cm)	6.5" (16.5 cm)	
Length of thumb (after gusset)	2.5" (6.5 cm)	2.5" (6.5 cm)	3" (7.5 cm)	

*Top shaping begins 2" (5 cm) from finished length.

GLOVES

Children	4–6 years	6–8 years	8–small adult
Hand circumference	6" (15 cm)	6.5" (16.5 cm)	7" (18 cm)
Cuff length	2" (5 cm)	2.5" (6.5 cm)	2.5" (6.5 cm)
Length from cuff to little finger	3" (7.5 cm)	3" (7.5 cm)	3.5" (9 cm)
Length of little finger	1.5" (4 cm)	1.5" (4 cm)	2" (5 cm)
Length of ring and index fingers	1.5" (4 cm)	2" (4 cm)	2" (5 cm)
Length of middle finger	2" (5 cm)	2.5" (6.5 cm)	2.5" (6.5 cm)
Length of thumb (after gusset)	1" (2.5 cm)	1" (2.5 cm)	1.5" (4 cm)
Women	Small	Medium	Large
Hand circumference	7" (18 cm)	7.5" (19 cm)	8" (20.5 cm)
Cuff length	2.5" (6.5 cm)	2.5" (6.5 cm)	3" (7.5 cm)
Length from cuff to little finger	3.5" (9 cm)	3.5" (9 cm)	4" (10 cm)
Length of little finger	2" (5 cm)	2" (5 cm)	2.5" (6.5 cm)
Length of ring and index fingers	2" (5 cm)	2.5" (6.5 cm)	2.5" (6.5 cm)
Length of middle finger	2.5" (6.5 cm)	3" (7.5 cm)	3" (7.5 cm)
Length of thumb (after gusset)	1.5" (4 cm)	1.5" (4 cm)	2" (5 cm)
Men	Small	Medium	Large
Hand circumference	8" (20.5 cm)	8.5" (21.5 cm)	9" (23 cm)
Cuff length	3" (7.5 cm)	3" (7.5 cm)	3" (7.5 cm)
Length from cuff to little finger	4" (10 cm)	4" (10 cm)	4.5" (11.5 cm)
Length of little finger	2.5" (6.5 cm)	2.5" (6.5 cm)	3" (7.5 cm)
Length of ring and index fingers	2.5" (6.5 cm)	3" (7.5 cm)	3" (7.5 cm)
Length of middle finger	3" (7.5 cm)	3.5" (9 cm)	3.5" (9 cm)
Length of thumb (after gusset)	2" (5 cm)	2" (5 cm)	2.5" (6.5 cm)

ABBREVIATIONS

beg	begin, beginning
ch	chain crochet
cn	cable needle
dc	double crochet
dec	decrease
hdc	half double crochet
inc	increase
K	knit
K2tog	knit 2 stitches together (1 stitch decreased)
K3tog	knit 3 stitches together (2 stitches decreased)
Kfb	knit into the front and back of stitch (1 stitch increased)
kwise	knitwise, as if to knit
m	marker
M1	make 1 stitch (see page 263)
M1L	make 1 stitch, left leaning (see page 264)
M1R	make 1 stitch, right leaning (see page 263)
P	purl
P2tog	purl 2 stitches together (1 stitch decreased)
P3tog	purl 3 stitches together (2 stitches decreased)
Pfb	purl into the front and back of stitch (1 stitch increased)
pm	place marker
psso	pass slipped stitch over last stitch on needle
pwise	purlwise, as if to purl
RS	right side
rsc	reverse single crochet
sc	single crochet
sl	slip from left to right needle without knitting
sl st	slip stitch crochet
sm	slip marker
sp	space made between crochet stitches
ssk	slip 1, slip 1, place left needle into front of slipped stitches and knit them together
ssp	slip 1, slip 1, place left needle into back of slipped stitches and purl them together
st(s)	stitch(es)
tbl	through back loop
tr	treble crochet
WS	wrong side
wyib	with yarn in back
wyif	with yarn in front
yo	yarn over needle

Guide to Yarn Weights

This system of categorizing yarn, gauge ranges, and recommended needle and hook sizes was developed by the Craft Yarn Council of America and was used to classify the projects in this book.

		STITCHES IN 4" (10 CM) STOCKINETTE STITCH	RECOMMENDED NEEDLE SIZE
0 LACE	0	33–40	000–1 (1.5–2.25 mm)
1 SUPER FINE	1	27–32	1–3 (2.25–3.25 mm)
2 FINE	2	23–26	3–5 (3.25–3.75 mm)
3 LIGHT	3	21–24	5–7 (3.75–4.5 mm)
4 MEDIUM	4	16–20	7–9 (4.5–5.5 mm)
5 BULKY	5	12–15	9–11 (5.5–8 mm)

GLOSSARY

Backstitch. With a threaded tapestry needle, anchor the yarn at the beginning of the seam. *Working from right to left, count over two stitches and pass the needle through both layers from back to front. Then count back one stitch to the right and pass through both layers from front to back. Repeat from * until seam is completed.

Backward loop cast-on/increase. Hold the end of the yarn and a needle in your right hand. Hold the working yarn in your left hand. Bring your left thumb over the top, down behind, and up in front of the yarn, creating a loop. Insert needle into loop on thumb as if to knit and slide loop onto needle. You may also use the backward loop cast-on to add stitches to the end of a row of knitting.

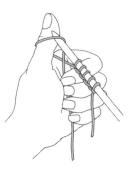

Bind off loosely. This method is sometimes called a suspended bind-off. Knit two stitches. *Lift the first stitch over the second stitch as for a regular bind-off but leave the lifted stitch on the left needle. Pass your right needle in front of the suspended stitch, knit the next stitch, and drop both from the left needle. Repeat from * until all stitches are bound off.

Buttonhole stitch. Reinforce a buttonhole by stitching around the opening as shown.

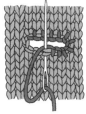

Cable cast-on. Make a slipknot and place it on your left needle. Follow Steps 1 and 2 for knitted-on cast-on (page 262).

1. Place the second needle between the two stitches on the first needle (see figure 1).

2. Knit a new stitch between the two stitches, pull it long, and place in on the first needle (see figure 2).

Continue in this manner, knitting between the last two stitches on the first needle, until you have the required number of stitches.

Chain (ch) (crochet). Begin with a slipknot on the hook. Wrap yarn over hook and pull the loop through the slipknot. Yarn over hook, pull loop through loop on hook to make second chain. Repeat for the required number of chain stitches.

Double crochet (dc). Yarn over hook. Insert hook through both loops of next stitch. Draw loop through stitch. Yarn over hook. Draw loop through first two loops on hook. Yarn over hook. Draw loop through two loops on hook.

Garter stitch. When knitting back and forth in rows, knit all rows. When knitting circularly, knit one row, purl one row.

Half double crochet (hdc). Yarn over hook. Insert hook through both loops of next stitch. Yarn over and draw loop through stitch. Yarn over hook and draw through all three loops on hook.

I-cord. Use two double-point needles to make I-cord. Cast on the required number of stitches. *Knit all stitches. Without turning work, slide the stitches to the other end of the needle. Pull the working yarn across the back. Repeat from * until cord is desired length. Bind off.

Kitchener stitch. This grafting technique is used to join two sets of live stitches invisibly. It is most often used for sock toes, but can be used to join shoulder seams or two halves of a scarf.

To begin, place the two sets of live stitches to be bound off on separate needles. Hold the needles parallel in your left hand with right sides of the knitted fabric together.

1. Insert the tapestry needle into the first stitch on the front needle as if to knit, and slip the stitch off the needle. Then insert the tapestry needle into the next stitch on the front needle as if to purl, and leave the stitch on the needle (see figure 1).

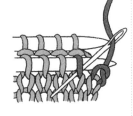

2. Insert the tapestry needle into the first stitch on the back needle as if to purl, and slip the stitch off the needle (see figure 2).

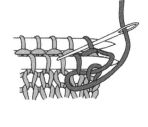

3. Insert the tapestry needle into the next stitch on the back needle as if to knit, and leave the stitch on the needle (see figure 3).

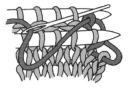

Repeat steps 1–3 until all stitches have been joined.

Knit the knits and purl the purls. This simply means that you work the stitches as they appear on your needles. For example, if a stitch was knitted on the right-side row, it appears as a purl on the wrong side and should be purled on the wrong-side row.

Knitted-on cast-on. Make a slipknot and place it on your left needle.

1. Knit a stitch into the slipknot, leaving the slipknot on the needle (see figure 1).

2. Place the new stitch onto left needle by inserting the left needle into the front of the new stitch (see figure 2).

3. Tighten stitch and continue until you have the required number of stitches.

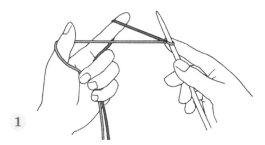

Knitwise (kwise). When a pattern says "slip the next stitch knitwise" or "slip the next stitch kwise," insert your needle into the next stitch from front to back as if you were going to knit it, then slip it to the right needle without knitting it.

Long-tail cast-on. Leaving a tail long enough to cast on the desired number of stitches (a generous guess would be 1" per stitch), make a slipknot, and place it on the needle.

1. Wrap one of the threads around your thumb and the other around your index finger. Hold the tails with your other three fingers (see figure 1).

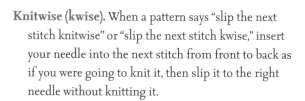

1

2. Insert the needle into the loop around your thumb from front to back and over the yarn around your index finger (see figures 2 and 3). Figure 2 shows the needle going into the loop on the thumb, and figure 3 shows the needle tip going over the yarn on the index finger.

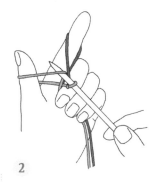

2   3

3. With the needle, bring the yarn from in front of your index finger down through the loop around your thumb (see figure 4).

4. Drop the loop off your thumb, tighten the stitch, and form a new loop around your thumb.

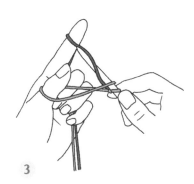

4

M1 (make 1) increase. This increase is worked into the strand between the current stitch and the next. Work in pattern to where you want to increase, lift the strand between the two needles, place the lifted strand on the left needle as shown below, and then knit or purl the stitch.

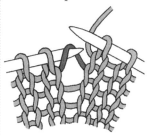
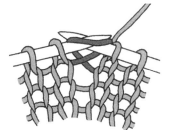

M1 R (right slant)

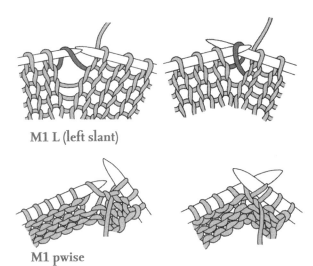

M1 L (left slant)

M1 pwise

Mattress stitch. For a half-stitch seam allowance, work through the horizontal bar at the base of the stitches in every other row (A). For a full-stitch seam allowance, work through two horizontal bars on either side of the stitches (B).

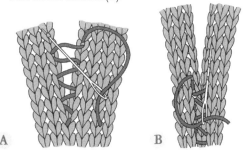

A

B

Pick up and knit. With right side facing, insert the needle under both strands of the edge stitch, then wrap the yarn around the needle and knit the picked up stitch.

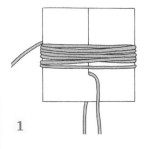

Pompoms. Cut a square of cardboard a little larger than the size of the pompom you want to make. Make a slit down the center, stopping just past the center point.

1. Center a 12" (30.5 cm) piece of yarn in the slit, leaving both ends hanging.

2. Wrap yarn around the cardboard to desired thickness of pompom (see figure 1). Cut the yarn.

3. Tie the wrapped yarn tightly together with the piece of yarn that's hanging in the slit.

4. Cut the wrapped yarn along both edges of the cardboard (see figure 2).

5. Remove the cardboard, fluff up the pompom, and trim any uneven ends.

1

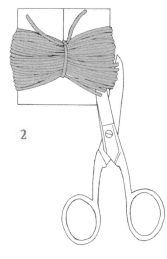

2

Provisional cast-on (crochet over needle).

1. Make a slipknot and place it on a crochet hook. Hold your knitting needle on top of a long strand of yarn (see figure 1).

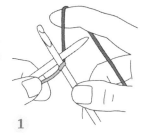

1

2. * With the crochet hook, draw the yarn over the needle and through the loop on the hook. To cast on another stitch, bring yarn behind knitting needle into position as for step 1, and repeat from * (see figures 2 and 3). Note: If you find it awkward to cast on the first couple of stitches, work a few crochet chain stitches before casting onto the needle so you have something to hold on to.

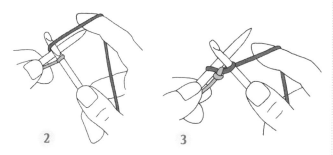

2   **3**

3. When the last stitch has been cast on, work two or three extra crochet chain stitches without taking the yarn around the knitting needle. Then cut the yarn, leaving a 10" (25 cm) tail, draw the tail through the last loop on the hook, and pull the tail to close the loop loosely — just enough so the tail can't escape.

4. To remove the scrap yarn when you've finished the knitting, pull the tail out of the last loop

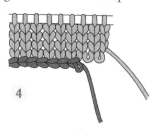

4

and gently tug on it to "unzip" the chain and carefully place the live stitches on a needle, holder, or separate length of scrap yarn as they are released.

Provisional cast-on (crochet chain).
Make a crochet chain with scrap yarn that is at least six chains longer than the number of stitches to be cast on (see page 261).

1

1. Cast on by knitting with the project yarn into the back loops of the chain.

2. To remove the scrap yarn when you've finished the knitting, pull out the crocheted chain and carefully place the live stitches on a needle.

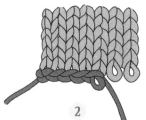

2

Purlwise (pwise). When a pattern says "slip the next stitch purlwise" or "slip the next stitch pwise," insert your needle into the next stitch from back to front as if you were going to purl it, then slip it to the right needle without purling it.

Reverse single crochet (rsc). This is worked the same as single crochet, only you work from left to right. Reverse single crochet creates a "braided" edge.

Seed stitch. This is an alternating K1, P1 stitch. When knitting back and forth, on wrong-side rows knit the stitches that were knit on the right side (they will look like purls on the wrong side) and purl the stitches that were purled on the right side (they will look like knits on the wrong side). When working circularly, purl the stitches that were knit on the previous round and knit the stitches that were purled on the previous round.

Single crochet (sc). Insert hook into next stitch, wrap yarn over hook and draw the loop through the stitch. You now have two loops on the hook. Yarn over hook and draw loop through both loops on hook.

Slip stitch crochet (sl st). Insert hook into next stitch, wrap yarn over hook, and draw the loop through the stitch and the loop on the hook.

Stockinette stitch. When knitting back and forth in rows, knit the right-side rows, purl the wrong-side rows. When knitting circularly, knit all rounds.

Three-needle bind-off. This technique is used to join two sets of live stitches.

1. Place the two sets of stitches to be bound off on separate needles. Hold the needles parallel in your left hand with right sides of the knitted fabric touching.

2. Insert the tip of a third needle into the first stitch on both needles and knit these two stitches together.

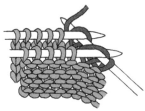

3. Repeat step 2. You now have two stitches on the right needle. With one of the needles in your left hand, lift the first stitch on the right needle over the second and off the needle as for a regular bind off. Repeat until all stitches are bound off.

3-stitch I-cord bind-off.

1. Cast on three stitches at the beginning of the row to be bound off.

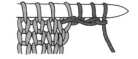

2. Knit two, slip one knit-wise, knit one.

3. Pass the slipped stitch over the last knit stitch and off the needle.

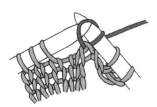

4. Slip three stitches back to left needle.

5. Without turning work, pull yarn across the back in position to knit the first stitch.

Repeat Steps 2–5.

Treble (triple) crochet (tr). Yarn over hook twice. Insert hook through both loops of next stitch. Draw loop through stitch. Yarn over hook. Draw loop through first two loops on hook. Yarn over hook. Draw loop through two loops on hook. Yarn over hook. Draw loop through remaining two loops on hook.

INDEX

Page numbers in *italics* indicate photographs; **bold** indicates charts.

OTHER STOREY TITLES YOU WILL ENJOY

2-at-a-Time Socks, by Melissa Morgan-Oakes.

An easy-to-learn new technique to banish Second Sock Syndrome forever!
144 pages. Hardcover with concealed wire-o. ISBN 978-1-58017-691-0.

101 Designer One-Skein Wonders, edited by Judith Durant.

More patterns for every lonely skein in your stash, from America's knitwear designers.
256 pages. Paper. ISBN 978-1-58017-688-0.

The Crochet Answer Book, by Edie Eckman.

All the information a crocheter could need to unsnarl any project.
320 pages. Flexibind with cloth spine. ISBN 978-1-58017-598-2.

The Knitting Answer Book, by Margaret Radcliffe.

Answers for every yarn crisis — an indispensable addition to every knitter's project bag.
400 pages. Flexibind with cloth spine. ISBN 978-1-58017-599-9.

One-Skein Wonders: 101 Yarn Shop Favorites, edited by Judith Durant.

One hundred and one projects for all those single skeins in your stash, collected from yarn shops across America.
240 pages. Paper. ISBN 978-1-58017-645-3.

These and other books from Storey Publishing are available
wherever quality books are sold or by calling 1-800-441-5700.
Visit us at *www.storey.com*.